SCRIPTURAL TRACES: CRITICAL PERSPECTIVES ON
THE RECEPTION AND INFLUENCE OF THE BIBLE

31

Editors
Matthew A. Collins, University of Chester, UK
Michelle Fletcher, King's College London, UK
Andrew Mein, Durham University, UK

Editorial board
Michael J. Gilmour, David Gunn, James Harding and Jorunn Økland

Published under
LIBRARY OF HEBREW BIBLE/
OLD TESTAMENT STUDIES

728

Formerly Journal for the Study of the Old Testament Supplement Series

Editors
Laura Quick, University of Oxford, UK
Jacqueline Vayntrub, Yale Divinity School, USA

Founding Editors
David J. A. Clines, Philip R. Davies and David M. Gunn

Editorial Board
Alan Cooper, Susan Gillingham, John Goldingay,
Norman K. Gottwald, James E. Harding, John Jarick, Carol Meyers,
Daniel L. Smith-Christopher, Francesca Stavrakopoulou, James W. Watts

WOMEN OF THE BIBLE

From Text to Image

Edited by
Guadalupe Seijas

Translated from the Spanish by
Mónica Ann Walker Vadillo

t&tclark
LONDON • NEW YORK • OXFORD • NEW DELHI • SYDNEY

T&T CLARK
Bloomsbury Publishing Plc
50 Bedford Square, London, WC1B 3DP, UK
1385 Broadway, New York, NY 10018, USA
29 Earlsfort Terrace, Dublin 2, Ireland

BLOOMSBURY, T&T CLARK and the T&T Clark logo are trademarks of
Bloomsbury Publishing Plc

First published in Great Britain 2022
Paperback edition published 2024

Chapters 1, 3, 4, 6 and 7 first published in Spain as *Mujeres del Antiguo Testamento: de los relatos a las imágenes* © Editorial Verbo Divino, 2015.
English translation, introductory and concluding matter, and Chapters 2 and 5 (first published for this edition) © Bloomsbury Publishing, 2022.

For legal purposes the Acknowledgements on p. xi constitute an extension of this copyright page.

Translated from the Spanish by Mónica Ann Walker Vadillo

Cover image: *The Mother of Sisera Looked out a Window*, Moore Albert Joseph
© Artepics / Alamy Stock Photo

All rights reserved. No part of this publication may be reproduced or transmitted in any form or by any means, electronic or mechanical, including photocopying, recording, or any information storage or retrieval system, without prior permission in writing from the publishers.

Bloomsbury Publishing Plc does not have any control over, or responsibility for, any third-party websites referred to or in this book. All internet addresses given in this book were correct at the time of going to press. The author and publisher regret any inconvenience caused if addresses have changed or sites have ceased to exist, but can accept no responsibility for any such changes.

A catalogue record for this book is available from the British Library.

Library of Congress Cataloging-in-Publication Data
Names: Seijas de Los Ríos-Zarzosa, María Guadalupe, editor. |
Vadillo, Mónica Ann Walker, translator.
Title: Women of the Bible : from text to image / edited by Guadalupe Seijas ; translated by Mónica Ann Walker Vadillo.
Description: New York : T&T CLARK, 2022. | Series: The library of Hebrew and Old Testament studies, 2513–8758 ; 728 | This English version presents edited versions of the five chapters of the revised and updated Spanish version, published in 2015 and incorporates two new ones (chapters 2 and 5), expanding the iconographic analysis to the New Testament with the representation of Mary Magdalene ... . |
Includes bibliographical references and index. | Summary: "The contributors present an interdisciplinary approach to the representations of women in the Hebrew Bible by focusing on texts, images and gender"– Provided by publisher.
Identifiers: LCCN 2022002291 (print) | LCCN 2022002292 (ebook) |
ISBN 9780567703606 (hardback) | ISBN 9780567703637 (paperback) |
ISBN 9780567703613 (pdf)
Subjects: LCSH: Women in the Bible. | Bible–Criticism, interpretation, etc.
Classification: LCC BS575 .W62 2022 (print) | LCC BS575 (ebook) |
DDC 220.9/2082–dc23/eng/20220208
LC record available at https://lccn.loc.gov/2022002291
LC ebook record available at https://lccn.loc.gov/2022002292

ISBN: HB: 978-0-5677-0360-6
PB: 978-0-5677-0363-7
ePDF: 978-0-5677-0361-3

Series: Scriptural Traces, volume 31
Library of Hebrew Bible/Old Testament Studies, volume 728
ISSN 2513-8758

Typeset by Newgen KnowledgeWorks Pvt. Ltd., Chennai, India

To find out more about our authors and books visit www.bloomsbury.com
and sign up for our newsletters.

CONTENTS

List of figures   vii
List of contributors   ix
Acknowledgements   xi

INTRODUCTION   1
   Guadalupe Seijas

Chapter 1
BIBLE, ART AND WOMEN: CRITERIA FOR ANALYSIS AND CRITICAL
INTERPRETATION   5
   Carmen Yebra-Rovira

Chapter 2
THE ICONOGRAPHIC REPRESENTATION OF THE BIBLE: THE
INTERACTION BETWEEN TEXT AND IMAGE   25
   Guadalupe Seijas

Chapter 3
BATHSHEBA IN MEDIEVAL MANUSCRIPTS: VISUAL ANALYSIS OF A
CONTROVERSIAL OLD TESTAMENT WOMAN   51
   Mónica Ann Walker Vadillo

Chapter 4
STRONG WOMEN OF THE BIBLE AND THEIR PERSISTENCE IN
SEVENTEENTH-CENTURY SPANISH PAINTING   85
   Amparo Alba Cecilia and Guadalupe Seijas

Chapter 5
MOSES'S MOTHER AND HER LITERARY AND VISUAL RECEPTION IN
THE NINETEENTH CENTURY   109
   Carmen Yebra-Rovira

Chapter 6
THE WOMEN IN THE BOOK OF JUDGES AND THEIR REPRESENTATION
IN NINETEENTH-CENTURY ENGRAVINGS   133
   Carmen Yebra-Rovira

Chapter 7
RUTH AND NAOMI: A STORY OF FRIENDSHIP IN IMAGES 159
    Guadalupe Seijas

CONCLUSIONS 183
    Guadalupe Seijas

Select bibliography 187
Index of Biblical characters 189
Index of references 192
Index of authors 196

FIGURES

2.1	*Bible of Saint Louis*, Toledo, *c.* 1226, vol. 1, fol. 94r	28
2.2	Rebecca, *The Flight into Egypt and Michal, Biblia Pauperum*, la Haya, *c.* 1405, fol. 4r	31
2.3	Matthias Stom, *Samson and Delilah, c.* 1630	37
2.4	Andrea Solari, *Saint Mary Magdalene, c.* 1524	43
2.5	Dante Gabriel Rossetti, *Mary Magdalene at the House of Simon the Pharisee*, 1858	45
3.1	Cycle of David and Bathsheba, *Book of Hours of Agnes of Bohemia*, Bamberg, Germany, *c.* 1204–19, fol. 17v	68
3.2	David rebuked by Nathan, *Homily of Gregory of Nazianzus*, Constantinople, Byzantine Empire, *c.* 879–83, fol. 143v	72
3.3	The intercession of Bathsheba, *Psalter of Queen Mary Tudor or Isabella of France*, London or Westminster, England, *c.* 1310–20, fol. 63v	75
3.4	Coronation of Bathsheba, Mary and Esther, *Biblia Pauperum*, The Hague, The Netherlands, *c.* 1405, fol. 28r	78
4.1	Chapel of the Virgin of Guadalupe, Convent of Las Descalzas Reales, Madrid	94
4.2	Iconography Scheme of the Chapel of the Virgin of Guadalupe	94
4.3	Cover of the *Elogios de mujeres ilustres del Viejo Testamento* by Martín Carrillo, 1627	96
5.1	G. Staal, *Eve*, 1846	114
5.2	Simeon Solomon, *The Mother of Moses*, 1860	125
6.1	H. Singleton, *Caleb and his daughter*, 1845; and A. Pascual, *The return of the prodigal son*, 1841	140
6.2	G. Staal and W. H. Mote, *Deborah*, 1850; and G. Doré, *Deborah*, 1871–73	143
6.3	J. Schnorr von Carolsfeld, *The woman of Thebez*, 1878–9	147
6.4	C. Oesterley, *Jephthah's daughter*, 1908; and G. Staal and W. H. Egleton, *Jephthah's daughter*, 1850	150
6.5	A. Pascual and R. Saez, *El ultraje hecho a la muger de un levita*, 1841	152
7.1	Sainte Chapelle (1248) *Orpah and Ruth/Naomi*	166
7.2	The Farewell, *Bible of Saint Louis*, Toledo, *c.* 1226, vol. 1, fol. 94r	167
7.3	Philip Hermogenes Calderon, *Ruth and Naomi*, 1886	173
7.4	Gustavo Doré, *Ruth and Naomi*, 1866	174
7.5	Jacob Symosz Pynas, *Ruth and Naomi*, before 1650	177

CONTRIBUTORS

Amparo Alba Cecilia is Tenured Professor at the Hebrew and Aramaic Studies Department of Complutense University of Madrid, Spain, and member of the Spanish Royal Academy of History. She teaches Hebrew language and literature, Kabbalah, Jewish science and mysticism. Among her research lines we can mention Medieval Hebrew Literature, Literature of the Judaeo-Christian controversy, Kabbalah, Jewish mysticism, Jewish liturgy, Hispano-Hebrew narrative and medieval Jewish science. She is the author of numerous publications, among which we can mention the books on medieval Hebrew stories: *Cuentos de los rabinos* (1991) and *El Midrás de los Diez Mandamientos y el Libro precioso de salvación* (1990), as well as numerous articles on Hebrew literature, liturgy and Kabbalah in books and specialized journals.

Guadalupe Seijas de los Ríos-Zarzosa holds a doctorate in Semitic philology and is Senior Lecturer at the Hebrew and Aramaic Studies Department of Complutense University of Madrid, Spain, where she teaches biblical Hebrew and Hebrew literature. She was the editor of *'Ilu. Revista de Ciencias de las Religiones* between 2007 and 2011. Her research focuses on the Bible, mainly in the syntax of prophetic texts, in the masorah and in the study of the cultural manifestations of the Bible. She is the author of *Las masoras del libro de Deuteronomio* (2002) and *Masora: La transmisión de la tradición de la Biblia Hebrea* (2010) in collaboration with E. Martín Contreras; she has co-edited *Computer Assisted Research on the Bible in the 21st Century* (2010) and a *History of Hebrew and Jew Literature* in Spanish (2014), of which she is editor and co-author. Currently she directs the research group *Bible: Texts and Iconography*.

Mónica Ann Walker Vadillo holds a PhD in medieval art history from Complutense University in Madrid, Spain, and an MA in medieval studies from the Central European University in Budapest. She is currently a tutor at the Department for Continuing Education at the University of Oxford, UK, and a freelance writer for National Geographic. Among her lines of research is the iconography of the women of the Old Testament, the representation of animals in medieval art and the influence of the Middle Ages on popular visual culture. She is the author of the monograph *Bathsheba in Late Medieval French Manuscript Illumination: Innocent Object of Desire or Agent of Sin?* (2008), among other publications on medieval iconography. She has co-edited a book entitled *Animals and Otherness in the Middle Ages: Perspectives Across the Disciplines* (2013) with María Victoria Chico Picaza and Francisco de Asís García García (UCM), and she is the series editor for 'Medieval History and Art' at Trivent Publishing where she has published the edited collection *Ambiguous Women in Medieval Art* (2019).

Carmen Yebra-Rovira has a PhD in theology with an MA in art history. She is Associated Professor of Bible and Hermeneutics at the Pontifical University of Salamanca, Spain. Her research focuses on the history of the reception and interpretation of the Bible through the arts – especially painting and engraving – and its influence on Western culture (nineteenth and twenty-first centuries). Her publications include *Biblia e imagen: Lectura gráfica de la Escritura Sagrada en la España del siglo XIX* (2012) and numerous articles in which she addresses the influence of biblical images in society, especially in the formation of women: 'French Biblical Engravings and the Education of the Spanish Woman in the XIX Century' (2013); 'Interpretación bíblica y formación moral de la mujer en el siglo XIX. El ángel del hogar' (2013).

ACKNOWLEDGEMENTS

This book is the result of the combined efforts of many people. First of all, I would like to thank Amparo Alba Cecilia, Mónica Ann Walker Vadillo and Carmen Yebra-Rovira for agreeing to participate in writing this book. The exchange of opinions and scientific discussions held with Carmen Yebra-Rovira have been particularly enriching and fruitful.

I would also like to thank Mónica Ann Walker Vadillo for translating the book and to Moleiro Editores, who published the facsimile edition of the *Bible of Saint Louis* in three volumes and who have, generously, allowed us to reproduce some of its miniatures in the book.

The financing provided by the Ministry of Science, Innovation, and Universities of the Government of Spain to the R+D Project *Transmission and Reception of the Bible: Texts and Iconography* (FFI2015-65610-P, 2016–2018) has made it possible to carry out research work, as well as to subsidize part of the costs of translation and editing.

The financing provided by Santander Bank & Complutense University of Madrid to the Research Project *Transmission and Reception of the Bible: Texts and Iconography* (PR87/19-22535, 2019) allowed us to finish the translation of the book.

My gratitude goes to the Editorial Verbo Divino who placed their trust in me and in the research work that I proposed, even though this area of knowledge was somewhat marginal in its editorial line.

My acknowledgement also goes to the T&T Clark Publishing House for publishing our research in the *Scriptural Traces* collection so we can present it to non-Spanish speaking countries.

Finally, I would like to thank my family, especially my husband and my sons, for their unconditional support.

INTRODUCTION

Guadalupe Seijas

The Bible and art are at the core of this book, which analyses the iconographic representation of several women of the Bible. The essays in this book consider the way in which the biblical texts have regarded these women, how they have understood them through time and the way in which they were represented. The answers that this book offers come from different areas of knowledge such as theology, philology or history of art, and they demonstrate a cross-sectional, plural and rich approach to the subject which provides clues to understand the history of the transmission and reception of the Bible in general and of the women of the Old Testament in particular.

The study of biblical representations must begin with the analysis of the biblical text, followed by the exegesis and the history of interpretation. It is necessary to know what values and concepts were associated in each era with the biblical story. This will be the starting point that will allow us to access the study of biblical iconography in order to answer questions such as what is represented, how it is represented, what is eliminated, what is emphasized or what is insinuated, just to name a few. A two-way road is iterated here: from text to image, that is the text that inspires the artist, and from the image to the text, that is, what is the degree of fidelity or independence of the representation with respect to the Bible?

This double perspective is the guiding thread of this book, which is located at the centre of the crossroads where different areas of knowledge converge. This requires an enriching dialogue among its scholars, since it is not possible to analyse the iconographic representation without taking into account the text on which it is based, its interpretation, the time and mentality surrounding the work, the artistic styles of the moment and so forth.

Mujeres del Antiguo Testamento: De los relatos a las imágenes was published in 2015 by the publisher Verbo Divino (Estella, Navarra). This work was part of the research project *Reception and Transmission of the Bible: Texts and Iconography*, funded by the Ministry of Science, Innovation and Universities of the Government of Spain. The second and seventh chapters, which are published for the first time in this English version, are the result of the work carried out for this project in the 2016–18 triennium (R+D projects: FFI2015-65610-P). Part of the expenses derived from editing and translating this volume into English have been financed by this project. Other scholarly results from the project include the organization of the workshop *Deborah, Jael and Delilah: Biblical Heroines and Their Reception in Literature, Arts, Music and Film in the 19th–21st Century* in the Annual Conference of the European Association of Biblical Studies (Warsaw 2019) led by Guadalupe Seijas and Susanne Gillmayr-Bucher.

The English version published by Bloomsbury T&T Clark (2022) presents edited versions of the five chapters of the revised and updated Spanish version and incorporates two new ones (Chapters 2 and 5), expanding the iconographic analysis to the New Testament with the representation of Mary Magdalene. In the chapter 'Bible, art and women: Criteria for analysis and critical interpretation', Carmen Yebra-Rovira analyses the difficulties inherent in interdisciplinary studies, the challenges that scholars face and the possibilities they offer. The author argues that images are an open window through the visual communication that is established between the author and the recipient, which allows scholars to know the context, concerns, mentality and prevailing ideology of the time. On the other hand, representations are divided between faithfully reflecting the biblical text and exploring new possibilities, such as recreation, innovation or new creation.

In 'Bathsheba in medieval manuscripts: Visual analysis of a controversial Old Testament woman', Mónica Ann Walker Vadillo focuses on the analysis of a single woman. Bathsheba is an ambiguous character who, depending on the biblical episode mentioned, can be branded as immoral and libidinous or, on the contrary, be praised as a woman who acts as an intercessor, and, as such, she becomes a prefiguration of the Virgin Mary. The study starts from the interpretation of this character from the perspective of the medieval exegesis and continues with the analysis of the images that appear in the manuscripts, which include the Homilies of Gregory of Nazianzus, Psalters, Books of Hours and the *Biblia Pauperum* and other typological manuscripts. Despite the tension that occurs between these two very different facets, Bathsheba is presented as a role model. This chapter is the final product of Walker Vadillo's PhD thesis.

In 'Strong women of the Bible and their persistence in seventeenth-century Spanish painting', the iconographic representation of a set of female characters that stand out for their initiative and courage are addressed. The starting point is the identification of the chapels and hermitages in which they are represented, because until now there was no monographic work on this subject. In a special way, the Chapel of Guadalupe stands out from the Convent of Las Descalzas Reales[1] in

---

1. Translator's Note: In *Women of The Bible: From Text to Image*, as a rule it was decided to keep the title of the publications in their original language and to translate into English the names of churches, convents and invocations to the Virgin and saints. As an exception we have decided to maintain the Spanish name of this convent (Descalzas Reales) because there is no logical English translation that can convey the meaning to the reader. 'Descalzas' means 'barefooted', in allusion to the religious order, and 'Reales' refers to the relationship of this monastery with the Austrian dynasty from the beginning. Joanna of Austria, Philip II's sister, was the founder of the convent.

Madrid, where twenty-one women from the Old Testament were represented. Among them are little-known women, such as Achsah (Noemá), and others who tradition has silenced, as is the case with the daughters of Job, whose relevance is evident in rabbinic traditions. Amparo Alba Cecilia and Guadalupe Seijas focus on finding out the message that the artist want to convey to those who see the paintings in this chapel through the use of very different women from the biblical tradition, all of them characterized by their determination and courage; women who took sides, intervened or understood correctly the reality in which they lived.

Yebra-Rovira is the author of 'The women in the book of Judges and their representation in nineteenth-century engravings'. The book of Judges is characterized by including among its pages a high number of female characters, mostly secondary or not very relevant; women who, in the last decades, have aroused the interest of numerous researchers, especially from literary and/or feminist studies, who have discovered in them new interpretations and contributions to their stories. Yebra-Rovira deals with the representation of the female characters of the book of Judges and the values associated with the engravings which appear in Bibles and Sacred Histories. The manner and purpose of their representation in the nineteenth century are some of the keys to this study.

'Ruth and Naomi: A story of friendship in images' by Seijas closes the book. This chapter analyses the iconography of the scene of Ruth 1.7-18 from a diachronic point of view, exploring the different values associated with the iconography of this passage from the Middle Ages to the twentieth century by looking at what aspects were emphasized and which were omitted in every time period.

The first of the new chapters is 'The iconographic representation of the Bible: The interaction between text and image'. In this chapter, Seijas analyses some considerations regarding biblical iconography and the close relationship that exists between the text and the images that reproduces its contents. The first part is centred on the text of the Bible, the text that inspires the image and how it has been understood and disseminated. The second part deals with its representation and how it affects the transmission of the biblical message. The third part illustrates the above by analysing the character of Mary Magdalene, focusing on how artists represented her and how they moved away from the biblical story and reflected new characteristics derived from exegetical commentaries and medieval legends.

The second addition is 'Moses's mother and her literary and visual reception in the nineteenth century', where Yebra-Rovira studies two characters: Moses's mother, Jochebed, and the Pharaoh's daughter. Hardly ever mentioned in Biblical Studies and rarely reported in visual studies, they had, however, a great influence in nineteenth-century Europe. Both women have been important role models in the formation of Catholic and Protestant women alike, as the numerous literary and artistic representations of the time testify. Such representations emphasize aspects that are present in the biblical narrative and other features that are never mentioned. Drawing on nineteenth-century gender roles, the resulting portrait of Jochebed is one of a sacrificial and heroic mother. The Pharaoh's daughter is presented as a model of beauty and kindness. In this chapter, Yebra-Rovira addresses which gender role models they embodied, how they evolved and what was genuinely specific of such nineteenth-century representations. She also presents the intertwining influence of literature and artwork, and how such confluence of different factors was used as a lens to interpret the biblical text, which, interestingly enough, results in interpretations where Catholicism and Protestantism converges.

Therefore, two chapters deal with theoretical and methodological issues with reflections on the problems and difficulties that have to be addressed in the iconographic study of the biblical characters, and the other five analyse the representation of women of the Bible in different periods.

The chapters that make up the book are intended to reflect the variety of possibilities offered by the study of biblical representations, centred, in this work, on the women of the Old Testament. Each of them studies one or several eras (Middle Ages, Baroque, the nineteenth century), each focuses on a technique (miniature, engraving, oil painting) and each one of them approaches the analysis of images from a certain perspective: the scholar who combines theology and art (Yebra-Rovira), the one that introduces the lens of the art historian (Walker Vadillo) and the philologist who analyses the texts in detail as a prior step to the iconographic study (Alba and Seijas). Each of the authors, from their field of knowledge, asks different questions and poses different problems. It is precisely this interdisciplinarity and plurality, the hallmarks of this book, that make this work attractive to an audience with various interests. Those who are studying philology and exegesis, people who study art and medievalists, those dedicated to theology or those who are interested in the process of transmission of culture in general and the Bible in particular will find in these pages aspects not contemplated in their own disciplines, which will enrich their understanding of the interaction between text and image.

We trust that this type of work contributes to a better understanding of the history of reception and hermeneutical study of the biblical text and to make known the research that is being developed in the Spanish scholarly world.

Chapter 1

BIBLE, ART AND WOMEN: CRITERIA FOR ANALYSIS AND CRITICAL INTERPRETATION

Carmen Yebra-Rovira

Presentation: The Metal Snake

The visit to a museum, the contemplation of the frescoes of a temple, the viewing of the works of an exhibition or the encounter with a simple illustration placed in a book are daily activities whose repercussion is much greater than what is usually thought. The canvas, the fresco, the photograph or the drawing imprint on the viewer, consciously and unconsciously, a set of values and a very particular way of approaching the story that is being narrated.

In a gallery you can see excellent works of art that show not only a history of painting by chronologically presenting different styles and artists, but also a history of society, politics or religion, to give some examples. Images are not mere objects to be looked at and, perhaps, contemplated. They reflect the context that creates them, and, at the same time, they are active agents in the formation of the society that observes them, contributing to build – or destroy – their values, their memories and their identity.[1] Therefore, they are also valid sources for knowing the structures of thought and the sociopolitical and religious foundations of a group. Iconic representation is a complex reality whose meanings and consequences can change depending on its use, location, viewers and contexts.[2]

The Prado Museum (Madrid) holds one of the early works of the Flemish painter Anton van Dyck, *The Metal Snake* (c.1618–20), which illustrates a little-known passage from the book of Numbers (21.5-9). The story tells how God, in response to the whispers and doubts of the people, sent a shower of poisonous

---

1. Cf. Jesusa Vega, *Pasado y tradición. La construcción visual del imaginario español en el siglo XIX* (Madrid: Ediciones Polifemo, 2016).

2. Cf. Manuel Núñez Rodríguez, *Casa, calle, convento: iconografía de la mujer bajomedieval*, Monografías da Universidade de Santiago de Compostela (Santiago de Compostela: Servicio de Publicacións e Intercambio Científico, 1997); Bernardo Riego, *La construcción social de la realidad a través de la fotografía y el grabado informativo en la España del siglo XIX* (Santander: Universidad de Cantabria, 2001).

snakes. To get rid of their deadly bite, the Hebrews had to raise their gaze to the top of a mast topped by a bronze serpent. A woman with a haggard face, kneeling and supported by another, stands out above the group and attracts the gaze of the person who is contemplating the painting. The painter chooses the moment in which she is rebuked by a group of men who seem to demand that she look at the banner. This object with the metal figure and with healing qualities is the symbol of God's goodness, while recalling the need to trust in His providence. The disposition of the figures and the use of colour make the viewer believe that only the woman has been mortally bitten and that only she needs divine help. The foreground of her body and face among so many men emphasizes her guilt and subtly makes her seen as an example of a sinner. This version differs substantially from others from the same period, for example, that of the Spaniard José Leonardo (1630–40, Museum of Fine Arts of San Fernando, Madrid), which shows men and women dead and a woman pointing her finger towards the serpent, but, far from van Dyck's version, she does not appear as a sinner but as a mediator for salvation.

When art historians analyse the work of van Dyck, they emphasize the novelty of the composition, the arrangement and anatomy of the figures, the texture or the stroke of the brushwork. When a biblical scholar contemplates it, he focuses his attention on different aspects. The first thing that is asked is why the artist has chosen this passage, why has he prioritized the book of Numbers versus that of Exodus – in which the stories of the people in the desert are narrated – and, above all, what image of the *People* is being transmitted. At the same time, the figure of the kneeling woman evokes the passage in which Miriam, sister of Moses, is punished with leprosy for having gossiped against her brother – 'Miriam noticed that she was leprous, white as the snow' (Num. 12.10) – and it raises the question whether, in fact, there is no conflation of the two stories in the work of the Flemish artist: Numbers 12 and 21. The Prado Museum, in the exhibition dedicated to this author, *The Young van Dyck* (20 November 2012–3 March 2013), placed the painting next to that of *Samson and Delilah* (c.1618–20, Dulwich Picture Gallery, London). The consecutive viewing of both works, with two women with very white skin and one of them, Delilah, considered a *femme fatale* throughout history, unconsciously reinforces in the viewer the fallacy that women have a greater tendency to be sinners. The exhibition, with several representations of 'penitents' and other biblical women, increased the perception that women are a 'danger' to society, with the sole exception of the Virgin Mary.

The choice of texts and their scenes, the way they are captured and their location in an exhibition convey a set of contents that are alien to the work itself, to a certain extent, which are of great importance for the socio-ecclesiastical construction and for the conception of women as a weak, sinful and dangerous subject. This introductory example allows us to appreciate the complexity of the image, its relation to a reference text, the distance between written and visual language, and the ability of visual art to evoke other biblical passages. At the same time, it demonstrates the repercussion that the election of one passage or another can have and its presentation in a concrete context when it is analysed from a gender perspective.

The following text intends to guide the reader in the understanding and analysis of biblical images and will try to offer ways of dialogue between art historians and biblical scholars. These guidelines aim to make possible a greater understanding of these compositions by analysing those structures that, consciously or unconsciously, erase or fix the status and performance of the biblical woman, and they present a critical study of the consequences for society, the churches that use them and the people that contemplate them.

The biblical scholar and his/her encounter with images

Since the seventies of the twentieth century, biblical studies have been enriched by a multiplicity of approaches from disciplines related to literature, history, sociology and anthropology. Feminist approaches and other liberating perspectives have also been an invaluable engine for the advances made in the last decades.[3] All these sciences and approaches have in common the centrality of the *written* biblical text – or of related sources – as a starting point for the study and knowledge of the context in which it arose and developed. Only in recent decades has our discipline entered into dialogue with other disciplines whose primary language is not the written word. This is the case of the sciences related to the image as a form of communication: art history, cinema, communication sciences, graphic illustration[4] – all of them value the iconic as a specific form of human language, and, therefore, the exegete may discover in them a specific way through which God can reveal himself, which makes the image worthy of analysis. This constitutes a challenge, especially if one considers that when a theologian or a biblical scholar uses the image, it is usually done as a decorative complement, to 'prove' his or her affirmations or to propose it as a pedagogical element. They do this without considering critically what the values are that each transmit, what the interpretation is that is made of the story and what the impact is it can have on the viewer.

---

3. In the document of the Pontifical Biblical Commission, *The Interpretation of the Bible in the Church* (Rome, 1993), the evolution and contributions of these methods and approaches within the Catholic Church are recorded. Mª. Elisa Estévez López, 'La Escritura en el centro de la evangelización', in *Biblia y nueva evangelización*, ed. Gabino Uríbarri Bilbao, Biblioteca de Teología Comillas 12 (Madrid: Universidad Pontificia Comillas – DDB, 2005), 109–58.

4. Studies in which the source of knowledge is sound also begin to emerge, albeit timidly. The analysis of music composed from the biblical stories reveals very interesting aspects of the history of transmission. The melodies and songs are also a source that help establish many stories. Cf. J. M. Bullard, 'Music, the Bible and', in *Dictionary of Biblical Interpretation*, ed. John H. Hayes (Nashville: Abingdon, 1999), 172–87; Robert Ignatius Letellier, *The Bible in Music* (Newcastle: Cambridge Scholars, 2017).

In the decade of the nineties of the twentieth century, British research, led by Professor Cheryl Exum within the framework of Cultural Studies, began a fruitful path to discover the possibilities that could be open for exegetes when they understand and analyse the image as a relevant source for biblical knowledge, especially for the history of its interpretation and transmission, and for the analysis of its influence on culture and society.[5] The assumption on which this research is based is to consider that an image of a biblical theme is more than a mere transposition from written to visual language; it is a new interpretation of unforeseeable consequences – in which both the artist and the viewer intervene – which is necessary to analyse as if it came from a theological treatise or an exegetical commentary.[6] Professor Exum's studies have created an important current, both in Europe and in the United States, which proposes new ways of approaching biblical images and, therefore, of understanding and welcoming the cultural heritage of a visual nature. At the same time, it invites us to investigate the influence that these artistic vestiges have had throughout history in the reading and interpretation of the Bible.[7] The studies of *Reception and Interpretation of the Bible* have undergone a great evolution in the last two decades, and in these studies the study of visual representations has been crucial.[8] This interest also opens ways of understanding and collaboration between art historians and biblical scholars. It requires an interdisciplinary work through which we can see the need that the latter have for the use of visual sources for their academic work and the enrichment that it supposes for art historians

---

5. Regarding the relation between *Cultural Studies* and *Biblical Studies*, cf. J. Cheryl Exum and Stephen D. Moore, 'Biblical studies/cultural studies', in *Biblical Studies/Cultural Studies: The Third Sheffield Colloquium*, ed. J. Cheryl Exum, Journal for the Study of the Old Testament Supplement Series 226 (Sheffield: Sheffield Academic Press, 1998), 19–45. In this chapter, the authors explain how in the interrelation between Bible and culture there is a process of constant redefinition and influence.

6. The beginning of this type of study was initiated by J. Cheryl Exum, *Plotted, Shot, and Painted: Cultural Representations of Biblical Women*, Journal for the Study of the Old Testament Supplement Series 215 (Sheffield: Sheffield Academic Press, 1996); J. Cheryl Exum, 'Beyond the biblical horizon: The Bible and the arts', *Biblical Interpretation* 6, no. 3 (1998): 259–65; J. Cheryl Exum (ed.), *Biblical Studies/Cultural Studies: The Third Sheffield Colloquium*, Journal for the Study of the Old Testament Supplement Series 226 (Sheffield: Sheffield Academic Press, 1998).

7. The bibliography of the last decades is very abundant, specially the works of Michaela Giebelhausen, *Painting the Bible: Representation and Belief in Mid-Victorian Britain* (Aldershot: Ashgate, 2006); Martin O'Kane, *Painting the Text: The Artist as Biblical Interpreter*, The Bible in the Modern World 8 (Sheffield: Sheffield Phoenix Press, 2007); Martin O'Kane (ed.), *Bible, Art, Gallery*, The Bible in the Modern World 21 (Sheffield: Sheffield Phoenix Press, 2011).

8. Emma England and William John Lyons (eds), *Reception History and Biblical Studies*, Library of Hebrew Bible/Old Testament Studies 615-STr 6 (London: Bloomsbury T&T Clark, 2018).

and iconographers the addition of a greater thematic, textual and content-wise precision to their work. When a historian or art historian analyses a work of a biblical nature, its interests, as indicated in the example with which this chapter opened, focus on the stylistic characteristics, the identification of the different iconographic elements, the influences and repercussions that the image has had throughout history, and its capacity to transform the environment. When a biblical scholar approaches his or her work, they often feel that there is a lack of greater refinement in the relationship with the text and its message, and they also feel – why not say it? – a certain negative prejudice towards the biblical image or religious tradition with explanations about the meaning and content of the stories that are not always well defined.[9] The iconographic identification is made from the biblical reference – the quote – but without taking into account the full story, the significance of the passage in the history of salvation or the repercussion that the selection of said scenes may have had on the social, cultural, political and religious configuration. On many occasions it has been perceived that in the analysis of the selected visual stories, scholars have considered neither the history of interpretation and transmission of the Bible nor other sources such as sacred stories, homilies, commentaries and so forth. These were the main bases throughout most of history for the transmission of biblical stories, and they could explain the spectator's reception and interpretation of the images.[10]

The common path: Art and Bible from a gender perspective

The paths that separate the two disciplines (biblical scholarship and visual culture) are shortened by the existence of common interests, approaches and methodologies, such as the use of gender perspectives. Both disciplines formulate questions that try to discover the structures, languages and strategies with which a patriarchal model is reinforced. In this model the woman is understood as a subject of inferior category to the man, and this position therefore restricts her

---

9. This can be seen, for example, in the work of Louis Réau, *Iconografía del arte cristiano: Iconografía de la Biblia. Antiguo Testamento*, trans. Daniel Alcoba (Barcelona: Ediciones del Serbal, 2007), or in the work of Erika Bornay, *Mujeres de la Biblia en la pintura del Barroco: imágenes de la ambigüedad*, Ensayos Arte Cátedra (Madrid: Cátedra, 1998). In the study of María López Fernández, *La imagen de la mujer en la pintura española, 1890–1914* (Madrid: A. Machado Libros, 2006), she speaks in a generic way of the 'usual misogyny of the Catholic Church' without reflecting on the importance that the feminine biblical image has had also for the visibility of women and to propose liberating and formative models.

10. The apocryphal literature or pseudo-biblical sources such as the 'biblical novels' have been the primary source for the construction of the image, but they also show the enormous importance that secondary works or literary commentaries have had and how they survive in time because they have survived through artistic representations.

possibilities of growth and her social and ecclesial participation.[11] For this purpose, since the beginnings of this type of analysis, researchers have tried to recover the experiences of silenced, invisible or unknown women. These stories allow us to identify the imprint that these women have left throughout history.[12] In this task of discovery, there has been a concern to rescue not only important women but also biblical characters, female artists, exegetes or theologians, a veritable *history of women*, which reflects a rich world of often forgotten female contributors. This *history of women* attests to the existence of parallel stories to those of traditional and official male-centred history and shows an unsuspected pluralism. Both sciences have also been asked about the image that men have given of women, their functions and their role in society. A critical perspective does not allow us to do this research without reflecting on the repercussions that all this has had and continues to have on social construction and ecclesial configuration inviting, many times, to recreate and rewrite a history written and drawn primarily by men.[13]

In the specific study of the biblical image from a gender perspective and in continuity with the aforementioned elements, a series of enriching paths could be postulated for the two disciplines that speak of a new way of understanding work with images from an exegetical point of view.

Recovering the memory of biblical women: The selection process

In the study of biblical transmission through images, the realization that not all scenes, biblical stories and characters have received the same treatment or iconographic weight is of great importance. It could be said that not every part of the Bible has been 'told in images'. Only a small part associated, generally, with certain narrative stories and dramatic scenes or with individual characters of special relevance (Abraham, Moses, David, some of the prophets, Paul and

---

11. For example: Katy Deepwell, *Nueva crítica feminista de arte: estrategias críticas*, Feminismos (Madrid: Cátedra, 1998); Marián López F. Cao (ed.), *Geografías de la mirada: género, creación artística y representación*, Instituto de Investigaciones Feministas (Madrid: Universidad Complutense – Asociación Cultural Al-Mudayna, 2001); Rosario Camacho Martínez and Aurora Miró, *Iconografía y creación artística: estudios sobre la identidad femenina desde las relaciones de poder* (Málaga: Diputación de Málaga (CEDMA), 2001); Patricia Mayayo, *Historias de mujeres, historias del arte*, Ensayos Arte Catedra (Madrid: Cátedra, 2003); María Jesús Godoy Domínguez, *La mujer en el arte: una contralectura de la modernidad* (Granada: Universidad de Granada, 2007); David Hidalgo Rodríguez, Noemí Cubas Martín, and María Esther Martínez Quinteiro (eds), *Mujeres en la historia, el arte y el cine: discursos de género, variantes de contenidos y soportes: de la palabra al audiovisual*, Aquilafuente (Salamanca: Ediciones Universidad de Salamanca, 2011).

12. Dorothee Sölle, Joe H. Kirchberger and Anne-Marie Schnieper, *Great Women of the Bible in Art and Literature* (Minneapolis: Fortress Press, 2006).

13. Griselda Pollock, *Generations and Geographies in the Visual Arts: Feminist Readings* (London: Routledge, 1996).

so forth) has been visually represented.¹⁴ These stories have also been treated in the same way because, once the iconographic model has been fixed, very few variations occur. Every modification, however small, becomes relevant for the exegete because it implies a variation in the interpretation of the text. The visual representation of the Bible, therefore, is based on a *selection process* that is motivated by literary, artistic (support, function, technical resources and so forth), aesthetic, sociopolitical, theological and liturgical reasons. In fact, using literary categories, one could talk about the existence of a 'visual canon within the Canon' of enormous repercussions in the processes of transmission and interpretation.¹⁵ In this sense, we cannot ignore that the access of many faithful to the Bible throughout history has been mediated, primarily, by images. The pre-eminence of some of these images over others and, therefore, of certain stories, conditions the transmission of the Revelation and the effectiveness of the communication with the spectator since, in fact, those texts/images that are sporadically represented can go unnoticed or are underestimated for not being recognized.

The analysis of the selection of stories that have gone down in the history of art undoubtedly allows to continue the recovery of the *visual history of biblical women*. The history of art has captured stories of women as a 'feminine visual canon' that has not only brought forth a constant feminine presence but also served as an incentive and counterpoint to the exegete, who is too used to reading and transmitting the history of salvation almost exclusively through its masculine protagonists. Far from corroborating the widespread statement of the practical disappearance of women in the Church, the image is offered as a witness of the relevance they have had in the evolution of figures such as the daughters of Noah, Miriam, the daughters of Job, the wives of David, Tabitha or Lydia throughout time. The image as an indelible testimony contributes to the recovery of the memory of those characters and their role in history.

In the study of each story from the point of view of this selection process, it is crucial to perceive how artistic representation, by its very nature, chooses only a specific moment in the narrative. Its concision is relevant to the interpretation and provides data on what passages were important for the reader and with what values these images were transmitted. In the case of Esther, for example, it is clear that the Catholic Church at the time of the Counter-Reformation emphasized the scene of the fainting of Esther before Ahasuerus. By choosing this scene, Esther's fragility, fear and submission are transmitted and reinforced, and other attributes

---

14. Martin O'Kane, 'The biblical King David and his artistic and literary afterlives', *Biblical Interpretation* 6, no. 3 (1998): 317.

15. With regard to the controversy about the relevance of some biblical stories over others – the existence of a 'canon within the Canon' – Clive Marsh ('Rembrandt the Etcher: Mission and commission as factors in the New Testament interpretation', *Biblical Interpretation* 6, no. 3 (1998): 401) postulates that the artistic representations constitute a palpable and visible proof of their existence and make possible the study of their composition and variations throughout the history of biblical transmission.

of the queen such as her ability to govern or her sagacity and courage in the accusation against the viceroy Haman (Est. 7.1-10) are ignored. The Protestant traditions, on the other hand, are not afraid to represent Esther signing the decree of revocation of extermination of the Jews or revealing the iniquity of Mordecai.[16] This has strong implications for the formation of women. In the story of Susannah (Daniel 13), the bath scene is selected more frequently than the protagonist's prayer or her defence in the trial, which shows the passivity of the protagonist.[17] In the farewell of Ruth, Naomi and Orpah, for example, the emphasis on the scene, even illustrating the same verse, can fall on Naomi and Ruth or Orpah. The choice is not irrelevant because the interpretation of the second is usually blameworthy, and so this includes nuances not explicit in the story.[18] In this same line, the multiplicity of versions offered by the artistic representation of each story, where each one of them can be seen as a new interpretation, reflect for the exegete the inherent plurality of the biblical characters and the multiplicity of nuances that they contain. In the representation of Eve, for example, it does not have the same repercussions to represent her as the 'origin of sin' and to do so by choosing the moment of dialogue with the serpent than to portray her as a mother of a family and as a working woman.[19] Both nuances are present in the biblical narrative. With the first example, especially if the figure of Adam is overlooked, the perception of Eve as a sinful woman is emphasized, and with the second, the focus is on a woman who anticipates the figure of Mary and the Church, also blessed and capable of overcoming difficulties.

As a counterpoint to this multiplicity and pluralism within the image, the exegete perceives very early on that artistic studies have prioritized the analysis of great works of art and within them the great heroines and virtuous women – Judith, Esther, Susannah, Mary – or those *femme fatales* whose examples are a paradigm of what a woman should not 'be' – Eve, Mary Magdalene, Jezebel, Job's wife. The abundance of these representations shows that the selection of these main characters follows a pattern or practically uniform structures (although in its manifestation important transformations take place). That uniformity is not always coincident with the plural history of Sacred Scripture. In addition, the student observes how the image sanctions certain types conferring a degree of reality that does not always fit the story, but whose interpretation crosses borders

---

16. Cf. Carmen Yebra-Rovira, 'La figura de Ester: plasmación y transmisión a través del arte', *Reseña Bíblica* 56 (2007): 57.

17. Victor I. Stoichita, 'Susana y los Viejos', in *Las imágenes de la Biblia*, ed. Francisco Calvo Serraller and Jesús María González de Zárate (Madrid: Fundación Amigos del Museo del Prado, 2016), 371–86.

18. Carmen Yebra-Rovira, 'El libro de Rut y su repercusión en el arte: Entre la fidelidad y la traición', *Reseña Bíblica* 71 (2011): 46.

19. For the study of this complex figure, cf. J. Cheryl Exum, 'Notorious biblical women in Manchester: Spencer Stanhope's *Eve* and Frederick Pickersgill's *Delilah*', in *Bible, Art, Gallery*, ed. Martin O'Kane (Sheffield: Sheffield Phoenix Press, 2011), 69–98.

and cultures. This is the case of the representation of Mary Magdalene as a sinner. This widespread iconography, that has no direct connection with any biblical, unconsciously conditions the reading of all those passages associated with this woman.[20] Regaining her identity as a privileged disciple is difficult due to the weight that these representations have in the collective visual memory, among other factors.

In the study of this selection process it is important to highlight how the choice of a scene and its detachment from the entire written source may involve the partial transmission of the theological content of the text or emphasize some concrete value that significantly distorts the general sense of the scene, the parable or the story. The figure of Miriam, the sister of Moses, for example, is diametrically different if you select the moment in which she initiates the canticle of salvation of ch. 15 of the book of Exodus, with which you can see her cultic and leadership functions, or if the moment chosen is the one where she is affected by leprosy (Num. 12.1-2), which has a clear message that the woman is deceitful, insidious and unreliable. The way of representing each scene can suffer such variations that the primary and theological meaning differ substantially from the final value. In this sense, the position of the image is also important: the location where it is placed can provide theological value and additional meaning or, on the contrary, be completely indifferent. The image of Ruth gleaning the fields at the door of a tabernacle in the Catholic sphere invites a Christological rereading of her figure and emphasizes her courage, dedication and universality as well as her role in the history of salvation. Its location in a group of strong women located around Mary alludes primarily to her fecundity, fidelity and obedience.[21]

Denouncing oblivion

The other side of this recovery in the history of biblical women is born when we see that there are figures who have hardly been represented or who, although they have been significant at some point in history, have suffered a gradual process of silencing and exclusion.[22] In other words, as important as making visible the main protagonists of the biblical story is, so too is the process of rescuing the silenced or invisible figures, as well as conferring a greater prominence to secondary female characters. The researcher must investigate the reasons that have led to the silence of the passages in which they appeared and the repercussion that this may have

---

20. For a further development, see the last part of Chapter 2.
21. See Chapter 4.
22. Max Engammare, 'Les Figures de la Bible. Le destin oublié d'un genre littéraire en image (XVIe–XVIIe s.)', *Melánges de l'Ecole française de Rome. Italie et Méditerranée* 106, no. 2 (1994): 566. It emphasizes the modifications that take place for moral reasons in the iconographic programmes of the illustrated holy stories (*Figures de la Bible*). In the series of the sixteenth century, violent images with sexual content disappear. It implies that the daughters of Lot, the wife of Potiphar or the wife of Uriah are silenced.

had (and has) on the social and ecclesial configuration. Examples of this are the silencing of Dinah or the denial of the women that accompanied Jesus with the Apostles. It is also symptomatic, for example, that in the representation of the history of the Canaanite woman, the image never illustrates the moment in which Jesus corrects his disciples (Mt. 15.23-24).

Among the reasons that explain the 'suppression' of characters and narrative sequences, some of the ones that have the most influence are the doctrinal dispositions, such as those emanating from the Council of Trent (1545–63), artistic treatises and religious or civil censorship. All of them are explained by the pedagogical-doctrinal, moral and propagandistic function of the image and by its sacred nature.[23] These images are then used to construct, modify or reaffirm a religious socio-historical reality and therefore 'must be controlled'. At the time of the Counter-Reformation, for example, the creation of images that differentiate Catholicism from the Reformation world was of great importance. The changes in Marian iconography and the elimination of many Old Testament women from the iconographic repertoires bring with them the stereotyping of the secondary role of women, the emphasis of their harmful role in society and the decrease in the importance of their stories. In the case of Esther, while the Protestant world prioritizes domestic, moral and educational elements of Esther, the Catholic world emphasizes the submission, obedience and fragility of the Jewish heroine. With this example, the differences between the Catholic and Protestant canons are also highlighted.

Changes in sensibility in the viewer and society must be equally considered in the analysis of this silencing process. Throughout history, it can easily be seen how an image or an iconographic model stops being used when it loses significance for those who contemplate it. Each period had not only certain aesthetic tastes but also biblical literary preferences. Each society and context require, therefore, some images that are meant to clarify and have a social, moral and aesthetic impact. Today's society, for example, rejects violent biblical texts and with them the stories in which women suffer or exercise violence. This results in the silencing of stories and images associated with the rape of Tamar by Ammon (2 Sam. 13.1-19) and the concubine of the Levite of Ephraim (Judges 19), or the invisibility of the dramatic story of the daughter of Jephthah (Judges 11). These stories were very successful in the nineteenth century in the framework of sociopolitical reconstruction. This sensitivity also implies the rejection of the more traditional iconography of Judith or Jael (Judges 4) and, therefore, of its literary work and its salvific meaning. The suppression of those scenes avoids their interpretation as a denunciation of how that violence continues to be exercised over women today and that it must be eradicated.

A third form of silencing biblical women, in consonance with what was said in the previous section, is provoked by the researchers and their hermeneutical

---

23. Cf. Juan Plazaola, *Razón y sentido del arte cristiano*, Cuadernos de Teología Deusto (Bilbao: Universidad de Deusto, 1998).

prejudices. In the iconographic analysis, certain formats or genres such as drawing, engraving, advertising, embroidery, goldsmithing or porcelain are not observed and studied. They are understood as works of less interest or quality and are often disdained. The works made in these media or with these techniques, and usually classified within the minor arts, have had, however, in many cases, a greater diffusion than large oil paintings or sculptures visible only to patrons, aristocrats or scholars. They, therefore, may have had a significant influence on the reception and transmission of the Bible. Reflection of the most traditional research habits is also the fact that in the analysis of texts and images, the main or best-known characters are prioritized and the secondary ones obviated. It is, however, in them where remains and traces of the role of women in society and their conception within sacred history can be found. A seemingly nondescript example of this is the iconographic cliché of *The Watercarrier* that appears in many of the images of the collection of engravings made by the French artist Gustave Doré to illustrate his Bible (*La Bible de Tours*, 1843) at the end of the nineteenth century. This character, the artist's invention, sneaks into scenes as important as the entrance of Abraham into Canaan, the wedding at Cana or the return of the prodigal son. Her inclusion as a participant or spectator in them not only brings them an element of daily life and reflects a woman's habitual work but also postulates her as a privileged witness of the action, while at the same time serving as a link between stories of the Old and New Testaments, helping to unify visually the story of salvation. The inclusion of Judith's servant in the scenes of the death of Holofernes is another clarifying example of this reality. Studies of narration and images often silence her and cause the group value of the action of the Jewish heroine to be lost. The salvation of her people is not done by the hand of a woman but through the complementarity and collaboration of both women.[24]

Recreating history

In the transition from text to image, in addition to the selection process and the question of the silencing of characters and narrative scenes, there is an amplification or expansion of the story. This is the result of the idiosyncrasy of the process of artistic creation in which the artist starts with a personal appropriation of the text.[25] In fact, some authors emphasize that what the biblical religious artist paints or draws is not the text but his own reading. This highlights the importance of creative action and shows that each new work recreates and, therefore, reinterprets the story. In each one, the narration is rewritten, narrated again, explained and commented on, passing through the filter of the author's

---

24. Andrea M. Sheaffer's work, *Envisioning the Book of Judith: How Art illuminates Minor Characters* (Sheffield: Sheffield Phoenix Press 2014), turns out to be an exception, arguing for the relevance of secondary characters both in the plot and in the ulterior tradition.

25. The following explanation focuses on the active role of the artist. The viewer has a similar role as a receiver of the image. At that moment he 'narrates it again'; he 'rewrites' it.

understanding, his historical, artistic, ecclesial and social contexts, his technical capacities and his own intentionality. The critic calls *visual exegesis* to this process that shows the interaction between the artist and the biblical source or other related sources.[26] From that perspective, he is a new biblical narrator or 'translator' who can introduce novel elements, alien to the story, which produce a *visual expansion* of the story. That is, in each image there may be, and in fact there are, important variations that may reflect and advance the interpretation of the narrative.

This process of visual expansion must be understood from the very nature of artistic creation, which is closely linked to the process of imaginative reading and the transition from verbal language to visual language. In every text, and specifically in the biblical narrative, there are numerous gaps, omissions and silences that the reader and the artist must complete to obtain a comprehensive and comprehensible visual discourse. The narrator does not explain everything; he does not give all the details, only those very few that serve to maintain the plot and create narrative tension. In those gaps or cracks is where, generally, a new interpretation or substantial changes on the previous tradition can take place. Faces, costumes, landscapes, decorations – they are elements that, in most cases, are not described by the biblical author. The artistic creator needs to capture them, and that is where they introduce modifications (almost always contextual to the author) so long they do not come into clear contradiction with tradition or when the memory has not given them a degree of 'reality' that makes their transformation impossible.[27] For example, in a parable, the characters involved can be clearly detailed and individualized. In that case, introducing new ones implies a substantial variation with respect to the source, and the artist may run into the ecclesiastical authority that accuses him or her of deviation. However, if we talk about a collective character – the people – this leads to the placement of different subjects and situations that, in many cases, will be taken from the socio-historical reality of the creator. The specific analysis of these elements provides

---

26. Paolo Berdini, *The Religious Art of Jacopo Bassano: Painting as Visual Exegesis* (Cambridge: Cambridge University Press, 1997); Martin O'Kane, 'The artist as reader of the Bible. Visual exegesis and the adoration of the Magi', *Biblical Interpretation* 13, no. 4 (2005): 337–73.

27. The importance of collective visual memory in reading the Bible has not been sufficiently taken into account in the analysis of the stories. Very recently, in a class, with a group of students, when proposing a reflection on Marian iconography, a student, when viewing the painting by Robert Campin, *The Annunciation* (1418–19, Museo del Prado), in which Mary is reading, said that this painting was pure invention because Mary did not know how to read and, therefore, did not serve as a real model. A companion responded sharply that we also did not know what Mary's gestures were when she prayed and yet we did give 'credit' to the *Immaculate* images in Murillo's style looking at the sky with their hands clasped on their chests that were used as a model of prayer and an object of devotion but that they transmitted a submissive and silent model of a woman.

important information about the reception and contextualization of the story in its time and environment.

A reading from a gender perspective invites to analyse in detail all those elements and to study the works of art by discussing the function, image, location and attitudes of women. Keeping in mind this perspective, it is not strange to find how the preaching of the prophets or of Jesus is in many cases directed exclusively to men. The analysis of the presence or absence of women in these scenes is a denunciation of how the preaching and its recipients are understood. This has had clear consequences in regards to leadership and ecclesial organization because, according to these images, the woman is 'not' a follower, is not taught by Jesus and does not need to be formed. The images reinforce their domestic and maternal function.

In this same line, the image constitutes a clear model for teaching (or reproach) the moral and social behaviour of women and reinforces patriarchal values that are not always in line with the liberating nature of the stories. In the analysis of the female image, and closely related to this process of visual expansion, it is necessary to pay special attention to the location, the gestures and the clothing with which the biblical women are represented. Regarding the former, the position, size and manner of placing themselves in front of the men are a clear reflection of what stereotypes are to be transmitted for women, what their real role is in the society to which they belong and what their accepted moral behaviour is. Regarding gestures – a clear reflection of feminine virtues and of modesty – it is relevant to analyse how they transmit and/or reinforce gender stereotypes. For example, through the position of the gaze it is possible to show how the virtuous woman should be. A biblical woman will not look directly at the viewer or at her interlocutor but at the ground or at the sky. The self-absorption and the low gaze are characteristics associated with feminine biblical iconography that aim to reinforce the values of submission, modesty, obedience, candour and silence. Regarding clothing, jewellery, ornaments – these determine how a woman should be by following the image of the biblical protagonists. The use of the nude or broad necklines is a form of complaint of unworthy behaviour, a way to blame the woman for the actions of men, or a reflection that seduction has been the weapon used to beat a male – the case, for example, of Jael – emphasizing the danger that females posed.[28]

Another important element is to perceive if the woman, the protagonist of a scene, is really an active subject or a passive subject, someone placed to be looked at.[29] The most outstanding example of this transformation is the figure of Susannah. The iconography betrays the story by making it an object to be observed when it

---

28. Colleen M. Conway, *Sex and Slaughter in the Tent of Jael: A Cultural History of a Biblical Story* (New York: Oxford University Press, 2017).

29. María Jesús Godoy Domínguez, 'Educar la mirada. Propuesta pedagógica del Arte para la igualdad entre géneros', in *Miradas desde la perspectiva de género: Estudios de las mujeres*, ed. Isabel de Torres Ramírez (Madrid: Narcea, 2005), 135–52.

focuses on a nudity that is not mentioned in the story of Daniel 13.[30] By doing that, the viewer becomes one more of the elders.

Learning from images

The enrichment that the biblical scholar gets from working with images goes beyond the reflection on the three presented processes: selection, silencing and expansion. These show how the text is read and interpreted by artists and spectators and point out key elements for biblical interpretation. However, the image reveals to the exegete other elements and values that make it an inestimable teacher and discoverer of the richness of biblical stories and salvific history.

The artistic representation helps to reveal or remind the biblical scholar of parallel texts, relationships between different narratives of Scripture and connected experiences that are more evident from a visual language than from the textual one. There are paintings and drawings whose theme, figuration, structure or artistic resources allow for a visual relationship with other images or similar passages. That is, an image comes out of itself to suggest another, although they are not always literary parallels or have similar meanings. Between the representation of Judith and her servant beheading Holofernes and Delilah and the acolyte cutting Samson's hair, there is a clear parallelism created by the inclusion of an extra-biblical character in the second case – the result of a modification of the story – and the representation of the secondary character in the first. Both scenes represent how the action of two women ends with the dominant male. In the first case, this is done with salvific consequences and in the second case with destructive implications. Another example is the artistic parallel that exists between some engravings that illustrate the lament of Rizpah before the corpses of her children (2 Sam. 21.10-12) and that of Mary at the foot of the cross of Jesus. These two stories of women mourning the death of a child are also associated with the stories of the martyrs of the Maccabees and the martyrdom of the seven children of Felicitas, a Roman matron and model in early Christianity. The rich patristic tradition that had already related these four passages comes to light now, quickly, thanks to these images.

Artistic resources also contribute to discover parallels between seemingly distant stories. This can be seen from the difficulty generated by the identification of some works of art when the iconographer asks: is it about Boaz and Naomi, Tobias and Sarah, Jacob and Rachel, Judah and Tamar, Isaac and Rebecca?[31]

30. Bornay, *Mujeres de la Biblia en la pintura del Barroco*, 125–49; Babette Bohn, 'Rape and the gendered gaze: Susanna and the elders in early modern Bologna', *Biblical Interpretation* 9, no. 3 (2001): 259–86; Demetria Ruiz López, 'La historia de Susana y los viejos a través de la pintura', in *Actas Congreso Internacional 'Biblia, memoria histórica y encrucijada de culturas'*, ed. J. Campos Santiago and V. Pastor Julián (Salamanca: Asociación Bíblica Española, 2004), 694–703; Stoichita, 'Susana y los Viejos'.

31. Svetlana Alpers, *Rembrandt's Enterprise: the Studio and the Market* (Chicago: University of Chicago Press, 1990), 6–8.

In the relationship between text and image and in the analysis of that process of visual exegesis, modern research has begun to highlight the valuable contribution done by the artists, which previous studies had disregarded. This is the function of illuminating or revealing elements or values that had gone unnoticed by the exegesis.[32] The artist appears as a true exegete who discovers and shapes aspects that are in the story, usually associated with feelings, but that are not as relevant from literary techniques as from their translation into the image. In the case of the aggression to Susannah, for example, the expression of fear shows her condition of victim, in perfect consonance with her history and contradicting all those portraits that made of her a woman to be gazed upon.[33]

Each image also contributes to perceive the use and importance of the different versions and traditions of the Bible and related texts, thus constituting an instrument of textual criticism. The use of the apocryphal gospels – both the Old and the New Testaments – and other literary sources is extensively reflected in the iconography.[34] The figures of the midwives of Bethlehem that help Mary in the birth, of Anne – the mother of Mary – or of the procuress in the scene of Samson and Delilah reflect the capacity of survival of those characters and how the canonicity or not of the texts is irrelevant in the process of construction, transmission and fixation of the image.

In clear connection with the aforementioned process of selection and silencing, the iconographic study presents to the exegete and to the current spectator little-known passages that nowadays are not fashionable – often by changes in sensitivity – and minor characters that have been less drawn, but which have survived as the woman with the flow of blood (Mk 5.24-34) or the midwives of the Exodus, Puah and Shiphrah (Exod. 1.15-21), showing their active participation in the survival of the people of Israel.

---

32. J. Cheryl Exum, 'Lovis Corinth's blinded Samson', *Biblical Interpretation* 6, no. 3 (1998): 410–25.

33. Mayayo, *Historias de mujeres, historias del arte*, 32–33, points out how in the work of Artemisa Gentilleschi, *Susannah and the Elders* (1610, Schloss Weissenstein, Pommersfelden),

> the young woman is no longer represented as an available and even complacent woman, but as an anguished young woman whose vulnerability is reinforced by the strange contortion of her figure. The expressive intensity of her face and the gesture of horror with which she rejects the advances of the elders convey the sensation of 'anxiety, terror and shame experienced by a victim forced to choose between rape or public derision.'

34. Joaquín Yarza Luaces, 'La Ilustración del Antiguo Testamento en la última Edad Media española', in *V Simposio Bíblico Español. La Biblia en el arte y en la literatura. II. Arte*, ed. José J. Azanza, Vicente Balaguer and Vicente Collado (Valencia – Pamplona: Fundación Bíblica Española – Universidad de Navarra, 1999), 31–80. He analyses the different iconographic variants and the traditions of the main Spanish illuminated Bibles.

Conclusions and open questions

The biblical image, regardless of the support or style, has multiple functions, which are not always conscious. Of all of them, the primary function is the religious one because a religious image transmits a set of contents related to God and to the history of salvation. Therefore, it is used from the origins of the Church with a pedagogical and anamnestic perspective, providing moral and doctrinal interpretations. An image translates, then, what the appropriate moral behaviour is even if it corresponds with the context of its creator and not with the biblical story. The sacred character that has been consciously or unconsciously attributed to the biblical image, and its degree of realism or verism, have conditioned the repercussion that these compositions have had on social and ecclesial constructions. The religious image is understood as a faithful reflection of what the sacred text affirms and therefore is left out of almost any criticism. However, as it has been shown in the development of this study, the image, as a specific form of discourse, is not irrelevant. Each one communicates a set of contents and emphasizes elements that must be critically analysed. The questions about what is illustrated, how it is done, what values it contributes, what elements it silences are enormously relevant. The selection of the passages responds to a concrete intentionality and has consequences for the spectator. The detailed analysis of the transformations, innovations, ellipses with respect to the original story or some narration derived from it leads to a better understanding of the uses and reading modes of the Bible and to analyse what their use and intentionality have been throughout history.

The encounter with images allows the scholar to appreciate how the representations can condition the reading modes of the stories or how they have contributed to configure the role and perception of the female biblical characters throughout history. Advances in artistic and biblical studies from a gender perspective lead to the questioning of an image to see not only if its representation is adjusted to the content of the text but also what the female model is that is being presented, her characteristics, virtues and attitudes, the elements of idealization or the denunciation of stereotypes. Behind any representation underlies a set of values that are not always in consonance with the biblical stories. The form of representation of a biblical woman or of her community of reference has an enormous repercussion in the face of the understanding of the revelation and the ecclesial construction. Each one reflects how the texts are read and understood at a certain moment, but it is also an example of how salvation, the church and the function of the woman are understood.

The study of images from a critical perspective prevents their ability to reinforce values and stereotypes that are often contrary to the liberating and humanizing message of the Christian word. Its repetition and uncritical pastoral use conditions the perception of the characters and their possibilities. The understanding of the figure of Mary is strongly determined in Spain by the abundance of the Immaculate Conception images created in the Baroque style. Through them, the mother of Jesus is sublimated and separated, and her purity, obedience, silence or ability to pray is emphasized. This representation removes the conception of an active, determined, courageous woman, educated in the Jewish tradition and committed to the project of Jesus which is present in the texts, or of a cultured woman, knowledgeable of the Law and a reader, a vision of Mary that was transmitted in the Renaissance.[35] Baroque iconography not only conditioned the way of being and being in the Church for women and society in the sixteenth, seventeenth and eighteenth centuries but also continues even today. Each image is formed by a set of signifiers, values, and intentions that do not always have to do with the biblical text but that are involuntarily associated with it, conditioning the way of reading it, understanding it and its transmission.

The image, even when it is not easy for the current spectator to identify it, is offered as a witness of situations unworthy of women and humanity that must be corrected or modified. Violent images, like their stories, are forms of denunciation that, presenting aberrations of the past, invite reflection on the performance in the present and on the evolution in the expansion of human rights.

The whole of the artistic tradition invites the reflection of the canon from a gender perspective. The analysis of books, scenes and characters and their way of expression invites us to ask ourselves if the artist has considered women as spectators and as recipients of his work. It is indisputable that the collections and works directed in a particular way to them consciously transmit a set of values that are not neutral, valued and represented in the same way as their masculine parallels. A pending task is the study of a specific biblical iconographic canon proposed for women, bearing in mind that they have been precisely responsible for transmitting the contents of sacred history. We would have to ask her if she reads and tells different stories for women and men, and what values she emphasizes in each one of them.

Bibliography

Alpers, Svetlana. *Rembrandt's Enterprise: the Studio and the Market*. Chicago: University of Chicago Press, 1990.

Berdini, Paolo. *The Religious Art of Jacopo Bassano: Painting as Visual Exegesis*. Cambridge: Cambridge University Press, 1997.

Bernárdez, Asunción. 'Pintando la lectura: mujeres, libros y representación en el siglo de Oro'. *Edad de Oro* 26 (2007): 67–89.

Bohn, Babette. 'Rape and the gendered gaze: Susanna and the elders in early modern Bologna'. *Biblical Interpretation* 9, no. 3 (2001): 259–86.

---

35. The transformations in the iconography of Mary from a woman reading to an Immaculate inert one can be seen in: Joaquín Yarza Luaces, 'La santa que lee', in *Luchas de género en la historia a través de la imagen*, ed. Teresa Sauret Guerrero and Amparo Quiles Faz (Málaga: Servicio de Publicaciones Centro de Ediciones de la Diputación Provincial de Málaga, 2001), 421–65; Asunción Bernárdez, 'Pintando la lectura: mujeres, libros y representación en el siglo de Oro', *Edad de Oro* 26 (2007): 67–89.

Bornay, Erika. *Mujeres de la Biblia en la pintura del Barroco: imágenes de la ambigüedad*, Ensayos Arte Cátedra. Madrid: Cátedra, 1998.
Bullard, J. M. 'Music, the Bible and', in *Dictionary of Biblical Interpretation*, edited by John H. Hayes, 172–87. Nashville: Abingdon, 1999.
Camacho Martínez, Rosario, and Aurora Miró. *Iconografía y creación artística: estudios sobre la identidad femenina desde las relaciones de poder*. Málaga: Diputación de Málaga (CEDMA), 2001.
Deepwell, Katy. *Nueva crítica feminista de arte: estrategias críticas*, Feminismos. Madrid: Cátedra, 1998.
Engammare, Max. 'Les Figures de la Bible: Le destin oublié d'un genre littéraire en image (XVIe–XVIIe s.)'. *Melánges de l'Ecole française de Rome. Italie et Méditerranée* 106, no. 2 (1994): 549–91.
England, Emma, and William John Lyons, eds. *Reception History and Biblical Studies*. LHBOTS 615-STr 6. London: Bloomsbury T&T Clark, 2018.
Estévez López, Mª. Elisa. 'La Escritura en el centro de la evangelización', in *Biblia y nueva evangelización*, edited by Gabino Uríbarri Bilbao, Biblioteca de Teología Comillas 12 109–58. Madrid: Universidad Pontificia Comillas – DDB, 2005.
Exum, J. Cheryl. 'Beyond the biblical horizon: The Bible and the arts'. *Biblical Interpretation* 6, no. 3 (1998): 259–65.
Exum, J. Cheryl, ed. *Biblical Studies/Cultural Studies: The Third Sheffield Colloquium*. JSOT Supplement Series 226. Sheffield: Sheffield Academic Press, 1998.
Exum, J. Cheryl. 'Lovis Corinth's blinded Samson'. *Biblical Interpretation* 6, no 3 (1998): 410–25.
Exum, J. Cheryl. 'Notorious biblical women in Manchester: Spencer Stanhope's *Eve* and Frederick Pickersgill's *Delilah*', in *Bible, Art, Gallery*, edited by Martin O'Kane, 69–98. Sheffield: Sheffield Phoenix Press, 2011.
Exum, J. Cheryl. *Plotted, Shot, and Painted: Cultural Representations of Biblical Women*, JSOT Supplement Series 215. Sheffield: Sheffield Academic Press, 1996.
Exum, J. Cheryl, and Stephen D. Moore. 'Biblical studies/cultural studies', in *Biblical Studies/Cultural Studies: The Third Sheffield Colloquium*, edited by J. Cheryl Exum, 19–45, JSOT Supplement Series 226. Sheffield: Sheffield Academic Press, 1998.
Giebelhausen, Michaela. *Painting the Bible: Representation and Belief in Mid-Victorian Britain*. Aldershot: Ashgate, 2006.
Godoy Domínguez, María Jesús. 'Educar la mirada: Propuesta pedagógica del Arte para la igualdad entre géneros', in *Miradas desde la perspectiva de género: Estudios de las mujeres*, edited by Isabel de Torres Ramírez, 135–52. Madrid: Narcea, 2005.
Godoy Domínguez, María Jesús. *La mujer en el arte: una contralectura de la modernidad*. Granada: Universidad de Granada, 2007.
Hidalgo Rodríguez, David, Noemí Cubas Martín and María Esther Martínez Quinteiro, eds. *Mujeres en la historia, el arte y el cine: discursos de género, variantes de contenidos y soportes: de la palabra al audiovisual*, Aquilafuente. Salamanca: Ediciones Universidad de Salamanca, 2011.
Letellier, Robert Ignatius. *The Bible in Music*. Newcastle: Cambridge Scholars, 2017.
Lobo F. Cao, Marián, ed. *Geografías de la mirada: género, creación artística y representación*, Instituto de Investigaciones Feministas. Madrid: Universidad Complutense – Asociación Cultural Al-Mudayna, 2001.
López Fernández, María. *La imagen de la mujer en la pintura española, 1890-1914*. Madrid: A. Machado Libros, 2006.

Marsh, Clive. 'Rembrandt the Etcher: Mission and commission as factors in the New Testament interpretation'. *Biblical Interpretation* 6, no. 3 (1998): 381–409.

Mayayo, Patricia. *Historias de mujeres, historias del arte*, Ensayos Arte Catedra. Madrid: Cátedra, 2003.

O'Kane, Martin. 'The artist as reader of the Bible: Visual exegesis and the adoration of the Magi'. *Biblical Interpretation* 13, no. 4 (2005): 337–73.

O'Kane, Martin, ed. *Bible, Art, Gallery*, The Bible in the Modern World 21. Sheffield: Sheffield Phoenix Press, 2011.

O'Kane, Martin. 'The biblical King David and his artistic and literary afterlives'. *Biblical Interpretation* 6, no. 3 (1998): 313–47.

O'Kane, Martin. *Painting the Text: The Artist as Biblical Interpreter*, The Bible in the Modern World 8. Sheffield: Sheffield Phoenix Press, 2007.

Plazaola, Juan. *Razón y sentido del arte cristiano*, Cuadernos de Teología Deusto. Bilbao: Universidad de Deusto, 1998.

Pollock, Griselda. *Generations and Geographies in the Visual Arts: Feminist Readings*. London: Routledge, 1996.

Réau, Louis. *Iconografía del arte cristiano: Iconografía de la Biblia. Antiguo Testamento*. Translated by Daniel Alcoba. Barcelona: Ediciones del Serbal, 2007.

Ruiz López, Demetria. 'La historia de Susana y los viejos a través de la pintura', in *Actas Congreso Internacional 'Biblia, memoria histórica y encrucijada de culturas'*, edited by Jesús Campos Santiago and Victor Pastor Julián, 694–703. Salamanca: Asociación Bíblica Española, 2004.

Sheaffer, Andrea M. *Envisioning the Book of Judith: How Art illuminates Minor Characters*. Sheffield: Sheffield Phoenix Press, 2014.

Sölle, Dorothee, Joe H. Kirchberger and Anne-Marie Schnieper. *Great Women of the Bible in Art and Literature*. Minneapolis: Fortress Press, 2006.

Stoichita, Victor I. 'Susana y los Viejos', in *Las imágenes de la Biblia*, edited by Francisco Calvo Serraller and Jesús María González de Zárate, 371–86. Madrid: Fundación Amigos del Museo del Prado, 2016.

Vega, Jesusa. *Pasado y tradición. La construcción visual del imaginario español en el siglo XIX*. Madrid: Ediciones Polifemo, 2016.

Yarza Luaces, Joaquín. 'La Ilustración del Antiguo Testamento en la última Edad Media española', in *V Simposio Bíblico Español. La Biblia en el arte y en la literatura. II. Arte*, edited by José J. Azanza, Vicente Balaguer and Vicente Collado, 31–80. Valencia – Pamplona: Fundación Bíblica Española – Universidad de Navarra, 1999.

Yarza Luaces, Joaquín. 'La santa que lee', in *Luchas de género en la historia a través de la imagen*, edited by Teresa Sauret Guerrero and Amparo Quiles Faz, 421–65. Málaga: Servicio de Publicaciones Centro de Ediciones de la Diputación Provincial de Málaga, 2001.

Yebra-Rovira, Carmen. 'El libro de Rut y su repercusión en el arte: Entre la fidelidad y la traición'. *Reseña Bíblica* 71 (2011): 41–51.

Yebra-Rovira, Carmen. 'La figura de Ester: plasmación y transmisión a través del arte'. *Reseña Bíblica* 56 (2007): 53–60.

Chapter 2

THE ICONOGRAPHIC REPRESENTATION OF THE BIBLE: THE INTERACTION BETWEEN TEXT AND IMAGE

Guadalupe Seijas

In this chapter I will present some considerations about biblical iconography and the close relationship that exists between the text and the image that is reproduced from it. For this I have divided this chapter into three sections. The first is centred on the text, that is, the text that inspires the image and how it has been understood and disseminated. The second deals with its representation and how it affected the transmission of the biblical message. In the third section, I will analyse the iconography of Mary Magdalene's character and the evolution she experienced both in the sources and in her representation. To conclude, I will make some final considerations.[1]

The biblical text and its message

To begin with, it is necessary to reflect on how the biblical stories have been accessed. Throughout many periods, the common people could not read the Bible directly. The books were expensive and were only available to the most affluent of people or were kept in centres of knowledge such as monasteries and universities. Also, illiteracy was widespread, so access to written knowledge was very restricted.

The Bible was often accessed through sermons, *Via Crucis* and catechesis within the framework of the liturgy.[2] In the Middle Ages, a literature was developed for use in the dominical service and for the prayers of the monks in monasteries

---

1. The preparation of this work has been possible thanks to the financing of the Ministry of Economy and Competitiveness of the Government of Spain (R+D Projects: *Reception and Transmission of the Bible: Texts and Iconography* FFI2015-65610-P).

2. The religious dramas of medieval theatre must also be included as a source of transmission of the biblical stories.

(Evangeliaries, Lectionaries of Gospels,[3] Psalters, etc.), which included a selection of biblical passages, with a predominance of episodes from the New Testament. Some medieval Bibles omitted the Gospels and the Psalter. This striking fact – since the New Testament was the most important part of the Scriptures and the Psalms were very much used in prayer – may have been due to the fact that these Bibles were seen as complementary texts to the liturgical manuscripts and they were all kept together near the altar or in the sacristy.[4] In addition, the liturgical dramas that were represented in the churches and streets during the Holy Week revealed the last moments of the life of Jesus Christ.[5]

Likewise, the question of exegesis is essential, that is, how the Bible has been read and interpreted in each period. Theological concerns as well as political and religious problems had a decisive influence on its understanding. The exegetical production is very abundant: the commentaries of the Fathers of the Church and of medieval authors like Alcuin of York, Rabanus Maurus and Nichola de Lyra, as well as compendiums like the *Glossa Ordinaria* and the *Historia Scholastica* of Petrus Comestor are just a few of the best known, but there are many others.[6] At the same time, we must also mention a religious literature oriented to the dissemination of the biblical message and devotion which appeared in medieval legends, catechisms, sacred stories, breviaries and Books of Hours among other works.[7]

Although this parallel literature had its own specific characteristics in each time period, it had a great impact on the understanding of the biblical story by stressing certain ethical aspects of the protagonists, selecting the most significant stories and, as a consequence, silencing other parts which led to a complete ignorance later on of some episodes, and by focusing attention on specific theological issues. Not all the characters or the passages that appear in the Bible have always received the same attention. Episodes in which a 'weak being' is chosen by God to overcome a very superior enemy, such as David's victory over the giant Goliath (1 Samuel 17) or Judith's victory in front of the powerful enemy Holofernes (Judith

---

3. They only contain the passages of the Gospel that are used in the liturgy in chronological order.

4. Christopher De Hamel, *The Book: A History of the Bible* (London: Phaidon, 2001), 75. The author makes a diachronic study of the Bible as a book.

5. On the relationship between Bible and theatre in the Counter-Reformation, see Maria Laura Giordano and Adriana Valerio (eds), *Reformas y Contrarreformas en la Europa católica (siglos XV–XVII)*, La Biblia y las mujeres 16 (Estella: Verbo Divino, 2016). The English version will be published soon by SBL Press.

6. For an overview on the interpretation of the Bible in history see Karen Armstrong, *The Bible: A Biography* (New York: Grove Press, 2008).

7. An example of how the study of written sources is crucial to understanding the composition of iconographic cycles can be seen in Frederic Chordá, 'Dios renovador del universo en el ábside de Sant Climent de Taull', *RACBASJ* 25 (2011): 15–38, where the author explains the programme of the apse using biblical, patristic and liturgical sources.

13), acquired special relevance in the context of the Republic of Florence during the Renaissance, when the city faced much more powerful enemies.[8] The account of the liberation of serfs in Egypt (Exodus 1–15) permeated the rhetoric of English emigrants who, aboard the Mayflower, settled on the coasts of Massachusetts in 1620, as well as the fight against slavery and against racial segregation. And we could also cite the rejection by contemporary readers of the violent passages of the Bible, for example, those of the book of Judges.

In this chapter, I will dwell on some key moments of biblical exegesis: The Middle Ages, the Reformation and the Counter-Reformation, and literature for a female audience.

Medieval exegesis of the Bible

To illustrate medieval biblical exegesis, I will describe some examples in which the relationship between image and text is very significant and close because both elements appear together in the folios of manuscripts: Moralized Bibles, *Biblia Pauperum* and *Speculum Humanae Salvationis* ('The Mirror of Human Salvation').

The Moralized Bibles are luxurious codices that appeared with great force in Paris at the beginning of the thirteenth century, in which the image plays a primordial role. Each page contains eight illustrations, either inside a medallion or in a square format, and eight texts arranged in a characteristic and exclusive compositional scheme of these Bibles. The biblical passage (in Latin or in French) does not reproduce the text literally but summarizes it, and it is accompanied by a brief commentary (moralization) that aims to show its contemporaries the historical significance and moralizing character of these biblical episodes. Each of the texts is accompanied by a miniature, so in each folio there are four images that represent the biblical text and many others that allude to the moralization (Figure 2.1).

Folio 94r of the *Bible of Saint Louis* (1226-34, Archives of the Cathedral of Toledo, vol. I) corresponds to Ruth 1.3-14.[9] The first scene corresponds to the death of Elimelech and represents, through a very frequent compositional scheme, the lament of Naomi and her two children before his corpse. Below, the moralization presents Christ carrying the cross. In the commentary, the meaning of the name of the deceased is interpreted as 'my God',[10] that is, Christ, who was obedient to die for us. The second scene corresponds to the marriage of the sons of

---

8. The interest that this episode provokes is seen in the sculptures of David by Donatello, Verrochio and Michelangelo, and of Judith by Donatello.

9. The facsimile edition was published by M. Moleiro Editor (Barcelona, 2000-2). The book of Ruth in the Moralized Bibles has been studied by John Lowden in *The Making of the Bibles Moralisées II: The Book of Ruth* (University Park: Penn State University Press, 2000), a reference work in which he analyses in detail the texts and images of seven of them. The scenes commented here correspond to chapters 3–6 of this work.

10. Although according to the Hebrew etymology it must be 'my God is king'.

Figure 2.1 *Bible of Saint Louis*, Toledo, *c.* 1226, vol. 1, fol. 94r.
Source: M. Moleiro Editor (www.moleiro.com).

Elimelech and Naomi with Moabite women, and for this the image of the *pallium* is used on the heads of the contracting parties.[11] The commentary presents the apostles, with their heads in the middle, and two different groups on both sides, Gentiles and Jews. That is, two peoples united by faith through the preaching of the apostles. The third scene describes the death of the two sons and the three widows lamenting before the bodies of the men, with a compositional scheme

---

11. Under which the contracting parties received the nuptial blessing, which reflects the medieval custom.

like that of the first scene with which, given the proximity, the reader establishes a clear visual parallelism. The vignette with the moralization presents two episodes of martyrdom. To the right, a man prays while behind his back the executioner raises his sword high. On the left, another apostle is thrown from a chair while holding an open book. The other executioner lifts a long cane. The innocent souls of the two martyrs are raised to heaven by the angels in the space between the two weapons. The scene reflects the death of the apostles who, after preaching, and having fulfilled the Ten Commandments, left this world and were lifted to the celestial kingdom. In this case, the visual connection between the text and moralization is not clearly perceived, a connection that is much more evident in the horizontal register between the death of Christ and the martyrdom of the apostles. The fourth and last scene on the folio corresponds to the moment when Naomi says goodbye to Orpah and continues her journey with Ruth.[12] At the centre of the moralization, a kind of fountain, like a baptismal font, welcomes two adults who are baptized by a priest. To the left and in the opposite direction, a man carries a bag of money in one hand while in the other he holds a golden disk. The allusion to usury and the elongated hood with which the head is covered point to a possible identification with the Jews. To the right and in the opposite direction, a monk holds a book in his hands as a sign of preaching or teaching. Both figures represent two different attitudes: those who after receiving baptism return to their gods (Orpah) and those who persevere maintaining their chaste body and a pure heart (Ruth).

The visual exegesis is adapted to the time, as can be perceived by the costumes of men and women alike, the tonsure and habits of the friars, the conical hats and the money bags of the Jews. The miniatures present the biblical story and its interpretation in a medieval context, showing elements and problems typical of the society of that time, so that the meaning of the illustrations was very significant and evident to the reader.

In the Late Middle Ages, typological interpretation[13] was widely used. According to typology, the events of the life of Christ had already been anticipated or prefigured in passages of the Old Testament. This type of interpretation was conditioned from the beginning by the idea that Jesus was the expected Messiah and, therefore, Christianity was the true religion and not Judaism.[14] The visual representation of this type of exegesis had its maximum expression in the fourteenth

12. The image is somewhat equivocal. At first glance, the two figures that embrace each other seem like Naomi and Ruth. However, the city gates to the left indicate the return of Orpah to Moab, while Ruth continues the trip to Bethlehem. The first interpretation fits better with the sense of the moralization. The close union between Naomi and Ruth would have as a parallel the behaviour of those who remain faithful to the grace received after baptism. Cf. Lowden, *The Making of the Bibles Moralisées II*, 86–7. Further development of this scene can be seen in Chapter 7.

13. This type of interpretation was used until the Council of Trent.

14. The understanding and the role that the Jewish Scriptures had in Christianity was complicated from the beginning. Already in the second century, Marcion understood

century with the *Biblia Pauperum* and the *Speculum Humanae Salvationis*, works that had a great diffusion, as shown by the high number of preserved manuscripts.

The *Biblia Pauperum* is not a Bible per se, but it presupposes a remarkable knowledge of the Sacred Text.[15] The *Biblia Pauperum* formed an iconographic tradition where, unlike the illustrated Bibles, in which the images were subordinated to the text, the illustrations were the central focus that concentrated the attention of the reader by relegating the word to a secondary role. The visual disposition of the images contributed to reflect, memorize and understand the selected biblical passages. They collected scenes from the life of Christ and the Virgin Mary[16] together with passages from the Old Testament that established a clear relation of anticipation or 'prefiguration'. Each scene presents the same compositional scheme, complex and elaborated.[17] The passage from the New Testament is located at the centre and around it there are four figures from the Old Testament, which are usually King David[18] and three prophets; each one of these figures have a phylactery or a balloon where quotes related to the central theme are inserted.

We will use as an example the episode of the Flight into Egypt of Joseph, Mary and Jesus, after fleeing from Herod's persecution (Mt. 2.13-16) (Figure 2.2). The description corresponds to folio 4r of a fourteenth-century *Biblia Pauperum* (Kings MS 519, British Library, London). This scene is on the centre of the folio. On the left, Rebecca sends her son to her brother Laban's house to escape the wrath of Esau, who has usurped his birthright (Genesis 27); and to the right, Michal helps David out the window, when he is persecuted by Saul (1 Sam. 19.11-12). In the three episodes there is an element of flight where Jesus is placed in relationship with Jacob and David, while establishing the association between Herod, Esau and Saul as the persecutors. In addition, in each scene there is a female character who is responsible for their salvation: Mary, Rebecca and Michal.

Surrounding the scene of the New Testament are the Old Testament prophets with Hosea and Isaiah occupying the upper part and in the lower part the prophets

---

that the God of the Old Testament, the God of law and justice, was incompatible with the merciful and redeeming God of the New Testament and, therefore, held that the Old Testament should not be accepted by Christians. In addition, some medieval heresies, like that of the Cathars, manifested their rejection of the Old Testament, denying its veracity.

15. De Hamel, *A History of the Bible*, 159.

16. The scenes correspond to the Annunciation, the infancy and public life of Jesus, the Passion, the Resurrection, the Ascension, Pentecost, the Coronation of the Virgin and the Final Judgment.

17. To identify the compositional scheme of each folio, I refer to Santiago Sebastián López, *Iconografía medieval* (San Sebastián: ETOR, 1988), 110–24, and to the website *The Internet Biblia Pauperum – Amasis* in http://amasis.com/biblia/ (accessed 17 January 2022).

18. The quote from David comes from the Psalter, given the ancient tradition attributed to him by the authorship of this collection of religious poems.

2. Iconographic Representation of the Bible

Figure 2.2 *Rebecca, The Flight into Egypt and Michal, Biblia Pauperum,* la Haya, c. 1405, London, @The British Library Board, Kings Ms. 5, fol. 4r.

Jeremiah and David. The inserted quotes (Hos. 5.6, Isa. 19.1, Jer. 12.7 and Ps. 54.8) are relevant in relation to the issue of flight.

Another typological work, although in this case with the text having more prominence than in the *Biblia Pauperum*, is the *Speculum Humanae Salvationis*. The *Speculum Humanae Salvationis* was aimed at achieving the salvation of man after original sin by means of the teachings of Christ and the Virgin Mary. Therefore, it had a didactic and edifying function. It also adopted its own compositional arrangement that occupied the verse of one folio and the recto of the next. Four scenes were represented, the first of which corresponded to an episode of the New Testament or images associated with the Virgin followed by three scenes of the Old Testament arranged one next to the other. Often the same iconographic schemes of the *Biblia Pauperum* are repeated. The Annunciation is related to the episodes of Moses and the burning bush (Exodus 3), Gideon before the fleece (Judg. 6.36-40) and Rebecca with Eliezer (Gen. 24.16-20).[19] The first two Old Testament accounts correspond to different theophanies, where God manifests himself to the human being in parallel with the presence of the archangel to Mary. In the third, Rebecca offers to give a drink to the servant and his camels, thirsty after a long trip. Rebecca's disposition is an anticipation of the attitude of Mary, who is willing to accept the proposal of the archangel to be the mother of Jesus. So, the presence of the divinity, the reception of the message and the disposition and offering towards this message go through the composition textually and visually.

---

19. We follow fols 12v–13r from a manuscript of the first half of the fourteenth century in a facsimile edition, O: *Speculum humanae salvationis: Codex cremifanensis 243 del monasterio benedictino de Kremsmünster* (Madrid: Casariego, 1998).

The Protestant Reformation and the Counter-Reformation

Another decisive moment in the history of reading and interpretation of the Bible was the sixteenth century. Luther, the greatest exponent of a broad reform programme, insisted on the need for the Church and theology to return to the Gospel of Jesus. Therefore, the Scripture acquired a prominent role (*sola Scriptura*). Protestants and Catholics held a very different position from this moment on. The Reformation emphasized the need for each believer to read the Bible directly and make his/her own interpretation, for which a strong impulse was given to vernacular translations. Taking advantage of a period of imprisonment in the castle of Watburg (Eisenach, Germany), Luther translated the New Testament, which was printed in 1522. In 1534, the translation of the complete Bible into German was published, a task he carried out together with other collaborators. Until the end of his life he worked tirelessly to clarify and improve his translation because he wanted the linguistic register used to be close to the speech of his contemporaries. His work exerted a great influence on the development of the German language and subsequent literature.[20]

The Bible was considered a literary work and, therefore, its interpretation had to be based on philology to understand the literal meaning of the biblical text. This positioning supposed the relinquishing of the allegorical and/or spiritual readings. On the other hand, the Catholic reaction, the Counter-Reformation, chose to emphasize the role of tradition in the face of the text and prohibited the direct reading of the Bible, restricting it to a minority of learned and pious men. This prohibition was in force until 1757 when Benedict XIV authorized its reading and translation into the vernacular languages. The Bible could not be read freely but had to be understood according to the hierarchical interpretation. For this reason, from the Council of Trent (1545–63), Scripture was accessed indirectly through sermons, catechesis and worship. In book format we find some passages included in devotional books, biblical quotations in missals and breviaries and lives of saints destined to promote religious fervour and piety. On the other hand, the Counter-Reformation promoted the visual element, seeing in the images a means to instruct and promote virtue through the senses and established a normative on the matter.

From the seventeenth century, we can speak of a double orientation in biblical hermeneutics, the 'devotional' and the 'romantic':

> He first studies the Bible as one more book from the ancient world in a purely historical perspective (in the manner of Wrede), as 'decontextualized' as possible from the presuppositions of the interpreter and completely removed from any application or 'actualization' through a biblical theology for the present day. Devotional and romantic hermeneutics cannot conceive, instead, a

---

20. The *King James Bible* published in 1611 came later and it exercised a similar influence in the field of English language and literature.

decontextualized interpretation, immersed rather in tradition and intended for practical use.[21]

These two ways of approaching exegesis will influence, in a remarkable way, the later understanding of the Bible.

Literature destined for a female audience

We cannot forget the fact that the Bible is a religious book with a remarkable impact on the way of life, so its practical application, that is, the behaviours that must be observed and the behaviours to be avoided, is of great importance. The Bible as a 'living text', as a dynamic revelation, must be updated and incardinated in each period of history.

In these brief lines on the dissemination of the biblical story, it is worthwhile to pause and take into consideration the creation of a biblical literature destined for women. This literature focused on transmitting the biblical stories associated with certain values, virtues and attitudes that often reinforced the female models of each time period.

Among them we can mention the *Libro de las virtuosas e claras mujeres* by Álvaro de Luna (1436), which includes twenty-three biographies of biblical women, and that of the French Jesuit, Pierre Le Moyne, *La galerie des femmes fortes* (1647), which was accompanied by illustrations. In addition to these publications, we can find the work of Martín Carrillo, *Historia o Elogios de mujeres ilustres del Viejo Testamento* (1627), in which he describes fifty-four women of the Bible, a work that was very well received and was reissued several times. Carrillo rewrote the biblical episodes and included new details that could attract women, and at the same time transformed the narrative passages into dialogues and included sonnets and poems. His intention was to create a text that aroused feminine interest and to form them by reading it. For this reason, he did not limit himself to narrating the biblical text, but in his story, he incorporated positive behaviour models to imitate and also some negative ones as examples of what should be avoided. Therefore, the biblical text is transmitted already interpreted, giving rise to an educative and edifying reading. Even though only the cover of the book contains engravings, this work served as inspiration to configure the iconographic programme of the Guadalupe Chapel in the convent of Las Descalzas Reales (Madrid), carried out by Herrera Barnuevo in 1653.[22]

This type of educative religious literature contributed in the nineteenth century to the diffusion of the feminine ideal of the 'angel in the house'. From

---

21. Julio Trebolle Barrera, *La Biblia judía y la Biblia cristiana* (Madrid: Trotta, 1993), 27. An English version of this text is available: *The Jewish Bible and the Cristian Bible: An Introduction to the History of the Bible* (Leiden: Brill, 1998), 23.

22. Regarding this chapel and the role played by the work of Carrillo, see Chapter 4 and the bibliography quoted therein.

biblical characters and the interpretation that is made of them in light of the time, a type of woman is built, a counterpoint to the man, based on virtues such as modesty, sweetness, prudence, discretion, obedience and caring.[23] This female ideal was communicated and spread through the collections of prints, illustrated Bibles and sacred stories where the biblical image has a special role to play.[24] The collections of prints hardly include any text, so the image constitutes the vehicle for the transmission of the biblical content while at the same time being loaded with a notorious pious and moralizing intention. The illustrated Bibles published every book of the Bible and present a complete account of the history of salvation accompanied by representations of different scenes.[25] The sacred stories presented a selection of passages from the creation of the world to the birth of the first Christian communities: Genesis and Exodus (since the rest of the books of the Pentateuch have a marked legal and/or exhortative character); the narrative books of historical character (Joshua, Judges, Ruth, Samuel, Kings, Tobit, Judith, Esther, Maccabees); some stories about Job, Jonah, Daniel and Susannah; references to Isaiah, Jeremiah, Baruch and Ezekiel; and the Gospels and the Acts of the Apostles that make up the story of Jesus.[26] With a clear educational purpose, these books made the biblical message known in schools and in public circles, enjoyed the acceptance of readers and were able to adapt to the tastes of the time.[27]

The representation of the Bible

If in any iconographic representation the space that it occupies, and the purpose/function assigned to it, is important, in the case of biblical iconography it is even more so.

---

23. Cf. Carmen Yebra-Rovira, 'French biblical engravings and the education of the Spanish Women in the XIX century', *Biblical Reception* 2 (2013): 397–416; 'Interpretación bíblica y formación moral de la mujer en el siglo XIX', *Moralia* 36 (2013): 405–26; and Chapter 6 of this book.

24. Although direct reading in the vernacular languages was already possible in the eighteenth century, it continued to read the sacred stories as an indirect form of knowledge of the Scriptures. Cf. Carmen Yebra-Rovira, *Las biblias ilustradas en España en el siglo XIX: Desarrollo, relevancia e interpretación teológica*, Col. Tesis 64 (Estella: Verbo Divino, 2015).

25. One of the most famous was that of Gustave Doré, author of its more than two hundred illustrations. Commonly known as *Doré's Bible*, it was published at the same time in France and England in 1866. In Spain, the collection of engravings of Doré appears in the third edition of the *Holy Bible* of Torres Amat (Barcelona: Montaner y Simon, 1871–73). Cf. Yebra-Rovira, *Las biblias ilustradas en España en el siglo XIX*, 181–90.

26. For example, *Historias del Antiguo y Nuevo Testamento* with images created by Antonio Pascual and other illustrators (Valencia: Ventura Lluch, 1841).

27. For more details about these books, see Chapter 6, 133–6.

The image may appear in a religious context: in churches or cathedrals, spaces devoted to worship; in refectories or convent cloisters, places where friars or nuns devote time to meditation; in private oratories[28] where the believer gathers to address God; in Bibles, Psalters and Books of Hours where the miniatures that illustrate them facilitate reflection and devotion. The representation can be oriented to evoke, suggest or facilitate introspection. In other words, it is not a matter of knowing the story through its representation, but of arousing in those who contemplate the image the previously acquired knowledge about it.

The representations can appear in other contexts with an ornamental function and to demonstrate the economic level of the owner: the paintings and tapestries that adorn palaces and houses of wealthy merchants, for example. Some medieval Bibles and other religious codices would sit between the two, which, through the splendour of their decoration, revealed the power of those who commissioned them and became a family inheritance. In other cases, the decorative intention is less pretentious and are used in everyday objects such as furniture, trays or stamps. The purpose of the biblical image therefore encompasses a wide range of intentions: instructing, educating, teaching, moving towards piety, accentuating devotion, facilitating reflection, attracting, delighting and so forth.[29]

When the artist paints a biblical scene, he projects his own gaze on it. His perception leads him to focus his attention on a specific aspect while silencing others, to introduce variants or to merge similar episodes resulting in the creation of a new scene. Their perception also echoes previous iconographic traditions either to reproduce them or to transform them. But even when the artist wants to reproduce them faithfully, he is faced with the difficulty presented by the conciseness and briefness of the biblical account regarding the physical and psychological descriptions of the characters, so the reader is obliged to fill in the narrative gaps with his imagination. An example of how the artist pretends to faithfully represent the biblical story is *Rebecca and Eliezer* by Murillo (*c.* 1660, Museo del Prado, Madrid). The painting deals with the moment when Rebecca offers water to Eliezer, but according to Gen. 24.15-21, Rebecca is alone and there is no mention of other women being present. Murillo takes advantage of the painting to introduce new elements that allow him to develop a genre scene that could take place in seventeenth-century Seville. Very often, the artist substituted

---

28. It seems fitting to mention the Polyptych of the Life of Christ of Juan de Flandes (1496–1504), of which only twenty-seven panels are conserved (fifteen of them in the Real Palace of Madrid) of the forty-seven that conformed the series. They are panels of reduced dimensions (21 × 16 cm) destined to the private oratory of Isabella, the Catholic, a private space in which the pictures would inspire the queen in her moments of devotion. The images are accessible from the following web page: https://www.patrimonionacional.es/en/node/345 (accessed 15 January 2022).

29. Other important issues, in which for reasons of space I cannot go into detail, are the relationship between image and text in the codices and printed books and the image as part of a broader iconographic cycle.

the original time of the story for his own contemporary perspective, integrating past and present in the same scene and in this way allowing for the biblical story to remain alive and current. In the *Expulsion of Hagar* by Rubens (c. 1615–1617, Hermitage Museum, St. Petersburg), the clothes that the characters wear are those of the time and the artist transforms the tent of the patriarchs, who were semi-nomadic, into a house whose door becomes the axis of the painting.

The artists use iconographic models that are later imposed and repeated successively. For example, in the episode of Isaac's sacrifice (Genesis 22), there is a series of recurring elements such as the absence of firewood, a makeshift altar and the hand of the angel that stops Abraham when he lifts the knife. But in the story, the wood that Isaac carries is a key element, because unknowingly he is collaborating in the fulfilment of the divine plan, while Abraham builds the altar piling stones, and it is not the hand, but a voice, which prevents the sacrifice.

There is also the combination and/or overlapping of different iconographic models. In the representations of Samson and Delilah, Erika Bornay[30] mentions that in some occasions the artists introduced the figure of an old woman. In *Samson and Delilah* by Rubens (1609, National Gallery, London), he places her behind Delilah, illuminating with a candle the barber who cuts Samson's hair. She points out the possible influence of the work by Caravaggio of *Judith and Holofernes* (1598–99, Galleria Nazionale d'Arte Antica, Rome). The triangular composition formed by the woman, the decapitated general and the elderly male is also repeated in the work of Tintoretto and Artemisia Gentileschi, who made several versions of the theme. At other times the triangular composition is maintained, but the body of Holofernes is replaced by his head as in the Judith versions with the head of Holofernes by Gentileschi (1618–19, Pitti Palace, Florence) and by Cristofano Allori (1615, Palazzo Pitti, Florence). In the depictions of Judith, she is very frequently accompanied by her maid who, according to the biblical story, was with her when they went to the enemy camp. This servant who can be represented as either old or young appears in the scenes of beheading and is an element that serves to distinguish her from *Salome with the Head of John the Baptist* (Mk 6.14-29 and Mt. 14.6-12). For Bornay, the old woman would be a procuress and would emphasize the status of the protagonist as a prostitute. This interpretation departs completely from the biblical account that in Judg. 16.4 introduces the character of Delilah without making any allusion to this interpretation: 'After this he fell in love with a woman in the valley of Sorek, whose name was Delilah.' In addition, Delilah carries out her seduction strategy alone. No one accompanies her in the room where she meets Samson. Tradition, however, has seen her as a prostitute, possibly because v. 1 of the same chapter mentions that Samson had an encounter with a prostitute, of whom the name is not given. Other painters, such as Matthias Stom (*Samson and Delilah*, c. 1630, Barberini Palace, Rome) (Figure 2.3), also include the figure of the

---

30. Erika Bornay, *Mujeres de la Biblia en la pintura del Barroco: imágenes de la ambigüedad*, Ensayos Arte Cátedra (Madrid: Cátedra, 1998), 98.

Figure 2.3 Matthias Stom, *Samson and Delilah*, c. 1630, Palacio Barberini, Roma. Source: Getty.

old woman in the scene of Samson and Delilah.[31] It seems clear that there has been a fusion of iconographic models. Judith, Delilah and other biblical female characters have been portrayed as dangerous women, capable of seduction and the cause of temptation, leading to the perdition of the male protagonist.

The Bible can serve the artist as a starting point that allows him to channel other types of interests. Sometimes the freedom of creation reached such extremes that, if it were not for the title, the viewer would not be able to establish the connection with the Bible. The pretexts for these choices may have different motivations. Subjects such as the Creation or the Flood allowed painters such as Brueghel or Bassani to show their skills in the representation of nature and animals.

At the end of his artistic career, Nicola Poussin painted the series of *The Four Seasons* (1660–64, Louvre Museum, Paris) inspired by the Bible: Adam and Eve in paradise for Spring (Genesis 3), Ruth and Boaz for the Summer (Ruth 2), spies returning from Canaan with giant grape clusters for Autumn (Numbers 13) and the Flood for Winter (Genesis 7).[32] Each scene is related to a stage of

31. It is common that in the scene, one or several men appear in allusion to the Philistines whom Delilah call when she discovered the secret of his strength.

32. Cf. Martin O'Kane, 'The four seasons: Nicolas Poussin's biblical landscape', in *Painting the Text, The Artist as Biblical Interpreter*, ed. Martin O'Kane, The Bible in the Modern World 8 (Sheffield: Sheffield Phoenix Press, 2007), 196–214, especially 202–14.

the seasonal cycle: the renewal of nature in the garden of Eden; the harvest is associated with the harvest of the book of Ruth, the harvesting of the grapes at the end of Summer and the Flood with the inexhaustible rain and the inhospitable environment of Winter. The landscape is the articulating element in all of them, but in each painting there is a predominance of a specific colour (green, yellow-golden, grey-brown and grey-black) and each one of them is situated at a different time of the day (morning, noon, afternoon and evening). At the same time, each scene is associated with a moment in the life cycle of a human being, from birth to death through youth and maturity. Through the selected episodes, the artist explores the parallels between the evolution of human life and the cycles of nature, a vision that reflects the words of the passage of Ovid's *Metamorphoses*.[33] The paintings show man at the mercy of nature, a nature capable of nourishing and feeding (Summer, Autumn), but also of destroying and killing (Winter). Poussin uses these scenes as a starting point to express his feelings and the ideas that arouse in him the passage of time and his philosophical conception, but the main objective is not the representation of the Bible. The visual reading of this iconographic cycle allows us to discover the connections that the painter establishes between independent biblical stories to present his own convictions: 'The unpredictable nature of fate can be countered only by virtue, justice and right-living.'[34]

Other artists will choose biblical themes as a subterfuge to show the female nude and erotic scenes or as an excuse to represent the attraction of the exotic and the fascinating but, at that moment, unknown world of the Near East. Before concluding this section, we must remember that the concept of ideal beauty is not timeless or immovable but has been changing over time, and even diverse aesthetic ideals have coexisted, as, for example, in England during the Victorian era. The 'beautiful-repulsive' opposition has played an important role in the representation of the Bible.[35] After what has been said, it is necessary to ask to what extent the artistic representations reflect the characters of the biblical text and how the different and even contradictory characterizations with which the artists have represented the men and women of the Bible can be integrated.

The case of Mary Magdalene: A character in evolution

Mary Magdalene is a good example to illustrate the complex relationship between the figure as it appears in the Bible and the understanding of this woman as transmitted by artistic production.

---

33. Ovid, *Metamorphoses*, Book XV (Oxford: Oxford World's Classics, 1986), 199–213.
34. O'Kane, 'The four seasons', 209.
35. Cf. Umberto Eco (ed.), *History of Beauty*, 2nd edn (New York: Rizzoli, 2010), and Umberto Eco (ed.), *On Ugliness* (New York: Rizzoli, 2011).

There are not many references to Mary of Magdala in the Gospels.³⁶ The first one is in Lk. 8.1-3, with an indirect reference in Mk 16.9. In his itinerant preaching, Jesus was accompanied by the Twelve Apostles and several women who had been cured of evil spirits and diseases and who helped them with their possessions. That is to say, they were women with sufficient economic means to take care of the logistics and lodging arrangements for the group. Three are mentioned by their names, but only Mary of Magdala is singled out as the one from whom Jesus had expelled seven demons. The current exegesis, with the help of contributions made by the social sciences, understands that the demons represented some kind of physical or mental illness that totally conditioned the individual's life and that led him or her to transgressive and unconventional behaviours, which excluded him or her from the group. The expression 'to expel the demons' (exorcisms) refers to a healing process that would allow the individual to recover a full existence and recognition of the community.³⁷

The second significant moment is situated around the cross. The four Evangelists echo this information.³⁸ Mary of Magdala along with other women accompany Jesus at the moment of his death, demonstrating her fidelity.

The third episode is the visit of the women to the tomb to complete the tasks of preparation of the corpse, for which they have acquired ointments beforehand. There, they are witnesses of the empty sepulchre (Mt. 28.1-10; Mk 16.1-8; Lk. 24.1-12), but in Jn 20.11-18 Mary of Magdala comes alone, when it has not yet dawned, and receives the appearance of the Risen One and the mission to transmit the news, revealing the special relationship between the two.³⁹ This passage is known as the *Noli me tangere* and has been represented very often in art. The translation

36. The name refers to the town of origin, on the shores of Lake Tiberias. I use the term Mary of Magdala when I analyse the texts that speak of the disciple of Jesus and Mary Magdalene to refer to the 'mixed' character that is subsequently constructed.

37. On the possession as a form of protest and resistance, I refer to Carmen Bernabé, 'María Magdalena: la autoridad de la testigo enviada', in *Mujeres con autoridad en el cristianismo*, ed. Carmen Bernabé (Estella: Verbo Divino, 2007), 28–33; Régis Burnet, *María Magdalena. Siglo I al XXI: de pecadora arrepentida a esposa de Jesús. Historia de la recepción de una figura bíblica*, trans. Santiago García Rodriguez (Bilbao: Desclée de Brouwer, 2009 [2006]), 60–61; Esther Miquel, *Jesús y los espíritus: Aproximación antropológica a la práctica exorcista de Jesús* (Salamanca: Sígueme, 2009); and the cited bibliography.

38. Matthew 27.56 and Mk 15.40 mentions the names of the women but do not mention the men. Luke 23.49 describes the scene more generally. He mentions the women as a whole and includes them within the group of acquaintances. The three Evangelists specify that they remained at a distance from the cross. On the contrary, John points out that at the foot of the cross were the mother of Jesus, Mary of Cleophas, Mary of Magdala and the preferred disciple (Jn 19:25).

39. This scene takes place in an orchard and garden, and in it there are allusions to other biblical texts: the Garden of Eden (Genesis 3) and the Song of Songs.

of the Latin version is 'Do not touch me', but according to the Greek text it should be better understood as 'Do not hold unto me'.

How then can these images in which Mary Magdalene appear as a courtesan or as a repentant and penitent woman be explained?

In the Gospels, the news about the followers of Jesus is scarce, especially when compared with the mentions to the Twelve Apostles, which are much more numerous. In addition, the fact that several of the disciples of Jesus carry the name of Mary has caused confusion and the subsequent merger of this character with two other women: Mary of Bethany and the repentant sinner.

Mary of Bethany is mentioned in three episodes. She, along with her siblings, Martha and Lazarus, maintained a close relationship with Jesus. In Lk. 10.38-42, the Evangelist contrasts the attitudes of Martha and Mary, actions versus listening and paying attention to the message of Christ, the profane versus the mystical. The contemplative character of this Mary will pass to Mary Magdalene. In Jn 11.1-44, Jesus resurrects Lazarus and Mary shows herself as a woman of deep faith who manifests full trust in the Teacher. The third episode is known as 'The anointing at Bethany' (Jn 12.1-11). While her family offers a dinner for Jesus, Mary anoints his feet with a very valuable perfume and dries them with her hair.

The account of the repentant sinner appears only in Lk. 7.36-50 and takes place in the context of the preaching of Jesus in Galilee. Knowing that he was going to eat at the house of a Pharisee, a woman, who is only said to be 'known as a sinner in the city', prostrated herself at the feet of Jesus. With her tears she wet his feet, dried them with her hair, covered them with kisses and finally shed perfume on them. The episodes of the anointing reveal the recognition of the figure of Jesus by these women. The banquet, the hair and the perfume facilitate the identification of the anointing by Mary of Bethany.[40]

The fusion of these three characters (Mary of Magdala, Mary of Bethany and the repentant sinner) has given life to Mary Magdalene, a libertine woman who led a dissipated life and who, after meeting Jesus, changed her life. From then on, she maintained a close relationship with Jesus, accompanied him in the last moments of his life and became a privileged witness to the Resurrection. At the end of the sixth century, Saint Gregory the Great had already formulated that these three women were the same.[41] However, this figure's transformation does not end here. It will be completed with medieval legends that will add new facets to her figure.

In the West, in the eighth century, the devotion to Mary Magdalene reached great popularity[42] and it was necessary to provide more information about her

---

40. There are two other anointing stories in Mt. 26.6-13 and in Mk 14.3-9. In addition, both scenes take place in Bethany, but in a different place, in the house of Simon, the leper. An unknown woman pours a very expensive perfume on Jesus's head.

41. At the same time that he interpreted that the devils referred to his life of sin in his *Homily on the Gospel* 33, I; *Patrologia Latina*. Edited by J.-P- Migne (Paris: Garnier, 1844–55), vol. 76, col. 1239.

42. In the Middle Ages, three were the biblical women par excellence: Eve, Mary the mother of Jesus and Mary Magdalene.

life. Medieval legends[43] filled the silences found in the Gospels and they built her biography as a prostitute, repentant, penitent and holy woman.[44] In the Greek-Oriental version, Mary Magdalene left with John the Evangelist and the mother of Jesus to Ephesus, where she lived until the end of her days. In the West, the legend tells that a group of infidels brought Mary, Lazarus, Martha, the maid of the later, Martila, Maximin, one of the seventy-two disciples of Christ and some others on a ship, and were sent to the high seas adrift. Providentially, and with the help of God, they arrived in Marseille. For a time, Mary Magdalene began to spread the word of God, but towards the end of her life she became a hermit:

> In this meanwhile the blessed Mary Magdalene, desirous of sovereign contemplation, sought a right sharp desert, and took a place which was ordained by the angel of God, and abode there by the space of thirty years without knowledge of anybody. In which place she had no comfort of running water, ne solace of trees, ne of herbs. And that was because our Redeemer did do show it openly, that he had ordained for her refection celestial, and no bodily meats. And every day at every hour canonical she was lifted up in the air of angels, and heard the glorious song of the heavenly companies with her bodily ears. Of which she was fed and filled with right sweet meats, and then was brought again by the angels unto her proper place, in such wise as she had no need of corporal nourishing.[45]

When the moment of her death arrived, she sent for Maximin, already a bishop, so that on Easter Sunday he would enter her oratory, where she would have been taken by the angels. This is what happened and after communion, the saint stretched out on the earth and her soul ascended to Heaven.

The figure of Mary Magdalene will assume the features of another saint, Mary of Egypt.[46] A woman who led a dissolute life in Alexandria, after her conversion, she donated all her possessions to the poor. She then went into the desert with only three loaves of bread and a cloth to cover her body, but over time it deteriorated

---

43. The popular traditions about Mary Magdalene appear in the *Vita Eremitica beatae Mariae Magdalanae* (ninth century) composed by Italian monks who led a retired life, and in which her life is highlighted as that of a hermit and, fundamentally, in the *Golden Legend* of Jacobus de Voragine (1264) that describes her life, death and miracles. Cf. Andrea Taschl-Erber, 'Apostle and sinner: Medieval receptions of Mary of Magdala', in *The High Middle Ages,* ed. Kari Elisabeth Børresen and Adriana Valerio (Atlanta: SBL Press, 2015), 301–26.

44. Regarding the role of saints in the Middle Ages, see George Dubay, *Damas del siglo XII. Vol I: Eloisa, Leonor, Iseo y algunas otras* (Madrid: Alianza, 1998), 46–47.

45. Jacobus de Voragine, *The Golden Legend or Lives of the Saints,* trans. William Caxton (1483), from the Temple Classics, ed. F. S. Ellis (first issue of this edition, 1900; reprinted 1922, 1931), vol. 4, 36. Available online: https://www.christianiconography.info/goldenLegend/magdalene.htm (accessed 15 May 2021).

46. Jacobus de Voragine, *The Golden Legend.*

so much that only her long hair hid her nudity. She dedicated her life to penance, repentance and meditation. The death of both saints will also have similarities. The nudity and abundant mane with which the penitent Magdalene is depicted most likely have their origin in this fusion.

The object of a deep popular devotion, the faithful venerated Mary Magdalene as an intercessor and they trusted her ability to perform miracles. Her relics were kept in Vezélay and Sainte-Baume, which became pilgrimage centres that were on the route towards Santiago de Compostela. The penitent facet of the Magdalene fits very well in the development experienced by the sacrament of confession in the twelfth century, especially in relation to the demands of repentance and penance.[47]

The iconographic representation will echo these characteristics,[48] especially in the stained-glass windows and altarpieces dedicated to the life of Mary Magdalene, which included evangelical scenes and episodes of the Golden Legend. Among the first we can mention those of the French cathedrals of Chartres, Bourges, or Auxerre created in the thirteenth century. Among the second, one of the most renowned altarpieces is the one found in the church of the same name in Tiefenbronn (Germany) made by Lucas Moser in 1431.[49] Less known but equally noteworthy is the altarpiece found in the Museum of Salamanca (Spain), among the funds of the Prado Museum. It is of Spanish-Flemish style by an unknown author and dated to the second half of the fifteenth century. Although of reduced dimensions, it stands out for its expressiveness and for the use of golden nimbus. On the central panel and in a prominent place, there is a portrait of the Magdalene enthroned. The above retables are dedicated to scenes from the canonical Gospels: *Noli me Tangere* on the left, the Virgin Mary and Mary Magdalene at the foot of the cross

---

47. Cf. Dubay, *Damas del siglo XII*, 58–62.

48. A selection of images can be seen on the personal page of Guadalupe Seijas at https://ucm.academia.edu/GuadalupeSeijas with the title 'The Iconographic Representation of Mary Magdalene'. On the iconography of Mary Magdalene, cf. the reference work by Louis Réau, *Iconografía del arte cristiano*, 2nd edn, trans. Daniel Alcoba (Barcelona: Ediciones del Serbal, 2001), Tome I, vol. 2, 293–306, and Tome 2, vol. 7, 338–43; and of Louis Goosen, *De Andrés a Zaqueo. Temas del Nuevo Testamento y la literatura apócrifa en la religión y las artes*, Tres Cantos (Madrid: Akal 2008), 226–35; and the monographic works by David Jasper, 'La Biblia en el arte y en la literatura: fuente de inspiración para poetas y pintores. María Magdalena', *Concilium* 1 (1995): 67–83; Odile Delenda, 'La Magdalena en el arte. Un argumento de la Contrarreforma en la pintura española y mejicana del siglo XVII', in *Actas del III Congreso Internacional del Barroco Americano: Territorio, Arte, Espacio y Sociedad: Universidad Pablo de Olavide, Sevilla, 8 al 12 de octubre de 2001* (Sevilla: Universidad Pablo de Olavide, 2001), 277–89; and Mª Leticia Sánchez Hernández, 'María Magdalena en el arte: entre el enigma y la fascinación', in *María Magdalena: de apóstol, a prostituta y amante*, ed. Isabel Gómez-Acebo and Carmen Bernabé (Bilbao: Desclée de Brouwer, 2009), 207–46. The latter is a detailed study that includes an extensive bibliography.

49. Cf. Réau, *Iconografía del arte cristiano*, Tomo I, vol. 2, 300. On the representations of the life of Mary Magdalane see, cf. Goosen, *De Andrés a Zaqueo*, 232–4.

2. Iconographic Representation of the Bible

Figure 2.4 Andrea Solari, *Saint Mary Magdalene*, c. 1524.
Source: Walters Art Museum, Baltimore, Maryland.

in the centre, and dinner at the Pharisee's house on the right. In the lower register and on both sides of her portrait, scenes of the Golden Legend: the assumption of Mary Magdalene on the left and the preaching of the Magdalene to the Kings.[50]

In the Renaissance we find the model of the Magdalene courtesan, a woman of high social status, elegantly dressed and holding between her hands or standing near her a bottle of perfume (Andrea Solari, *c.* 1524, Walters Art Museum, Baltimore, Maryland) (Figure 2.4) or jewels (Caravaggio, 1597, Palazzo Doria Pamphilj, Rome). Caravaggio presents her asleep as another mode of expression of beauty. Sometimes a book is included, a sign of her being a noble and cultured woman.

In the Baroque period this scene is still represented, although they are less frequent. In the *Assumption of Mary Magdalene* by Ribera (1636, Royal Academy of Fine Arts, San Fernando, Madrid), she is taken to heaven by the angels while

---

50. In this scene there seems to be represented the Catholic Monarchs, who felt great devotion for this saint, and something separate from the group: their son, Prince John, is accompanied by his nanny. This fact would make this altarpiece a real document. Cf. Mercedes Moreno Alcalde, *Museo de Salamanca: Sección de Bellas Artes* (Valladolid: Junta de Castilla y León, Consejería de Cultura y Turismo, 1995), 26.

looking upwards with her hands crossed over her chest in a contemplative attitude. It is a Magdalene in ecstasy, dressed in ragged clothes and long hair, elements that refer to her last years as a hermit, highlighting the red mantle, the colour of passion and love.

The iconography of the penitent Magdalene developed above all in the context of the Counter-Reformation, which established new guidelines on how to represent the saint.[51] The images had to insist on her facet as a repentant woman rather than a licentious woman. Objects of daily life, loaded with symbolism, appeared next to her and lead the viewer to meditation and prayer: the skull is a reminder of vanity and humility, the hourglass symbolizes the fleeting life, the crucifix and the jewels remember the life of sin. Other elements such as the mirror, the candle or the cave contribute to reinforce the full iconography.[52] This is the case of the *Penitent Magdalene* of Pedro de Orrente (seventeenth century, Corpus Christi College, Valencia), showing a woman with tormented expression, ragged clothes and long blond hair, surrounded by a skull and a crucifix. In the *Meditation of the Magdalene* by Zurbarán (seventeenth century, Museo de San Carlos, Mexico City), she is no longer a beautiful and richly dressed woman, but she wears a habit and with a pensive expression renounces worldly pleasures, represented by an hourglass, and dedicates her life to prayer and penance, symbolized by the skull and the candle.

Another common theme in the Counter-Reformation is Martha reprimanding Mary Magdalene, where the characters of Mary of Bethany and Mary Magdalene merge. In the painting by Andrea Vaccaro (seventeenth century, Museum of Fine Arts, Utah), Martha, with a mantle on her head and raised hand, rebukes her sister for her libertine and sinful life. Mary wears a low-cut dress, her head is uncovered and her face shows a sad expression. The jewels that allude to her love of pleasures are located on the table. The scene has an instructive purpose that highlights the importance of conversion in the life of Christians.

Even though the iconography of Mary Magdalene is not as popular from the nineteenth century onwards, her character continues to arouse the interest of some artists although the issue of repentance is left aside. Francesco Hayez painted in 1825 *Magdalene Penitent* (Municipal Gallery of Modern Art, Milan). Represented in the nude, she is sitting on a white canvas in the middle of nature against the background of a powerful landscape. She carries a crucifix in her hand and next to it there is a skull. However, neither eroticism nor repentance are the dominant themes. Her self-absorbed gaze and ambiguous beauty show her as a mysterious woman. Pre-Raphaelite painters were very interested in biblical themes, especially characters and scenes from the New Testament. Mary Magdalene became an important object of their attention. In some paintings she is still represented with a perfume jar and loose and abundant hair, which is an allusion to her reputation as a prostitute. These were done in half-length

---

51. Cf. Delenda, 'La Magdalena en el arte', 279–81.

52. A list of the attributes of Mary Magdalene and their meanings can be found in Delenda, 'La Magdalena en el arte', 283–4.

Figure 2.5 Dante Gabriel Rossetti, *Mary Magdalene at the House of Simon the Pharisee*, 1858. Source: © The Fitzwilliam Museum, University of Cambridge, UK.

portraits of the Magdalene which exuded a certain sensuality despite being fully dressed.[53] However, these artists reflect a new understanding of her character that goes beyond the erotic and emphasize either her conversion experience (Dante Gabriel Rossetti, *Mary Magdalene at the House of Simon the Pharisee*, 1858, The Fitzwilliam Museum, University of Cambridge, UK)[54] (Figure 2.5) or her role as witness of the Resurrection (Edward Burne-Jone, *The Morning of the Resurrection*, 1884, Tate Gallery, London).[55] In this sense, the Pre-Raphaelites left aside the dominant iconographic models and ventured to explore other facets of her person, anticipating contemporary exegesis.

We can say that in the history of biblical exegesis, Mary Magdalene has not always been accepted unanimously as the fusion of the three characters in one, fluctuating

---

53. Dante Gabriel Rossetti, *Mary Magdalene* (1877, Delaware Art Museum, USA) and Frederick Sandy, *Magdalene* (c. 1857, Delaware Art Museum, USA).

54. The drawing was accompanied by a sonnet. The artist made several versions of the theme.

55. Cf. Ernest Fontana, 'Mary Magdalene and the Pre-Raphaelites', *Journal of Pre-Raphaelite Studies* 9 (2000): 89–100.

between multiplicity and uniqueness. Especially in the East, the existence of the three women was maintained, while in the West the presentation of a single figure was frequent, as reflected in the artistic representations – although there was no lack of discrepant voices. The current exegesis, which has devoted great efforts to the recovery of the female characters of the Bible, has vindicated Mary Magdalene and her role as an authority figure among the first followers of Jesus.[56] In the first centuries of the Common Era (first to second centuries) arose a series of writings coming from the diverse currents that conform early Christianity, part of which received the label of 'Apocryphal' because they were not part of the biblical canon. Of particular relevance are the Nag Hammadi manuscripts discovered in 1945, among which are very significant texts related to Mary Magdalene from Gnostic Christianity such as the *Gospel of Philip*, the *Gospel of Thomas* or *Wisdom of Jesus Christ*, among others.[57] Another very significant work is the *Gospel of Mary*[58] (from the end of the second century) of which copies had been found at the end of the nineteenth century, but the academic world disagrees about its Gnostic character. In these works, a dialogue is reproduced between Jesus and his disciples in the period between the Resurrection and the Ascension, in which Mary Magdalene has a very prominent role as favourite of the Teacher and as recipient and transmitter of the secret teachings of Jesus to a restricted group of initiates. In these texts, the rivalry between Peter and Mary of Magdala, who was seen as an agent of authority, was obvious. In this polemic, which goes back to the origins of Christianity,[59] lies the question of apostolic authority (i.e. directing, teaching, interpreting) and the role of women in the community.[60] The fact that she accompanied Jesus in his life and at the time of his death, that she witnessed the appearance of the Risen One and received the mission of witnessing, were key elements in recognizing her apostolic authority. Still in the third century the figure of Mary of Magdala was still highly valued as follows from the expression of Hippolytus of Rome, who considers her 'apostle (in feminine) of the apostles', but from the fourth century her figure was gradually replaced for Mary, the mother of Jesus, or by Peter. Contemporary studies and especially feminist critics have wanted to recover and claim her importance in the development of early Christianity.

56. Bernabé, 'María Magdalena', 19–47. To support the access of women to the priesthood, cf. Burnet, *María Magdalena. Siglo I al XXI*, 135, n. 51.

57. Cf. Mar Marcos and Juana Torres, 'El Evangelio de María Magdalena y la literatura gnóstica', 19–150, and Carmen Bernabé, 'María Magdalena y los siete demonios', 37–40 and 44–48, both in *María Magdalena: de apóstol, a prostituta y amante*, ed. Isabel Gómez-Acebo and Carmen Bernabé (Bilbao: Desclée de Brouwer, 2009).

58. Although the title of the work is the *Gospel of Mary*, it refers to Mary Magdalene.

59. The term 'origins of Christianity' refers to the first followers of Jesus. In its beginnings, this movement remained very close to Judaism and it is not possible to mark a clear distance between both religions until at least the third century.

60. It is not only a theological question but also a gender issue, since the role of teaching and leadership of women in the Church is considered.

A final reflection

The representation of biblical scenes should not presuppose that the artist knows the text through a direct reading. The knowledge of these comes from diverse sources such as orality (sermons, *Via Crucis*, catechesis), tradition, theatrical performances, devotional works or sacred stories. Even the knowledge of the episodes can be based on previous iconographic sources. In each time period, the political, economic and social circumstances and the prevailing ideology have conditioned the interpretation of the biblical episodes and the relevance of some over others at different times. All this is essential to identify the sources that have inspired the artists, the message, the values that convey their representations and the empathy with the visual readers who contemplated their works.

The biblical stories are like paintings on which time has deposited a patina of dust and new varnishes, darkening or modifying the original colours. Knowing the Bible, that is, the original meaning of the texts in their original context and distinguishing it from the later interpretation that has developed from the first centuries of Christianity to the present day, as well as the legends that have been emerging around the biblical episodes and their protagonists, is essential to understand the text that underlies the biblical representations.

Bibliography

Armstrong, Karen. *The Bible: A Biography*. New York: Grove Press, 2008.

Bernabé, Carmen. 'María Magdalena: la autoridad de la testigo enviada', in *Mujeres con autoridad en el cristianismo*, edited by Carmen Bernabé, 19–48. Estella: Verbo Divino, 2007.

Bernabé, Carmen. 'María Magdalena y los siete demonios', in *María Magdalena: de apóstol, a prostituta y amante*, edited by Isabel Gómez-Acebo and Carmen Bernabé, 21–59. Bilbao: Desclée de Brouwer, 2009.

Biblia de San Luis: cuyo original … se conserva en el Tesoro de la Santa Iglesia Catedral Primada De Toledo. Edición facsimile, 3 vols. Barcelona: M. Moleiro Editor, 2000-2.

Bornay, Erika. *Mujeres de la Biblia en la pintura del Barroco: imágenes de la ambigüedad*, Ensayos Arte Cátedra. Madrid: Cátedra, 1998.

Burnet, Régis. *María Magdalena. Siglo I al XXI: de pecadora arrepentida a esposa de Jesús. Historia de la recepción de una figura bíblica*. Translated by Santiago García Rodriguez. Bilbao: Desclée de Brouwer, 2009 [2006].

Carrillo, Martín. *Historia o Elogios de mujeres ilustres del Viejo Testamento*. Huesca: Pedro Blusón, 1627. Available online: https://books.google.es/books?id=ELy2wTaOksYC (accessed 15 January 2021).

Chordá, Frederic. 'Dios renovador del universo en el ábside de Sant Climent de Taull', *RACBASJ* 25 (2011): 15–38.

De Hamel, Christopher. *The Book: A History of the Bible*. London: Phaidon, 2001.

De Voragine, Jacobus, *The Golden Legend or Lives of the Saints*. Translated by William Caxton (1483), from the Temple Classics, edited by F.S. Ellis (first issue of this edition 1900; reprinted 1922, 1931). Available online: https://www.christianiconography.info/goldenLegend/ (accessed 15 May 2021).

Delenda, Odile. 'La Magdalena en el arte. Un argumento de la Contrarreforma en la pintura española y mejicana del siglo XVII', in *O: Actas del III Congreso Internacional del Barroco Americano: Territorio, Arte, Espacio y Sociedad: Universidad Pablo de Olavide, Sevilla, 8 al 12 de octubre de 2001*, 277–89. Sevilla: Universidad Pablo de Olavide, 2001.

Dubay, George. *Damas del siglo XII. Vol I: Eloisa, Leonor, Iseo y algunas otras.* Madrid: Alianza, 1998.

Eco, Umberto, ed. *History of Beauty*, 2nd edn. New York: Rizzoli, 2010.

Eco, Umberto, ed. *On Ugliness*. New York: Rizzoli, 2011.

Fontana, Ernest. 'Mary Magdalene and the Pre-raphaelites'. *Journal of Pre-Raphaelite Studies* 9 (2000): 89–100.

Giordano, Maria Laura, and Adriana Valerio, eds. *Reformas y Contrarreformas en la Europa católica (siglos XV–XVII)*, LBLM 16. Estella: Verbo Divino, 2016.

Goosen, Louis. *De Andrés a Zaqueo. Temas del Nuevo Testamento y la literatura apócrifa en la religión y las artes*, Tres Cantos. Madrid: Akal, 2008.

The Internet Biblia Pauperum – Amasis. Available online: http://amasis.com/biblia/ (accessed 17 January 2022).

Jasper, David. 'La Biblia en el arte y en la literatura: fuente de inspiración para poetas y pintores. María Magdalena'. *Concilium* 1 (1995): 67–83.

Lowden, John. *The Making of the Bibles Moralisées II: The Book of Ruth*. University Park: Penn State University Press, 2000.

Marcos, Mar, and Juana Torres. 'El Evangelio de María Magdalena y la literatura gnóstica', in *María Magdalena: de apóstol, a prostituta y amante*, edited by Isabel Gómez-Acebo and Carmen Bernabé, 19–150. Bilbao: Desclée de Brouwer, 2009.

Miquel, Esther. *Jesús y los espíritus: Aproximación antropológica a la práctica exorcista de Jesús*. Salamanca: Sígueme, 2009.

Moreno Alcalde, Mercedes. *Museo de Salamanca: Sección de Bellas Artes*. Valladolid: Junta de Castilla y León, Consejería de Cultura y Turismo, 1995.

O: *Speculum humanae salvationis: Codex cremifanensis 243 del monasterio benedictino de Kremsmünster*. Madrid: Casariego, 1998.

O'Kane, Martin. 'The four seasons: Nicolas Poussin's biblical landscape', in *Painting the Text, The Artist as Biblical Interpreter*, edited by Martin O'Kane, 196–214, The Bible in the Modern World 8. Sheffield: Sheffield Phoenix Press, 2007.

Ovid, *Metamarphoses*, Book XV. Oxford: Oxford World's Classics, 1986.

Patrologia Latina. Edited by J.-P. Migne, 217 vols. Paris: Garnier, 1844–64.

Réau, Louis. *Iconografía del arte cristiano*, 2nd edn. Translated by Daniel Alcoba. Barcelona: Ediciones del Serbal, 2001.

Sánchez Hernández, Mª Leticia. 'María Magdalena en el arte: entre el enigma y la fascinación', in *María Magdalena: de apóstol, a prostituta y amante*, edited by Isabel Gómez-Acebo and Carmen Bernabé, 207–46. Bilbao: Desclée de Brouwer, 2009.

Sebastián López, Santiago. *Iconografía medieval*. San Sebastián: ETOR, 1988.

Taschl-Erber, Andrea. 'Apostle and sinner: Medieval receptions of Mary of Magdala', in *The High Middle Ages*, edited by Kari Elisabeth Børresen and Adriana Valerio, 301–26. Atlanta: SBL Press, 2015.

Trebolle Barrera, Julio. *La Biblia judía y la Biblia cristiana*. Madrid: Trotta, 1993. English version: *The Jewish Bible and the Cristian Bible: An Introduction to the History of the Bible*. Leiden: Brill, 1998.

Yebra-Rovira, Carmen. 'French biblical engravings and the education of the Spanish women in the XIX century'. *Biblical Reception* 2 (2013): 397–416.

Yebra-Rovira, Carmen. 'Interpretación bíblica y formación moral de la mujer en el siglo XIX'. *Moralia* 36 (2013): 405–26.

Yebra-Rovira, Carmen. *Las biblias ilustradas en España en el siglo XIX: Desarrollo, relevancia e interpretación teológica*, Col. Tesis 64. Estella: Verbo Divino- Asociación Bíblica Española, 2015.

Chapter 3

BATHSHEBA IN MEDIEVAL MANUSCRIPTS: VISUAL ANALYSIS OF A CONTROVERSIAL OLD TESTAMENT WOMAN

Mónica Ann Walker Vadillo

Introduction and methodology

Among the many women who appear in the Old Testament, one of the most ambiguous was possibly Bathsheba, wife of King David and mother of King Solomon.[1] Her ambiguity arises not only from the biblical narrative but also from her visual representation in the Middle Ages, especially in the field of manuscript illumination. These sources present a woman trapped between the two opposite poles of femininity in the Middle Ages: that of the seductress or temptress and that of the woman who after becoming queen mother could obtain redemption through her actions. To understand this historical and artistic characterisation of Bathsheba, it would be necessary to start at the beginning, with her biblical narrative.

---

1. This study is based on my PhD thesis titled *Betsabé en la Miniatura Medieval* (Madrid: Universidad Complutense de Madrid, 2013), under the supervision of Dr. Matilde Azcárate Luxán and Dr. Irene González Hernando. While a more in-depth discussion of the previous scholarship done on Bathsheba can be found in my dissertation, from the first monograph done by Elisabeth Kunoth-Leifels, *Über die Darstellungen der 'Bathseba im Bad': Studien zur Geschichte des Bildthemas; 4. bis 17. Jahrhundert* (Essen: Verlag Richard Bacht, 1962), going through the present study to the more contemporary approach by David M. Gunn, 'Bathsheba goes bathing in Hollywood: Words, images, and social locations', in *Biblical Glamour and Hollywood Glitz*, ed. Alice Bach, Semeia 74 (Atlanta: Scholars Press, 1996), 75–101, Bathsheba continues to be a popular subject of scholarly inquiry and fascination even today.

Many of the images that have been analysed in the chapter can be seen by following this link: http://sites.google.com/site/betsabeenlaminiaturamedieval/home (accessed 15 October 2021).

Bathsheba in the Old Testament

The story of Bathsheba appears in a series of episodes related to King David and King Solomon and narrated in 2 Sam. 11, 2 Sam. 12.24-25, 1 Kgs 1.11-31 and 1 Kgs 2.19.[2] Her story begins with the episode of the bath (2 Samuel 11). One afternoon David was strolling on the terrace of his palace when from above he saw a woman bathing. Her beauty aroused his curiosity, so he asked about her. A servant who accompanied him told him that the woman was Bathsheba, daughter of Eliam and wife of Uriah the Hittite. Then David ordered that she be brought before him, and when she arrived at the palace, he lay with her and then sent her home. The story would have ended here, in a mere case of adultery, had it not been for the letter that Bathsheba sent shortly after with the following words: 'I am pregnant' (2 Sam. 11.5). This led to disaster, as King David, trying to hide his actions, ended up committing an even greater crime. He ordered General Joab to send him Uriah. When he arrived before him, he asked him about the siege and urged him to go to his house and enjoy the company of his wife. However, instead of lying with Bathsheba, Uriah ended up sleeping at the palace's gates, arguing that if his men on the battlefield could not enjoy their wives, he would not do so either. Finally, David managed to provoke the death of Uriah through a letter that Uriah himself delivered to Joab in which David ordered his general to place Uriah in the most dangerous part of the front lines so he would die during one of the assaults on the city; and that is how it happened. Bathsheba mourned the death of her husband, but after a while David sent for her and made her his wife. Bathsheba gave birth to a son, the consequence of the adultery. David's actions were not pleasing to the eyes of God, who sent the prophet Nathan to reproach him for his conduct. As punishment, David's son died on the seventh day after his birth. Neither David's supplications nor his prayers saved his son's life (2 Sam. 12.1-19). After his death, David consoled Bathsheba and lay with her again. Bathsheba became pregnant once more and gave birth to a son whom he named Solomon, and God loved him.

The story continues during David's old age when the problem of succession to the throne of Judah became an issue. Adonijah, son of Haggith, another of David's wives, was preparing to ascend to the throne by gathering his followers around him and organising a sacrifice of cattle. All but the priest Benaiah, the prophet Nathan and his brother Solomon were invited to the event. Nathan spoke with Bathsheba, Solomon's mother, and said to her,

> Have you not heard of Adonijah, the son of Haggith, who has become king, and our lord does not know? Now, I want to give you some advice to save your life

---

2. Other episodes which are related to Bathsheba, even though she does not appear on the text, are David rebuked by Nathan (2 Sam. 12.1-14), Solomon on a mule after being crown king (1 Kgs 1.32-35) and the death of King David (1 Kgs 2.10-12). When these scenes were depicted in the Middle Ages, on occasion the figure of Bathsheba was included in them.

and the life of your son, Solomon. Go to King David and say: 'Oh my lord king! Did you not swear to your servant, saying, truly, Solomon, your son, will reign after me, and he will sit on my throne? Why then has Adonijah become king?' And behold, while you are talking there with the king, I will go in after you and emphasise your words (1 Kgs 1.11-14)

And so, Bathsheba and Nathan proceeded to do exactly that. When David heard her words, he was outraged and promised Bathsheba that Solomon would sit on the throne. David sent for the priest Zadok, Nathan and Benaiah and told them to look for court officials and to mount Solomon on his own mule to take him to Gihon and anoint him there as king of Israel. After the ceremony, the trumpets were played and the people acclaimed Solomon as king.

When Adonijah learned that it would be Solomon and not him who would sit on the throne of Israel, he feared for his life and begged his brother not to kill him. Solomon said that if there was no evil in him, he would not carry on the sentence and sent him home. Shortly after David died and was buried in the city, his son Solomon succeeded him on the throne, just as he had arranged. However, Adonijah did not give up on his pretensions and tried to recover the throne. He went to Bathsheba so that she would intercede on his behalf with her son. Adonijah wanted to take as his wife one of King David's concubines, the young Shunamite Abishag.[3] With this request Adonijah was trying to take over the place of his father, King David, by marrying one of his women because the tradition established that whoever owned the king's women would inherit the throne. Bathsheba, ignorant of these pretensions, went in search of Solomon. Arriving before her son to speak to him on behalf of Adonijah, 'the king rose to meet her, and bowed down to her; then he sat on his throne, and had a throne brought for the king's mother, and she sat on his right' (1 Kgs 2:19).[4] Bathsheba told her son not to deny her what she was going to ask, to which he agreed. However, Solomon realized Adonijah's stratagem and had him killed.

This narrative will not only be the basis for the visual representation of Bathsheba, who appeared in medieval art as either the object of desire of King David or as queen and mother, but it will also have important repercussions in the interpretations of the text that were made throughout the Middle Ages. It is for this reason that it is necessary to review the medieval exegesis before proceeding to study her iconography.

---

3. Leila Leah Bronner, *Stories of Biblical Mothers: Maternal Power in the Hebrew Bible* (New York: University Press of America, 2004), 51.

4. Susan Ackerman, 'The queen mother and the cult in ancient Israel', *Journal of Biblical Literature* 112, no. 3 (1993): 385–401. The queen mother, or *gebirah*, occupies the highest position in the Israelite court, to the right of the king. It seems that this is a custom of Hittite origin that was preserved in Israel, Assyria, Ugarit and so forth.

Bathsheba in medieval exegesis

The Christian exegesis that developed in the first centuries of Christianity and became one of the main systems of biblical interpretation throughout the Middle Ages offered two types of readings for Bathsheba: the first one symbolic and the other historical. These will be the basis for the different interpretations of Solomon's mother. To interpret the Sacred Scriptures, medieval exegesis admitted several levels of meaning: (1) the literal or historical; (2) the allegorical; (3) the tropological or moral; and (4) the anagogical or mystical-eschatological.[5] These levels could be divided into two different categories related to the way in which the biblical text was read: literally or symbolically (the latter encompassing the allegorical, tropological and anagogical meanings). Medieval exegetes also made a distinction between the extrinsic meaning and the intrinsic meaning of Scriptures. The extrinsic meaning had to do with the historical reality of the Old Testament as understood by the Jews, while the intrinsic had to do with the hidden meaning of the Old Testament that would later be 'revealed' by Christian exegetes. As a rule, these symbolic and intrinsic explanations were related above all to the Old Testament and their function was to harmonise the Hebrew Scriptures with the Christian ones so that there would be a concordance between the two. This relationship was of great importance to Christian exegetes because if the New Testament coincided point by point with the Old Testament, it could easily be inferred that 'both [were] the authentic expression of the same divine thought'.[6] Therefore, both the Old and New Testaments convey the same divine message, but what 'appears veiled in the Old Law, is revealed in the Gospels'.[7] Or as Augustine of Hippo said, 'the shadow projected in the pages of Old Testament history by a truth whose incarnation or anti-type is found in the New Testament revelation'.[8] In this way, the history of humanity from Adam and Eve and original sin has been no more than a long wait for Christ, the Saviour, whose sacrifice redeemed human beings from original sin. For medieval exegetes, this history of humanity was essentially the history of salvation where everything and every event until the

---

5. Louis Réau, *Iconografía del arte cristiano: Iconografía de la Biblia, Introducción General*, Vol. 3, trans. José María Sousa Jiménez (Barcelona: Ediciones del Serbal, 2000), 231–39; Bert Cardon, *Manuscripts of the Speculum Humanae Salvationis in the Southern Netherlands (c. 1410–c. 1470): A Contribution to the Study of 15th Century Book Illumination and of the Function and Meaning of Historical Symbolism* (Lovania: Uitgeverij, 1996), 13–41; Raymond Clemens and Timothy Graham, *Introduction to Manuscript Studies* (Ithaca: Cornell University Press, 2007), 181. This division of the different types of interpretations was primarily developed by Augustine of Hippo, who is the author which most of these researchers refer to.

6. Réau, *Iconografía del arte cristiano*, Vol. 3, 230. According to Réau, the concordance of the testimonies was always considered as a test, or at least, a presumption of the Divine Truth.

7. Réau, *Iconografía del arte cristiano*, Vol. 3, 231.

8. Everett F. Harrison, Geoffrey W. Bromely and Carl F. H. Henry, *Baker's Dictionary of Theology* (Grand Rapids: Baker Book House, 1987), 533.

Last Judgment had a fixed and predestined place and meaning.⁹ Time was divided into the time before Christ, the time of Christ and the time after Christ. All the characters and events prior to the arrival of Christ are designated by the name of types or prefigures and their counterparts in the New Testament are designated with the name of anti-types or figures. This exegetical method to understand Scriptures is called typology, but in this study, it will be referred to as symbolic narration.

The origin of this typological doctrine goes back to Christ who said, 'Do not think that I have come to abolish the law or the prophets; I have come not to abolish but to fulfil. For truly I tell you, until heaven and earth pass away, not one letter, not one stroke of a letter, will pass from the law until all is accomplished' (Mt. 5.17-18). In the New Testament, there are several references to Old Testament characters and stories that were later on applied to the figure of Christ: 'And just as Moses lifted up the serpent in the wilderness, so must the Son of Man be lifted up' (Jn 3.14); 'For just as Jonah was three days and three nights in the belly of the sea monster, so for three days and three nights the Son of Man will be in the heart of the earth' (Mt. 12.40). In the first example, the elevation of the cross is prefigured by the elevation of the bronze serpent, 'so Moses made a serpent of bronze, and put it upon a pole; and whenever a serpent bit someone, that person would look at the serpent of bronze and live' (Num. 21.9), and in the second example, the Resurrection of Christ appears prefigured by Jonah in the belly of the whale. And Paul of Tarsus also mentions, 'These are only a shadow of what is to come, but the substance belongs to Christ' (Col. 2.17). Taking into consideration these biblical precedents, the typological doctrine was developed and subjected to a greater refinement throughout the Middle Ages. Nevertheless, the new exegetes were not limited to the typological examples already described in the New Testament.¹⁰ Medieval exegetes found a way to expand the number of allusions between the two Testaments by multiplying the comparisons with greater subtlety. This will lead to the creation of typological manuscripts such as the *Biblia Pauperum*, the *Speculum Humanae Salvationis* or the *Concordantiae Caritatis*.

Within this typological system, Bathsheba appears as a prefiguration not only of *Ecclesia* but also of the Virgin Mary, a relationship that was, above all, a creation of the Fathers of the Church.

Thus, Ambrose of Milan (c. 339-397) mentioned in his *Apologia Prophetae David* (390) that Bathsheba's union with David was a figurative union where she

---

9. Cardon, *Manuscripts of the Speculum Humanae Salvationis*, 2-3.

10. Cardon, *Manuscripts of the Speculum Humanae Salvationis*, 13-14. The typological doctrine began to develop with the text *Concordantia Veteris et Novi Testamenti* and other texts as in the *Tituli* of Ambrose of Milan (c. 339-397), now disappeared, or in the *Dittochaeon* or *Tituli Historiarum* by Prudentius (348-c. 410). This theory became very popular in the following centuries, even influencing Alcuino of York who wrote the *Glossa Ordinaria* considering this exegetical method.

represents the Church of the Nations and he represents Christ.[11] This union was not a legal union, but a union of faith. In this way, Ambrose intended to give a positive meaning to an act, that of adultery, which historically was not only frowned upon but also entailed the death penalty for those who perpetrated such a sin.

Following in the footsteps of Ambrose of Milan, Augustine of Hippo (354–430) mentions in his *Contra Faustum Manichaeum* (404–5) that David was the prefiguration of Christ.[12] For him, the etymology of the names of David and Bathsheba was sufficient indication to demonstrate this typology. On the one hand, David can be translated as 'strong hand' or 'desirable', which reinforces the prophecy 'The desired one of all the nations will come' (Hag. 2.7). On the other hand, Bathsheba translates as 'well of satiety' or 'seventh well', which connects with the Song of Songs where the Church appears as the wife called the 'well of living water' (Song 4.15). The allegorical interpretation in this case is important, since there are other ways to read this book. Jerome of Stridon in his *Epistle* LXIX, 419, spelled the name of Bathsheba as 'Bersabee', a region of southern Palestine where the source of water mentioned in Gen. 21.13 miraculously appeared. Augustine replaced the name of Bathsheba (as it appeared in Jerome's Vulgate) by that of Bersabee to establish that connection with the etymology of 'Bathsheba'. Considering this etymology, Augustine of Hippo affirms,

> He who is the desire of all nations loved the Church when washing herself on the roof, that is, when cleansing herself from the pollution of the world, and in spiritual contemplation mounting above her house of clay and trampling upon it; and after commencing an acquaintance, He puts to death the devil, whom He first entirely removes from her, and joins her to Himself in perpetual union.[13]

Thus, Bathsheba must be interpreted as *Ecclesia* or the Holy Church, the object most desired by Christ in the Song of Songs. David sinned for desiring Bathsheba. However, this desire should be understood as the prefiguration of Christ's desire for all the nations that will later culminate in his union with the Church, just as David will join Bathsheba.

Augustine of Hippo also mentions David and Solomon as prefigurations of Christ in *The City of God*: 'The things that are said about Solomon are uniquely for Christ, and in such a way that what we see figuratively in him, we find in Christ realised.'[14] Bathsheba appears as the prefiguration of the Virgin

---

11. Ambrose of Milan, *De Apologia Prophetae David*, ed. Pierre Hadot (Paris: M. Cordier, 1977), 73–4.

12. Augustine of Hippo, *Contra Faustum Manichaeum*, I, XXII, chap. 87, trans. Richard Stothert, in Philip Schaff (ed.), *Nicene and Post-Nicene Fathers*, first series, vol. 4 (Buffalo, NY: Christian Literature,1887). Available online: http://www.newadvent.org/fathers/140 622.htm (accessed 10 July 2021).

13. Augustine of Hippo, *Contra Faustum Manichaeum*, 629.

14. Augustine of Hippo, *De Civitate Dei*, XVII, 9, trans. Marcus Dods, in Philip Schaff (ed.), *Nicene and Post-Nicene Fathers*, first series, vol. 4 (Buffalo, NY: Christian Literature,

Mary. Their connection is established through certain related events: just as Bathsheba gave life to Solomon, so did the Virgin Mary give life to Christ; Christ performed his first miracle at the Wedding of Cana when he transformed the six water jugs into wine at the request of his mother, while Bathsheba ensured her son's ascension to the throne of his father, King David, through her intercession.[15] Therefore, the intercessory function of Bathsheba will be seen as the prefiguration of the Virgin Mary as an intercessor for all humanity. Likewise, the moment in which Solomon commands to bring a seat for his mother and had it placed on his right will be seen as the prefiguration of the coronation of the Virgin Mary by her Son in Heaven.[16] In Psalm 45 there is also a mention to a coronation and it was immediately placed in relation not only to Bathsheba's coronation but also to the Virgin Mary's,[17] 'daughters of kings are among your ladies of honour; at your right hand stands the queen in gold of Ophir' (Ps. 45.9). This would serve as inspiration to Adam de Saint-Victor (d. 1146), poet and composer of Latin hymns and musical sequences, who at the beginning of the twelfth century wrote a poem where he directly related Bathsheba with 'the queen at the right hand':

Bersabee sublimatur
Sedis consors regiae
Haec regi varietate
Vestis astat deauratae
Sicut regum filiae.[18]

(Bathsheba after being enthroned,
the king appears standing [before her]
who appears in gold clothing
as the daughter of kings.)

1887). Available online: http://www.newadvent.org/fathers/120117.htm (accessed 10 July 2021). In this chapter, Augustine of Hippo also indicates that Christ is descended from David through his mother, the Virgin Mary.

15. Lydwine Saulnier-Pernuit, *Les Trois Couronnements Tapisserie du Trésor de la cathédrale de Sens* (Belgium: Mame, 1993), 94–5.

16. Matilde Azcárate Luxán, 'La coronación de la Virgen en los tímpanos góticos españoles', *Anales de la Historia del Arte* 4 (1994): 353–4.

17. In fact, in Song 3:11 another coronation related to Bathsheba is mentioned, although it is she who crowns her son. The text reads as follows: 'Look, O daughters of Zion, at King Solomon, at the crown with which his mother crowned him on the day of his wedding, on the day of the gladness of his heart.'

18. Eugene Mittet and Pierre Aubry, *Les proses d'Adam de Saint-Victor* (Paris, 1900), 180–81, cited by Phillipe Verdier, *Le couronnement de la Vierge: les origines et les premiers développements d'un thème iconographique* (Montréal: Institut d'études médiévales Albert-le-Grand, 1980), 106.

Therefore, Psalm 45 appears as the source of inspiration through which Bathsheba appears crowned queen just like the Virgin Mary would later. However, this poem is not the only one that relates in some way the image of 'the queen at the right hand' with Bathsheba. Hildebert of Tours (1055–1133), in his first sermon dedicated to the assumption of the Virgin Mary, based in part on the same psalm, reflects this same idea.[19]

The original text reads as follows:

Si enim Salomon matri ad se venienti pro petitione Adoniae, thronum sibi collaleralem stravit, probabilius est [Christum] matrem statuisse ad dexteram secundum illud: 'Astitit Regina a dextris tuis (Sal. XLIV, 10)'. Et siont in die Ascensionis Domini: Dixit Dominus Domino meo, sede a dextris meis (Sal. CLX, 1).[20]

(If Solomon placed his mother on his right according to this 'the queen sat at your right hand (Ps 45:9)', so let it be known on the day of the Ascension of the Lord: 'The Lord said, Lord, sit at my right hand (Ps 160, 1)').

Therefore, Bathsheba and the Virgin Mary seem irremediably connected through the literature of the twelfth century, and from the thirteenth and fourteenth centuries this connection will continue with the development of the Marian cult and the creation of moralising and typological texts such as the *Bibles Moralisées*, the *Biblia Pauperum*, the *Speculum Humanae Salvationis* and the *Concordantiae Caritatis*. The visual nature of these works makes it difficult to separate the text from the image that accompanies it and therefore its textual analysis will be postponed.

These texts are just one example of the way in which medieval exegetes used the figure of David and Bathsheba within the typological system. According to this exegesis, medieval theologians could demonstrate that the arrival of Christ was part of a divine plan long before his arrival on earth and that, even without knowing it, all the Gentiles wanted it. The cycle of David and Bathsheba was one of the resources that these theologians used to prove it.

Although this type of interpretation of the Holy Scriptures is probably one of the most important in relation to the interpretation of Bathsheba, we must also consider the importance of the historical or literal interpretation of the Old Testament, which presents the facts as they appeared, in chronological order, with a beginning and an end, and which also had a great influence on the artistic representations of the Middle Ages.

Bathsheba is framed within a narrative that was believed to be true during the Middle Ages, since the events of the Old Testament were considered historical. Adam, Moses, Noah, Saul, David and Solomon were historical figures whose life

---

19. Verdier, *Le couronnement de la Vierge*, 104.

20. *Patrologiae Latinae*, ed. J. J. Bourassé and J.-P. Migne (Turnholt: Brepols, 1990), vol. 171, cols 630–31. Free translation by the author.

had been recorded by the authors of the Old Testament and whose veracity was unquestionable. One of the most influential figures during the Middle Ages was David, not only because he was chosen by God to lead his people, but because according to the evangelist Matthew, David was one of the ancestors of Christ, and through Bathsheba, his son Solomon too (Mt. 1.1). This relationship made David and Solomon the prefiguration of Christ and they appeared as his direct ancestors. Montague Rhodes James, in one of the first studies carried out on the iconographic repertoire of the Old Testament, mentions that to some extent the entire Old Testament illustration has a symbolic but not necessarily typological character. According to Rhodes James, if it had not been this way, the artists would not have bothered to represent the Old Testament.[21] In any case, the interest that these stories exerted made the artists try to represent them in an attractive and realistic way.

On the other hand, throughout the Middle Ages, the idea of the *imitatio David regis* can be found in the great royal houses of the time.[22] King David appears as the 'type' of perfect monarch, the envoy of Christ and the model recommended by the popes to Christian kings. His figure, activities and conquests were of great importance to medieval royalty. Since the eighth century, David's physical characteristics resemble those of Christ, but from the ninth century the pictorial formulas to represent David changed and made him a medieval monarch. Charles the Bald, Charlemagne and Louis the Pious, among others, identified themselves with the monarchs of Israel, ancestors of Christ through Jesse. Alcuin of York (c. 735–804), in his biblical commentary, or *Glossa Ordinaria*, written in the eighth century, promulgated a return to the Old Testament in an attempt to unify all Western Christendom, including those parts that had not yet been Christianised, urging monarchs, especially Charlemagne, to follow the model of Jerusalem during the time of the great kings and priests.[23] In this way, Charlemagne was considered a New David or a Josiah of Judah, and the anointing of the princes as early as the seventh century was intended to be a reflection of the anointing of Old Testament kings such as those of Saul, David or Solomon. In his analogy between King Louis the Pious and King David, Amalarius of Metz (c. 775–c. 850), disciple of Alcuin of York, emphasised the difference between the emperor as an individual and his eternal prototype: *Divo Hludovico vita. Novo David perennitas*.[24] With this he wished long life to the divine Louis and eternity to that new David embodied in the figure of the emperor of the Carolingian dynasty. In this context, the sanctity

---

21. Montague Rhodes James, *Illustrations of the Old Testament* (London: Roxburghe Club, 1927), 1–2.

22. Hugo Steger, *David Rex et Propheta: Köning David als vorbildliche Verkörperung des Herrschers und Dichters im Mittelalter, nach Bilddarstellungen des achten bis zwölften Jarhundents* (Nürnberg: Verlag Hans Carl, 1961), 124–5.

23. Cardon, *Manuscripts of the Speculum Humanae Salvationis*, 14–16.

24. Ernst H. Kantorowicz, *The King's Two Bodies: A Study in Medieval Political Theology* (Princeton: Princeton University Press, 1957), 81.

of Louis was not a synonym of the 'divine' epitaph but was manifested through the eternity corresponding to the king of Israel in whom the idea of the Carolingian empire as *regnum Davidicum* culminated and became manifest. This return to the Old Testament had a great impact on the religious mentality and the spiritual life of that new medieval society. There is no doubt that the Old Testament model favoured the Christianisation of Western Europe.[25] In fact, the identification of the Carolingian and then the Ottonian dynasty, followed by successive generations of European monarchs, with the kings of the Old Testament symbolises the materialisation of David's reign, or *Regnum Davidicum*, through the figure of Christ, to whom the king or emperor represents on Earth. In other words, the historical events that happen at a certain moment are inscribed within the history of salvation which begins with Christ and ends at the end of times. This historical or literal reading of the texts of the Old Testament, understood also in a symbolic way, will be of vital importance in the interpretation of the visual narrative of Bathsheba, since if David and Solomon could appear as examples to follow for a masculine royalty, on several occasions so can Bathsheba appear as an archetype in which different royal women can be reflected.

Methodology for a visual analysis of Bathsheba

For the visual analysis of the images of Bathsheba, this work will follow a traditional methodology within the framework of the studies of the history of art, especially that of the field of iconography.[26] Although there are different opinions on the definition of iconography, in this study we have chosen to follow the one that Erwin Panofsky outlined at the time in 1955 in his study on iconography and iconology.[27] For Panofsky, the study of art objects and images could be systematised following three different levels of interpretation: the first has to do with the identification of objects and figures through the familiarity of the viewer with them and is descriptive.[28] The second one deals with the area of iconography

25. Cardon, *Manuscripts of the Speculum Humanae Salvationis*, 16. In this context we can speak of a spiritual climate where the Church, as a community, is assimilated to the 'people of God' of the Bible.

26. Réau, *Iconografía del arte cristiano*, vol. 3, 13–22. A traditional definition of iconography is the science that studies the origin and formation of images, taking into account their relationship with the allegorical and the symbolic, as well as their identification through the attributes that almost always accompany them. However, this definition falls short for the study of a complex figure such as Bathsheba.

27. Erwin Panofsky, 'Iconography and iconology: An introduction to the study of Renaissance art', in *Meaning in the Visual Arts: Papers in and on Art History* (New York: Doubldeday Anchor, 1955), 51–67.

28. Panofsky, 'Iconography and iconology', 53–4. When looking at the Last Supper picture a viewer would first see thirteen men sitting around a table in a room. Panofsky explained that this first identification, or pre-iconographic description, was subdivided into the factual and the expressive. The understanding of the factual and the expressive can vary

proper, that is, the linking of artistic motifs and composition with conventional themes, concepts or meanings.[29] It is at this level that images, stories and allegories are identified. The third refers to the iconological interpretation and takes into account the intrinsic meaning or content of the work.[30] This level considers the personal history of the artist, the techniques used in the artistic creation and the cultural environment in which a work was created. Art is seen not as an isolated incident, but as the product of a historical, sociological, economic and religious environment.[31] In this way, it is possible to discern several attitudes, ideas or beliefs related to the way in which medieval society viewed women in general, and for this study, Bathsheba in particular.

Although Panofsky's theories have been criticised, his methodology is still today one of the best tools for the study of images in the history of medieval art and the one that best allows us to do justice to the object within its complex historical particularities. Although the three phases proposed by Panofsky will not be specified in each case, his considerations about the interpretation of the images will be the guide through which this study will be developed.

Bathsheba: Iconography study

Even though Bathsheba is a secondary character within the great biblical narratives of David and Solomon, in the visual arts her figure had a great iconographic development. Medieval artists represented all the biblical scenes where her story was told, and she was included in other scenes in which the biblical text

greatly depending on the individual experience. In this way, a viewer could recognize the loaves and fishes that were on the table during the Last Supper or could recognize the facial expressions of surprise and disbelief of the figures.

29. Panofsky, 'Iconography and iconology', 54–5. At this level, the image of thirteen men eating around a table can already be identified as a representation of the Last Supper. This second level of interpretation would imply a non-interpretative descriptive analysis and would be responsible for the identification, description and classification of the images.

30. Panofsky, 'Iconography and iconology', 55–6. According to Panofsky, this level can be understood once 'the underlying principles that reveal the basic attitude of a nation, a period, a class, a religious or philosophical belief, qualified by a personality and condensed into a single work' has been determined.

31. Panofsky, 'Iconography and iconology', 65–7. In order to face an iconographic and iconological study, we must always bear in mind that identifications and interpretations will be subject to the subjective knowledge of the art historian and that, for that same reason, it is necessary to supply and correct them through knowledge of historical processes, or what Panofsky called 'history of tradition'. Each of the three levels has its own correction principle: the pre-iconographic description has the history of styles; the iconographic study has the history of types; and finally, the iconological study has the history of symbols (or cultural symptoms).

says nothing about her. However, only four scenes were relevant enough to be represented assiduously during the Middle Ages: Bathsheba's bath, David rebuked by Nathan, the intercession of Bathsheba and Bathsheba sitting on the right side of Solomon. The first two scenes are directly related to the sin of adultery committed by David and Bathsheba, while the last two are directly related to Bathsheba's role as queen mother and her role as a key instrument in the ascension to the throne of her son Solomon. These four scenes developed more or less stable iconographic models that were able to cross the borders of space and time in medieval Europe. The creation of these models responded to the two types of narrations mentioned above, the historical and the symbolic narratives, each one conditioned by the type of manuscript in which the iconography of Bathsheba was found, an iconography that presents a myriad of interpretations that place Bathsheba between the two opposite poles of women in the Middle Ages, as will be seen in the iconology section of this study.

Bathsheba's bath

The first scene in which Bathsheba makes an appearance in the Old Testament is in 2 Sam. 11.2-4:

> It happened, late one afternoon, when David rose from his couch and was walking about on the roof of the king's house, that he saw from the roof a woman bathing; the woman was very beautiful. David sent someone to inquire about the woman. It was reported, 'This is Bathsheba daughter of Eliam, the wife of Uriah the Hittite.' So David sent messengers to get her, and she came to him, and he lay with her. (Now she was purifying herself after her period.) Then she returned to her house.

The text offers the facts but leaves many aspects without clarification such as the physical reality in which the main characters were. Exactly where was Bathsheba bathing? In a bathroom in her house or in a pool in the garden? What was her degree of nudity? Was she alone or accompanied by other women? What the Old Testament ignores will be supplied by the imagination of the artists.

Bathsheba's bath scene may appear alone or as part of a more complex iconographic cycle (see figures 1–4 of the link cited on footnote 1). When the bathroom appears next to other episodes of David's life, these usually include the battle between David and Goliath, David playing the harp in the presence of Saul, David sending Uriah to certain death and the battle where he dies. In some examples, this last scene is the only one that accompanies the bath scene.

The iconographic origin of Bathsheba's bath could be found in Graeco-Roman scenes from the bath of Venus or Diana, whose typology could have easily been transferred to the biblical scene. Due to the scarce information found in the Bible about the place and the figures that were present, the artists of the Middle Ages created various iconographic models based on the degree of Bathsheba's nudity and the physical space where the bath took place. Thus, Bathsheba can appear either in undergarments, covered by a veil, or completely nude. Regardless of her degree of nudity, Bathsheba can be found inside an architectural space, sometimes bathing in a wooden tub, or she can be outdoors in a garden within a pond or inside/next to a fountain of very different typologies. Some examples merge the bath episode with that of the messenger that David sent to take her to the palace, so it is possible to find an emissary carrying or delivering a letter to Bathsheba in some bath scenes. In the background of these images, one can see King David dressed in robes that denote his position, even wearing the mantle with the *fleur-de-lys* typical of the French monarchy in some cases. As a rule, David usually wears a crown and is represented as a mature man with a beard. In many images, the king is usually accompanied by his servants, perhaps referring to the moment when he asks about Bathsheba.

The last iconographic element to be considered is that on many occasions Bathsheba, whether dressed, covered by a veil or in the nude, is attended by one or several servants or ladies-in-waiting, who are usually dressed. Sometimes these women hold the dress or shoes of Bathsheba; in others they present a mirror, a comb and a tray or glass with red fruits; and in some examples they look towards David while pointing to Bathsheba.

David rebuked by Nathan

The biblical reference to David rebuked by the prophet Nathan is found in 2 Samuel 12. In this narrative, Nathan rebukes King David for his adultery with Bathsheba, aggravated by the murder of Uriah the Hittite, by using a parable. A rich man steals the only sheep that a poor man had to feed it to an unexpected visitor, even though the rich man had a large number of livestock. David, upon hearing this story, became angry and asked that this man be punished, but Nathan identified him with David and then communicated the punishment that God had decided: the son whom he had fathered would die on the seventh day after his birth. In this story, Bathsheba is not expressly mentioned.

Although there are two well-differentiated iconographic traditions on this subject, the Eastern and the Western, it is possible that both had a very well-defined archetype that probably was common for both (see figures 5–8 of the link in footnote 1). Some researchers like Kurt Weitzmann have considered the probable existence, already in the fourth century, of early Christian iconographic cycles that represented the life of David.[32] This iconography would have been based on the appropriation of Graeco-Roman compositions and typologies when the first Christian artists faced the novel and difficult task of illustrating the Bible.[33] The image of David sitting on his throne, or standing, listening to the accusations of Nathan

---

32. Kurt Weitzmann, *Late Antique and Early Christian Book Illumination* (London: George Braziller, 1977), 13.

33. Kurt Weitzmann, *Byzantine Book Illumination and Ivories* (London: Ashgate, 1980), 55.

standing can be related to Graeco-Roman images of dialogue between a seated figure and a standing figure, or even between two standing figures.[34] Subsequent modifications have to be sought directly in the Bible, biblical commentaries or in Christian practices. Thus, when the kneeling figure of David appears in the East, it is no more than the visualisation of the Byzantine confessional practice and does not require the search for an extra-biblical source as Leslie Brubaker has rightly highlighted in her study of vision and meaning in Byzantium.[35] The origin of the introduction in some iconographic examples of the lifeless body of Uriah or the parable of the rich man who steals the poor together with the rebuke of Nathan can be found directly in the texts and biblical commentaries already mentioned. Taking these considerations into account, medieval artists sometimes included an angel, the allegory of repentance (*Metanoia*) and Bathsheba. The figure of Bathsheba is the only one common to the two traditions, the Eastern and Western, the angel and Metanoia being examples that can only be found in the Byzantine Empire. These figures were introduced even though they were not mentioned in the biblical narrative. The difference between these two traditions is given by the place that Bathsheba occupies in the composition: in the Eastern examples, Bathsheba appears seated under an architectural structure separated from the scene of the rebuke. In the Western examples, Bathsheba is standing or sitting holding her son, in front of an architectural structure, but located behind David. This scene can also appear isolated or as part of a more complete narrative cycle.

Bathsheba's intercession

There are two different moments in the story of Bathsheba in which she appears as an intercessor: one before David and the other before her son, Solomon. Both scenes will be represented with assiduity in medieval manuscript illumination.

The first intercession takes place when Bathsheba intercedes to David on behalf of her son Solomon to be his successor (1 Kgs 1.11-27) (see above) and the second intercession takes place when Adonijah asks Bathsheba to speak in his favour before Solomon (1 Kgs 2.19-25) (see above). From these chapters will come two iconographic formulas for Bathsheba as queen, which are different since there are two different moments contemplated: the intercession and Bathsheba sitting to the right side of Solomon.

Intercession scenes usually represent the intervention of one person in favour of another.[36] An act of intercession implies, on the one hand, the presence of

---

34. Hugo Buchthal, *The Miniatures of the Paris Psalter: A Study in Middle Byzantine Painting* (London: The Warburg Institute, 1938), 27.

35. Leslie Brubaker, *Vision and Meaning in 9th Century Byzantium* (Cambridge: Cambridge University Press, 1999), 352.

36. Jean-Marie Moeglin, 'L'Intercession du Moyen Âge à l'époque modern: Autour d'une practique sociale', *École practique des Hautes Études, Sciences Historiques et philologiques V: Hautes études médiévales et modernes* (Géneve: Droz, 2004), 113–202.

at least two or three people (the one who intercedes, the person to whom one intercedes to and the person who is seeking the intercession). On the other hand, it implies a relationship of mediation established by the intercessor with its referents and, finally, a request or demand for something that is not for the intercessor, but for another person. Above all, intercession is a practice rather than an institution and therefore obeys principles, rituals and unwritten rules. There are two types of intercession, religious[37] and socio-political. The latter will be the type of intercession that Bathsheba will perform and as such it is possible that her representation reflects fully accepted social practices.

Considering these aspects of the practice of intercession, this will be represented in various ways in relation to Bathsheba (see figures 9–12 of the link). On the one hand, Bathsheba appears before David standing or kneeling. David, on the other hand, appears either on a throne, or convalescent on a bed. Some examples show Bathsheba standing before King David's bed. In several cases Bathsheba appears accompanied by the prophet Nathan as indicated in 1 Kgs 1.24-27. These two figures are usually represented standing in front of the throne of David or located next to the bed of the convalescent king. In other cases, the figure of Abishag, the Shunamite, is included, following the text of 1 Kgs 1.15, although she only appears in the scenes where an old King David is in bed. Some examples include courtiers surrounding either the throne or King David's bed. Finally, Solomon is also included being crowned and/or anointed with Bathsheba. That is, the result of the request of Bathsheba is included in the scene. In the few surviving examples of Bathsheba's intercession before Solomon, they follow the same iconography, but Solomon is usually portrayed as a young or mature man, thus distinguishing this iconography from that of Bathsheba's intercession before an elderly King David.

This is a very variable iconography that does not have an established model or a linear evolution from a simple iconography model to a more complex one. All these elements can be found at any time. Like Nathan's rebuke, the image of David sitting on his throne listening to the request of Bathsheba standing or kneeling can be related to Graeco-Roman images of dialogue.[37]

Bathsheba seated to the right of King Solomon

The biblical reference of Bathsheba sitting on the right of Solomon appears in 1 Kgs 2.19 and is part of the life cycle of King Solomon (see above). This is the last scene in which Bathsheba appears in the Bible. Nothing else is known about her.

The iconography of Bathsheba sitting to the right of Solomon was codified rather quickly, although with slight variations that will be considered below.[38]

---

37. Buchthal, *The Miniatures of the Paris Psalter*, 27.

38. Louis Réau, *Iconografía del arte cristiano: Iconografía de la Biblia. El Antiguo Testamento*, vol.1, trans. José María Sousa Jiménez (Barcelona: Ediciones del Serbal, 2000), 337.

Bathsheba can appear either on the right or on the left of Solomon on a bench or individual thrones of the most diverse typology (see figures 13-16). It is possible that the artists wondered if Bathsheba had to be to the right of the composition or to the right of Solomon, in which case Bathsheba could appear both on the left and on the right within the composition. When the thrones appear separated, Solomon is usually seated on a high throne with a high back, and Bathsheba in a smaller and less elaborate one. In the case of benches, these tend to be simpler. Solomon usually has his index finger raised as an address and Bathsheba appears with hands raised at chest level, in a gesture of supplication or acceptance. In some cases, Bathsheba does not wear a crown, but her clothes and headdress indicate her position as a lady of high birth. However, in other examples, Bathsheba appears crowned queen or being crowned by her son Solomon. An iconographic variation on this last model is that of Bathsheba crowning his son Solomon, although it is not a very common iconography (see note 19). The Bible does not include the scene of Bathsheba crowned by Solomon possibly because Bathsheba was already a queen after her wedding with King David, and when David died, she became the queen mother of Solomon.[39]

The iconography of Bathsheba sitting to the right of Solomon could have its origins in representations of the gods of classical antiquity, especially the images of Hera/Juno enthroned with Zeus/Jupiter,[40] of the emperors during the Roman Empire and later of the Byzantine emperors, whose representations were widely disseminated in numerous artistic media (see note 19).

Bathsheba: Iconology study

Following Panofsky's methodology, we will contextualise the scenes that have been described in the previous section. These images do not appear isolated but are part of the material culture of the medieval era, and as such they had a very specific form and purpose. Due to the finite space available in this study, we have chosen to use four representative examples. The four examples that have been chosen will be organized following the biblical narrative and each of them will represent a particular type of manuscript. Although this approach is fragmentary, the study of these four cases will allow us to identify the multiple interpretations to which Bathsheba was subjected to in the Middle Ages.

---

39. Réau, *Iconografía del arte cristiano*, vol.1, 337. As already mentioned, Reáu describes the iconography of Bathsheba seated to right side of Solomon and relates it to the iconography of the Coronation of the Virgin Mary but does not mention the coronation itself or the multiple interpretations to which this scene may be subject to.

40. There are numerous examples of these two gods enthroned alone or together with the rest of the Olympian deities. An example appears in the frieze of the Parthenon of Greece or in the metopes of the temple of Selinunte in Sicily.

Bathsheba's bath and Books of Hours

The Book of Hours is a small-format devotional codex that was created for the private use of secular society and was extremely popular during the Late Middle Ages.[41] The central text of this prayer book is the Little Office of the Virgin Mary, also known as the Hours of the Virgin. This text presents a shorter version of the prayers and devotions that were made during the eight canonical hours (Matins, Lauds, Prime, Terce, Sext, Nona, Vespers and Compline) and that were recited first by the monks and the clergy, and then by a secular society eager to imitate their religious lives.[42] Apart from the Hours of the Virgin, the Book of Hours also incorporates other auxiliary texts such as, for example, the litany of the saints, the suffrages, the Office of the Dead, the Seven Penitential Psalms, the Gradual Psalms and other prayers chosen by the patron of the manuscript. At the beginning of each Book of Hours, there is usually a liturgical or occupational calendar that helps identify the region or geographical area in which that manuscript was used.[43] Manuscripts containing the Hours of the Virgin can already be found in the eleventh century. Later, during the twelfth and thirteenth centuries, these Hours were incorporated into the Psalter, the most popular devotional book among secular society at that time, and soon after a type of manuscript called the Psalter-Hours was formed. However, the Hours became so important that towards the end of the thirteenth century they became a separate book from the Psalter. It was at this moment that the other auxiliary texts that formed the Book of Hours that we know today began to be incorporated. This book was one of the great bestsellers of the Middle Ages, staying as one of the great favourites for more than 250 years. This popularity must be associated with the devotion to the Virgin Mary, who through the mystery of the Incarnation, becomes the great mediator of humanity before God. The Book of Hours symbolised in a tangential way that relationship between the one who prays and the Virgin Mary, and ultimately Christ/God.[44]

Within this context, Bathsheba appears as a very complex figure capable of assuming different meanings within the Book of Hours. The iconography of

---

41. For a more detailed description of Books of Hours, see Christopher De Hamel, *A History of Illuminated Manuscripts* (London: Phaidon Press, 1986), 168–98.

42. Michelle P. Brown, *Understanding Illuminated Manuscripts: A Guide to Technical Terms* (Los Angeles: The J. Paul Getty Museum, 1994), 23–4.

43. Brown, *Understanding Illuminated Manuscripts*, 123. By 'use', we refer to the type of liturgy that was practiced in a geographic region or by a certain group of people. During the Middle Ages, some 'uses' were specific to a cathedral or to the most important religious orders and could sometimes appear beyond their region of origin. Many Books of Hours have been identified according to 'use'.

44. John Harthan, *The Book of Hours* (New York: Thomas Y. Crowell, 1977), 14. Harthan mentions that the Virgin Mary was the substitute mother of all, the new Eve, the intercessor before God. In his book he quotes the famous historian Eileen Power, who says of the Virgin Mary that she was more powerful than the saints and less fearful than God. As a mother, she exercised a great influence on Christ, and her position between man and his creator was

Figure 3.1 *Cycle of David and Bathsheba, Book of Hours of Agnes of Bohemia*, Bamberg, Germany, c. 1204–19, New York, The Pierpont Morgan Library, Ms. M. 739, fol. 17v.

Bathsheba as queen that appears in this type of manuscript is the intercession of Bathsheba before King David on behalf of Solomon to be his successor and Bathsheba sitting on the right side of her son. The number of occasions in which these representations appear pale in comparison to the number of iconographic examples of Bathsheba's bath, that is, from the first moment in which King David, from the top of his palace, gazes the figure of Bathsheba in the bath[45] (Figure 3.1).

In this study I have chosen one of the oldest known Books of Hours where this story is represented, the Book of Hours of Agnes of Bohemia,[46] currently in New York at the Pierpont Morgan Library with the accession number Ms. M. 739. Originally

described by Bernard of Clairvaux when he says that Christ wants us to have everything through Mary.

45. For a complete study of this iconography, see Mónica A. Walker Vadillo, *Bathsheba in Late Medieval French Manuscript Illumination: Innocent Object of Desire or Agent of Sin?* (Lampeter: Edwin Mellen Press, 2008).

46. Meta Harrsen, *Central European Manuscripts in the Pierpont Morgan Library* (New York: Pierpont Morgan Library, 1958), 34. The official title of this manuscript is that of *Cursus Sanctae Mariae*. It was preceded by a calendar for the use of a nun in a convent

commissioned by Kunegunda of Swabia in the first quarter of the thirteenth century, it ended up being a gift for her niece, Agnes of Bohemia, daughter of King Ottokar I of Bohemia. For Agnes, educated in Cistercian and Premonstratensian convents, this Book of Hours played a very important role in her spiritual education.[47] The manuscript itself contains a calendar, the Hours of the Virgin combined with the Hours of the Trinity, the Hours of the Holy Spirit, the Hours of the Cross and the Hours of All Saints. Also included are the Office of the Dead (which follows the Premonstratensian ritual), the Litany, the Suffrages and an abbreviated Psalter, to end with some miscellaneous prayers. Although the suffrages contain historiated initials, it is the prefatory cycle that carries all the decorative load. With a total of thirty-two miniatures representing stories from the Old and New Testaments, the prefatory cycle follows the tradition of other similar cycles in the Psalters and is placed at the beginning of the manuscript, behind the calendar and several prayers. Other scholars have been able to identify the hand of three different artists in the decoration of this manuscript which seem to follow, although very superficially, the style of the miniaturist schools of Regensburg, Bamberg and Salzburg.[48] The folios, made in yellowish vellum, were divided into two, three and up to four horizontal registers. On this division of the space are drawn with sepia and red ink figures in backgrounds using two colours that divide the image (green-red, yellow-red and blue-green). The images are accompanied by inscriptions describing the stories in the vernacular language, in this case in Middle High German. The story of Bathsheba appears in folios 17v and 18r.

The visual representation of Bathsheba begins in the second horizontal register of folio 17v with David watching Bathsheba bathing, next to the scene of Bathsheba lying with King David. In this case, the bath scene takes place outside, next to a stream, and Bathsheba appears in her undergarments washing her feet. These elements present Bathsheba as the tempter of David because if she did not want to be observed by the king, why was she outdoors where anyone could look at her? Behind her, a maid points a finger at David who appears inside a tower spying on her. In this case there is no doubt about the sin that is represented, that of lust, consummated in the next scene, where David and Bathsheba appear directly in bed. In the next horizontal register is David rebuked by Nathan and David composing the *Miserere mei*. In the first horizontal register of folio 18r, Bathsheba appears, interceding before David so that Solomon would become his successor,

in Bohemia. Then followed a prayer, the *tituli* and the rubrics in Middle High German. It is believed that it was created in the monastery of Luka, near Znaim.

47. Roger S. Wieck, *Painted Prayers: The Book of Hours in Medieval and Renaissance Art* (New York: George Braziller, 1997), 21. See also Harrsen, *Central European Manuscripts in the Pierpont Morgan Library*, 34–5. Harrsen indicates more specifically the reasons why this manuscript has been attributed to the royal family of Bohemia.

48. 'Descriptions of medieval and renaissance manuscripts. MS. 739', *Corsair: The Online Research Resource of the Pierpont Morgan Library*. Available online: http://corsair.morgan library.org/msdescr/BBM0739.htm (accessed 10 July 2021).

accompanied by the anointing and coronation of his son Solomon. Both the images and the texts that accompany them seem to have a didactic value designed to offer the young princess the most important facts of the Bible in a visual format that is easy to understand and remember.[49] The two chosen moments of the story of Bathsheba make clear the position of this figure within the historical narrative. On the one hand, Bathsheba is the origin of David's sin, adultery and the death of Uriah the Hittite. However, the inclusion of the composition of the *Miserere mei*, after the great sin, redeems Bathsheba in a certain way since it was because of her that not only Psalm 51 was created but also the whole Psalter. This relationship can be found in the legends of the Holy Cross (*De ligno sancte crucis*) that proliferated in Latin and vernacular languages in Europe during the twelfth and thirteenth centuries. This legend offers a very complex series of medieval narratives based on the Old Testament that told the story of the wood of the cross on which Christ died, which was made with a tree whose genealogy could be traced back to the Tree of Knowledge in the Garden of Eden. The title that accompanies Psalm 51 ('To the Leader. A Psalm of David, When the Prophet Nathan Came to Him after He Had Gone in to Bathsheba'), may have been the origin of an extra-biblical story that was incorporated into these legends.[50] Later, Bathsheba interceding with David to make Solomon his successor shows the most important facet of Queen Bathsheba since it is through her influence that one of the great kings of the Old Testament not only manages to reign but will become one of the ancestors of Christ (Mt. 1.6-7). Probably the most important lesson that Agnes of Bohemia could learn about this story is that all sin, including that of lust, can be forgiven through the grace of God if repentance is sincere as the story of David and Bathsheba demonstrates.[51]

David rebuked by Nathan and the Homilies of Gregory of Nazianzus

After the restoration of the cult of images in 843 in the Byzantine Empire, the depictions of Bathsheba became more numerous. Thus, Bathsheba is represented in a manuscript that contains, among others, the *Homilies* of Gregory of Nazianzus (329–389), one of the Fathers of the Church. Gregory was Archbishop of Constantinople and a very prolific writer whose eloquence and theological explanations were so appreciated by the Byzantines that they produced many copies of his sermons throughout the history of Byzantium. This has allowed many Byzantine manuscripts containing the liturgical version of his homilies

---

49. Wieck, *Painted Prayers*, 21.

50. Claire L. Costley, 'David, Bathsheba and the penitential psalms', *Renaissance Quaterly* 57, no. 5 (2004): 1235–77.

51. For a more detailed discussion on the connection between the story of David and Bathsheba and the Seven Deadly Sins, see Monica Ann Walker Vadillo, 'Bathsheba's bath and the seven deadly sins: A new interpretation of a visual narrative strategy in late medieval Books of Hours', in *Ambiguous Women in Medieval Art*, ed. Monica A. Walker Vadillo (Budapest: Trivent Publishing, 2019), 56–82.

to have survived to this day,[52] although there are only three complete editions. Of the three copies, the most important and most studied is that found in the Bibliothèque Nationale de France with the signature Codex Graecus 510 created in the ninth century.[53] The Codex Graecus 510 is a large manuscript whose pages contain numerous miniatures and an extensive use of gold leaf. It contains a total of forty-six full-page miniatures with about two hundred scenes divided into vignettes with golden frames. Although the hands of several scribes and three miniaturists have been identified, the consistency with which this manuscript was carried out suggests that there was only one person in charge of supervising the project. According to Brubaker, the identification of this person has been possible considering not only the choice of text but also the choice of the images that accompany it, the high cost of the manuscript and the recipient. All these elements indicate that it was Photius, Patriarch of Constantinople, who commissioned, supervised and paid for this manuscript as a gift for Emperor Basil I, whose portrait and that of his family appears on the frontispiece of the manuscript. These images allowed us to date it between the end of 879 and 882, a crucial moment for the Byzantine annals which was marked by a rapid economic recovery and religious consolidation after the last iconoclastic period that prohibited the use of images between 813 and 843. The Codex Graecus 510 is the only Byzantine manuscript of the second half of the ninth century that can be dated safely and the only one we know that was produced especially for a Byzantine emperor by the patriarch of the Orthodox Church (Figure 3.2).

The represented themes encompass not only portraits but also biblical, hagiographic and historical cycles. The biblical scenes of the Old and New Testaments are represented in the same proportion, although the scenes of the Old Testament tend to be longer and more autonomous, while those of the New Testament are shorter and organized thematically. Not all the scenes are represented in chronological order: historical events and hagiographic scenes can be interspersed with the biblical scenes, and there are even episodes of the Old Testament combined in the same folio with episodes of the New Testament. Despite this supposed disorganisation, the images have been chosen with extreme care and relate to the text they accompany in four ways: to illustrate the historical circumstances under which Gregory delivered his sermons; to represent the main theme of the homily following its title; to show some scene mentioned in the homilies; or, finally, to teach topics parallel to the sermon in an exegetical

---

52. Leslie Brubaker, *Vision and Meaning in Ninth-Century Byzantium: Image as Exegesis in the Homilies of Gregory of Nazianzus* (Cambridge: Cambridge University Press, 1999), 13. A selection of Gregory of Nazianzus's homilies were recited throughout the liturgical calendar of the Byzantine Church. These liturgical editions contained illustrations.

53. For a codicological study, see Brubaker, *Vision and Meaning in Ninth-Century Byzantium*, 1–13. In fact, this book is the best study done to date of this manuscript in question and it is to which we will refer to in the following pages. The pages to which we will refer are 1–12 and 201–25.

Figure 3.2 *David rebuked by Nathan, Homily of Gregory of Nazianzus, Constantinople, Byzantine Empire*, Paris, c. 879–83, Paris, Bibliothèque nationale de France, Codex Graecus 510, fol. 143v.

manner without relying on the examples given by Gregory in the text. However, apart from the fact that the miniatures respond, more or less literally, to the text they accompany, the choice of certain themes had an underlying purpose. Some miniatures of this manuscript responded mainly to the imperial character of the addressee, Basil I. Photius chose a series of themes destined to legitimise and praise the power of the new Macedonian dynasty, emphasising the connections between Emperor Basil I and Constantine the Great as well as with Old Testament characters such as Joseph, Samson, David and Joshua. Of all these the most interesting to this study is that of David.

David was the ideal ruler of the Old Testament and therefore frequently was connected to the Byzantine emperors.[54] In spite of this, David only appears in two scenes of the *Homilies* of Gregory of Nazianzus: the anointing of David represented

---

54. Anthony Cutler and Nicolas Oikonomides, 'An imperial Byzantine casket and its fate at a humanist's hands', *The Art Bulletin* 70 (1988): 77–87. The comparison between King David and Emperor Basil I obtained visual form through an ivory chest found in the Palazzo Venezia in Rome. In this chest you can see the imperial couple, Basil and Eudokia, on the lid. On the body of the chest, the scenes of the life of David were chosen to symbolically show some events of the life of Emperor Basil I. This association was intended to flatter the emperor.

in folio 174v and the repentance of David after Nathan's rebuke represented in folio 143v. Bathsheba appears in the latter image. This scene would visualise the theme of forgiveness developed in the sermon it accompanies. Although Gregory does not seem to allude specifically to David's penance, he does mention his pain and his liberation through God's forgiveness.[55] The inscription that accompanies the scene is one of the clearest and brightest of the entire manuscript. David says, 'I have sinned before the Lord,' to which Nathan responds, 'And the Lord has forgiven your sins.' This scene does not properly represent the rebuke, a theme that will be much more frequent in Psalters, but repentance. In this manuscript, David, dressed as a Byzantine emperor, kneels before Nathan to ask for forgiveness. Behind is an archangel, who must be Michael, although the text does not state it explicitly. It is possible that Photius did not want to include the name of the archangel because it is the same name of the Emperor Michael III who was murdered by Basil I. Moreover, the archangel Michael does not appear in any biblical text related to this scene. Its inclusion is due to a Byzantine and anonymous paraphrase called *Historical Palaia*. In this commentary, when David confesses his crimes and repents, the archangel Michael, whose name appears in other examples, stops the sword of God's punishment. In the later part of the scene, Bathsheba appears richly dressed in Byzantine robes under a dome behind the throne of King David. In this scene Bathsheba is a secondary character. The texts never mention that Bathsheba was present in this scene, so that her inclusion in this episode could be understood as *fons et origo mali*, the source and origin of evil, as Louis Réau suggests.

The choice of this scene by Photius highlights one of the most important issues that appears throughout the manuscript: the proper behaviour that sovereigns must have and, particularly, the importance place on sovereigns following the recommendations of their religious advisors. The scene of David's repentance is likely to imply, by extension, a scene of repentance by Basil I. Just as David wished Bathsheba, Uriah's wife, Basil I married the mistress of Michael III, Eudokia Ingerina. In the same way that David sent Uriah to certain death, Basil I obtained the throne through the assassination of Emperor Michael III. Likewise, just as the prophet Nathan forgave David his sins in the name of God, so could Photius exercise forgiveness as patriarch and, consequently, representative of God on earth. Despite the secular symbolic content that can be given to this manuscript and especially the scene of David's repentance, most of the scenes follow a historical narrative linked to biblical events. In any case, the scene of repentance includes the figure of Bathsheba as the origin of sin and a witness to his repentance.

Bathsheba in the Queen Mary Psalter

The Queen Mary Psalter was created between 1310 and 1320 in England and given to Queen Mary Tudor in 1553, hence its name, although it has recently been

---

55. Brubaker, *Vision and Meaning in Ninth-Century Byzantium*, 193 and 413.

proposed to change it to that of Isabella of France's Psalter.[56] The work is kept in the British Library with the signature Ms. Royal 2 B VII. Its importance is due to the delicate and courtly style of its illustrations, which influenced many English manuscripts of the fourteenth century. Like other Psalters of its time, it contains the 150 Psalms preceded by a calendar and followed by canticles (including the Athanasian Creed) and by a litany of the Saints in Latin.[57] The decoration of this manuscript can be divided into three parts. The first is a pictorial book of 223 scenes with Anglo-Norman vernacular descriptions of the Old Testament, ranging from the Fall of the Angels and Creation to the death of King Solomon; the second is a series of genealogical tables and a calendar; and in the third, the images that accompany the 150 Psalms are included. These images appear in three places: at the beginning of each division of the Psalter, a complete folio appears with the events of the New Testament from the Annunciation to the Last Judgment; an initial story with a cycle of the life of King David follows after the incipit (the first words of a text) of each section of the Psalter, and in all the Psalms there is a large number of marginal illustrations ranging from a bestiary to a mirror of courtly life, to the miracles of the Virgin and the martyrdom of the saints. There is a total of eight hundred images distributed throughout the manuscript, many of them executed in ink and painted with very green, grey and red colours.

Most of the themes that decorate this manuscript highlight the actions that must be carried out by the rulers, the importance of family and the crucial role of women.[58] Among these women is Bathsheba, whose history is included in the Old Testament cycle. Her story begins with David seeing Bathsheba through a window, although in this case Bathsheba is neither naked nor bathing. The next scene in which she appears is in that of the adultery proper. In this case, David and Bathsheba are together in a bed covered by a sheet, but it is Bathsheba instead of David who appears as the active figure in adultery since it is she who hugs him. Here begins the misfortune of David, whose family will pay the consequences of his adultery.[59] Finally, Bathsheba redeems herself as queen and mother when she intercedes on behalf of her son Solomon (Figure 3.3).

56. Ann Rudloff Stanton, 'The Queen Mary Psalter: A study of affect and audience', *Transactions of the American Philosophical Society* 91, no. 6 (2001): 12.

57. George Warner, *Queen Mary's Psalter: Miniatures and Drawings by an English Artist of the 14th Century Reproduced from Royal Ms. 2 B. VII in the British Museum* (London: The British Museum, 1912), 3–4. Neither the textual nor the stylistic analysis has allowed the researchers to identify the precise place where the manuscript was produced, although it is believed that it originated in London or Westminster.

58. Ann Rudloff Stanton, 'From Eve to Bathsheba and beyond: Motherhood in the Queen Mary Psalter', in *Women and the Book: Assessing the Visual Evidence*, ed. Jane H. M. Taylor and Lesley Smith (London: British Library, 1995), 172–3.

59. The next scene is the rape of his daughter Tamar by his son Amnon, and the description in Anglo-Norman explains that this violation is a consequence of the adultery of David and Bathsheba. For more information, see Stanton, 'From Eve to Bathsheba and beyond', 179.

Figure 3.3 *The intercession of Bathsheba, Psalter of Queen Mary Tudor or Isabella of France*, London or Westminster, England, c. 1310–20, London, @The British Library Board, Ms. Royal 2 B VII, fol. 63v.

Bathsheba is but one among many other mothers who are represented in the Queen Mary Psalter.[60] Just as these other women, the actions of Bathsheba will determine the life of her son and through these actions she redeems her own sins, because she assures him of the throne even though he did not have the right to reign. The emphasis on the mother figures of the biblical story indicates that this work was probably created for a woman of the English court. The high cost of the materials, the number of images and the presence of an exceptional master artist reinforces this hypothesis. Stanton proposes as possible recipient, Isabella of France, queen consort of Edward II of England.[61] The daughter of King Philippe IV of France and Joan I of Navarre, in 1308, when she was twelve years old, she travelled to England to marry Edward II.[62] She was known throughout Europe for her beauty, diplomatic skills and intelligence. As queen of England, she bargained with the English barons, as well as with the Scots and the French on behalf of her

---

60. Other important female figures that appear in the Old Testament are Eve, Sarah, Haggar, Rachel, Hannah and Delilah, among others; the Virgin Mary appears in the New Testament, to which the mothers of the saints of Christian hagiography are added.

61. Stanton, 'The Queen Mary Psalter', 231–43.

62. See Alison Weir, *Queen Isabella: She-Wolf of France, Queen of England* (London: Pimlico Books, 2006), for a historical vision of Isabella of France.

husband who, in the opinion of historians, was very incompetent. At no time did she neglect her maternal role as she gave birth four children despite her husband's homosexual inclinations. Her first child, the future Edward III, was born in 1312. Later, she would adopt drastic measures against her husband to safeguard the interests of her son, imitating what other mothers of the Old Testament had done before. In 1327, Isabella and her lover, Roger Mortimer, invaded England with a mercenary army and deposed Edward II in the name of his son and the couple reigned as regents for three years. Later, Edward III would seize power and condemn Mortimer to the gallows. However, his mother suffered no punishment and was allowed to live comfortably in the castle of Rising in Norfolk. If the Queen Mary Psalter were the first manuscript that Isabella's children learned to read while they were still under her supervision, it would explain the reasons why she was not punished for usurping the throne. The Psalter would thus serve to educate the princes, insisting on the importance of being advised by maternal figures to govern with wisdom.[63] It is possible that Edward III saw in the story of Bathsheba a mirror of the story of his own mother, also a queen and an adulteress but who fought for the interests of her son. Thus, the Psalter that later belonged to Mary Tudor would legitimise the actions of Isabella of France, Bathsheba being a mirror on which she herself could be reflected.

Bathsheba seated to the right of Solomon and the Biblia Pauperum

The *Biblia Pauperum*[64] is the name that is traditionally given to a type of manuscript that consists, as a general rule, of a series of images showing the Life and Passion of Christ, together with the Pentecost and the Coronation of the Virgin, supported by prophecies and the prefigurations of the Old Testament.[65]

---

63. Stanton, 'The Queen Mary Psalter', 241–3. If this theme of the correct way of governing is taken into account, following the models of the kings of the Old Testament, this Psalter could also be considered a *Speculum Principis*.

64. The term *Biblia Pauperum*, or Bible of the Poor, has had different definitions depending on the time. First, the *Biblia Pauperum* is mistakenly used to call manuscripts that were used to teach the illiterate and the poor who did not know how to read and who needed images to understand the biblical story. On the other hand, in the Middle Ages, the term *Biblia Pauperum* was used for manuscripts written in Latin that were not illuminated and that belonged to clerics and students. Finally, in the nineteenth century, the name began to be used to refer to a specific type of manuscripts of typological character, which is the term that is going to be used in this study. For more information, see Gerhard Schmidt, 'King Ms. 5 and its place in the history of the *Biblia Pauperum*', in *Biblia Pauperum: The 'Golden Bible Picture Book'*, ed. Janet Blackhouse, James H. Marrow and Gerhard Schmidt (Switzerland: Faksimile Verlag Luzern, 1993), 21–3, among others.

65. Brown, *Understanding Illuminated Manuscripts*, 21; and Janet Backhouse, 'The "Golden Bible Picture Book" *Biblia Pauperum*', in *Biblia Pauperum: The 'Golden Bible Picture Book'*, ed. Janet Blackhouse, James H. Marrow and Gerhard Schmidt (Switzerland: Faksimile Verlag Luzern, 1993), 8–9.

There were about fifty copies of this manuscript created between the fourteenth and fifteenth centuries. More than two-thirds of these manuscripts are illuminated, while a third contain only textual components such as titles, lessons and prophecies. All these manuscripts originate from a prototype of the now-disappeared *Biblia Pauperum* created in the mid-thirteenth century, probably in southern Germany. It is an anonymous manuscript, although it is quite possible that its author was either a Benedictine monk or an Augustinian canon since the *Biblia Pauperum* circulated first among these orders. This prototype consisted of thirty-two groupings of images where the anti-types represented were the most important of the Life and Passion of Christ (from the Incarnation to the Ascension), along with two additional scenes, the miracle of the Pentecost and the Coronation of the Virgin Mary as *Maria Ecclesia*.[66] These last two scenes made reference to the Church founded by Christ (Pentecost represents the inspiration to create the Church through the Holy Spirit, and the Coronation of the Virgin represents how that Church was elevated to the status of the Saviour's wife in the figure of *Maria Ecclesia*). These anti-types were flanked by two types of the Old Testament (one scene before *legem* and another *sub legem*, as a rule) with two prophets at the top and two at the bottom holding phylacteries or surrounded by inscriptions, to which several additional texts are added making reference to the scenes that are represented and the relationship between them. The thirty-four groups were organized in such a way that they occupied only nine folios originally,[67] although over time this number increased to thirty with the addition of other New Testament episodes.

Taking this manuscript as a prototype, in the fourteenth century there were already three families of the *Biblia Pauperum*, the Austrian, the Bavarian and the Weimar, which differed in slight textual nuances, variations in the number and

66. Schmidt, 'King Ms 5 and its place in the history of the *Biblia Pauperum*', 31.

67. Schmidt, 'King Ms 5 and its place in the history of the *Biblia Pauperum*', 31–2. Schmidt mentions that the first folio was left blank and the scenes began in the verso of folio 1 of the manuscript. Then followed the thirty-two scenes of the Life and Passion of Christ divided into eight chapters each composed of four scenes. Chapter one includes the Annunciation, the Nativity, the Adoration of the Magi and the Presentation of Christ in the Temple; chapter two, the Flight to Egypt, the Fall of Idols, the Slaughter of the Innocents and the Return from Egypt; chapter three, the Baptism of Christ, the Temptations of Christ, the Transfiguration, the Penance of Mary Magdalene and Supper at the House of Simon; chapter four, the Resurrection of Lazarus, the Entrance of Christ into Jerusalem, the Purification of the Temple and the Last Supper; chapter five, the Conspiracy of the Jews, the Thirty Silver Coins, the Kiss of Judas and Christ before Pontius Pilate; chapter six, the Crowning of Thorns, Christ Carrying the Cross, the Crucifixion and Longinus thrusting the spear on the side of Christ; chapter seven, the Burial of Christ, the Anastasis, the Resurrection and the Three Marys before the Tomb of Christ; chapter eight, *Noli me tangere*, Christ appearing before his disciples, Doubting Thomas and the Ascension of Christ. The last folio has the Pentecost and the Coronation of the Virgin Mary.

Figure 3.4 *Coronation of Bathsheba, Mary and Esther, Biblia Pauperum*, The Hague, The Netherlands, *c.* 1405, London, @The British Library Board, Kings Ms. 5, fol. 28r.

order of groups of images that were represented and in the overall design of the folio. The first two refer to the geographical origin of the monasteries from which most of the manuscripts come, while the third refers to the library where the most famous manuscript of this family were found[68] (Figure 3.4).

During the fourteenth century, the original system which was very systematic in the three families of the *Biblia Pauperum* began to decline and subsequent examples simplified the organisation of the folio to show only one pictorial group per folio instead of two. This is the case of the manuscript found in the British Library with the signature Kings MS 5, where each folio contains the New Testament scene in the centre in a rectangular frame with the half-bust prophets located in each of the four corners. Flanking this scene are the prefigurations of the Old Testament with the texts located on the sides of the pictorial group.[69] Already in the fifteenth century, the *Biblia Pauperum* began to be reproduced in woodcut printing quickly and inexpensively. Because the plates could be used indefinitely since they were easy to transport, similar xylographic examples can be found throughout Europe so that the reproduction of this manuscript became the proliferation of it.[70] In these examples, such as the *Biblia Pauperum* of the Library of the Archdiocese of Esztergom (Hungary) or the British Library in London (England), each folio has a single pictorial group developed in the centre with the prophets at the top

---

68. Henrik Cornell (ed.), *Biblia Pauperum* (Stokholm: Thule-tryck, 1925), 89. It is important to bear in mind that the three families in turn are divided into many others.

69. Backhouse, 'The "Golden Bible Picture Book"', 9–21.

70. Albert C. Labriola and John W. Smeltz, *The Bible of the Poor: A Facsimile and Edition of the British Lirary Blockbook C.9 d.2* (Pittsburgh: Duquesne University Press, 1990), 5.

and bottom flanked by the texts, and everything appears organized within an architectural framework.[71]

In this context, the figure of Bathsheba usually appears in the last folios of the *Biblia Pauperum* next to the Coronation of the Virgin Mary and to Esther before Ahasuerus. The texts that usually accompany Bathsheba in all the examples are the title that says 'Solomon enthroning Bathsheba' followed by the text from 3 Kgs 2.19-20:

> We read in the Third Book of Kings, chapter 2, that when Bathsheba, the mother of Solomon, went to see him at his palace, King Solomon ordered that the throne of his mother be placed next to his. Bathsheba represents the glorious Virgin whose throne was placed next to the throne of the true Solomon, Jesus Christ.

Together with these texts you can read 'Your face is praised by the rich of the people' (Ps. 45.13) and the verses 'Solomon places his mother who has just entered to his side' (3 Kgs 2.19-20) and 'The glory of Lebanon shall be given to it, the majesty of Carmel and Sharon' (Isa. 35.2).

Bathsheba seated to the right side of Solomon is the only scene in the Bathsheba cycle that is represented in all the examples of the *Biblia Pauperum*. In most cases, Bathsheba sitting to the right of Solomon appears as the prefiguration of the Virgin Mary crowned by her son Jesus Christ in the Heavens, although in others the Dormition of the Virgin appears, with Christ in the centre holding the already crowned soul of the Virgin Mary.

To finish contextualising Bathsheba in the *Biblia Pauperum*, it is necessary to understand the function of this manuscript. As a rule, this type of typological work has an apologetic and didactic motivation. According to Albert Labriola and John Smeltz, it was conceived with the idea of educating the poor and illiterate in the unity of the Sacred Scriptures,[72] although it is possible that this didactic function had an alternative agenda since it seems that it was directed to one or several of the numerous heresies that were revived throughout the Late Middle Ages, especially that of the Cathars that spread rapidly through northern Italy, France and Germany during the time when the *Biblia Pauperum* was created.[73] The Cathars held, among other beliefs, that the Old Testament and some texts of the Fathers of the Church were written by Satan. For them, the Gospels were the only reliable and authentic

---

71. Other *Biblia Pauperum* that follow this same scheme are those of The Hague, Rijkmuseum Meermanno Westreenianum, Ms. 10 A 15, fol. 37v; Istanbul, Serai Museum, Rotulus Seragliensis Nr. 52; and Heidelberg, University of Heidelberg, Cod. Pal. Germ. 59, fol. 37r.

72. Labriola and Smeltz, *The Bible of the Poor*, 5. According to Labriola and Smeltz, not only was the audience to which the *Biblia Pauperum* addressed poor and illiterate, but those who taught with these manuscripts were also poor since they belonged to the mendicant orders.

73. Schmidt, 'King Ms 5 and its place in the history of the *Biblia Pauperum*', 26–7.

source about Christ and, hence, to refute the Cathar Heresy's false doctrines, the Church gave added importance to the connection between the Old Testament and the New Testament. Another possible didactic use of the *Biblia Pauperum* could have been a tool to help in the conversion of the Jews.[74] In order to carry out this type of conversion, it was much easier to visually present the reconciliation of the Jewish Old Testament with the new Christian texts.

Bathsheba seated to the right side of Solomon has a clear didactic function that relates the typological connections between the Old Testament and the New Testament. The scene of Bathsheba sitting to the right of Solomon, next to the figure of Esther before Ahasuerus, would be the prefiguration of the Coronation of the Virgin Mary as *Maria Ecclesia*. Both this scene and that of the Pentecost try to show the establishment of the Church as an organ predetermined by Christ and prophesied in the Old Testament. Therefore, Bathsheba would be the prefiguration not only of the Virgin Mary but also of the same *Ecclesia* which takes its place at the right hand of Solomon – Christ in the Heavens. If we contextualise this function within the framework of the heresies of the fourteenth century, this pictorial group would demonstrate the importance of the Church to affirm the orthodox doctrine about the Trinity, the miraculous birth of Christ, the double nature of Christ, his Resurrection, the Second Coming of Christ and the Last Judgment.

Conclusions

Different iconographic models of Bathsheba will coexist at the same time in the same place, showing Bathsheba between the two opposite poles of femininity in the Middle Ages: on the one hand, the seductive Bathsheba and, on the other, the Bathsheba that appears as a queen and mother. These two aspects can be understood literally following the historical narrative where Bathsheba appears as a woman who knew how to fight for the interests of her son despite the adverse circumstances that in some way characterised the beginning of her relationship with King David. However, these same aspects can be interpreted through the symbolic or typological narrative where the seductive Bathsheba becomes the prefiguration of *Ecclesia*, and the queen and mother Bathsheba becomes the prefiguration of both *Ecclesia* and the Virgin Mary. At first glance, this may seem to be a contradiction, since Bathsheba covers two opposite meanings, one negative and one positive. However, that contradiction might not be so in the Middle Ages where the sacred and the profane, the literal and the symbolic are intermingled at almost all cultural levels. The existence of a seductive, profane or literal Bathsheba of the Books of Hours does not seem to condition at all the sacred and symbolic reading of the Bathsheba Queen Mother. Bert Cardon, in his book on the *Speculum* emphasises the fact that the compiler of this manuscript, when choosing a prototype, only made use of those elements that were useful

---

74. Labriola and Smeltz, *The Bible of the Poor*, 5.

for the purpose that had been entrusted to him: to establish parallels between the Old and New Testaments. That is to say, for this compiler the adultery of David and Bathsheba was no impediment when it came to choosing Bathsheba as a prefiguration of the Virgin Mary in her role as intercessor in favour of her son Solomon. It is a contradiction with which the different artists and patrons coexisted in the Middle Ages. For this reason, the character of Bathsheba is the object of various iconographic interpretations/representations that place her at the centre of ambiguity throughout the Middle Ages.

Bibliography

Ackerman, Susan. 'The queen mother and the cult in ancient Israel'. *Journal of Biblical Literature* 112, no. 3 (1993): 385–401.
Ambrose of Milan (*c.* 400). *De Apologia Prophetae David*, edited by Pierre Hadot. Paris: M. Cordier, 1977.
Azcárate Luxán, Matilde. 'La coronación de la Virgen en los tímpanos góticos españoles'. *Anales de la Historia del Arte* 4 (1994): 353–63.
Backhouse, Janet, James H. Marrow and Gerhard Schmidt, eds. *Biblia Pauperum: The 'Golden Bible Picture Book'*. Switzerland: Faksimile Verlag Luzern, 1993.
Banning, Knud. *Biblia Pauperum: Billedbibelen fra Middelalderen*. Copenhaguen: G.E.C. Gad, 1991.
Bourassé, J. J., and J.-P. Migne, eds. *Patrologiae Latinae*, vol. 171. Turnhout: Brepols, 1990.
Bronner, Leila Leah. *Stories of Biblical Mothers: Maternal Power in the Hebrew Bible*. New York: University Press of America, 2004.
Brown, Michelle P. *Understanding Illuminated Manuscripts: A Guide to Technical Terms*. Los Angeles: The J. Paul Getty Museum, 1994.
Brubaker, Leslie, 'Every cliché in the book: The linguistic turn and the text-image discourse in Byzantine manuscripts'. In *Art and Text in Byzantine Culture*, edited by Liz James, 58–82. Cambridge: Cambridge University Press, 2007.
Brubaker, Leslie. *Vision and Meaning in Ninth-Century Byzantium: Image as Exegesis in the Homilies of Gregory of Nazianzus*. Cambridge: Cambridge University Press, 1999.
Buchthal, Hugo. *The Miniatures of the Paris Psalter: A Study in Middle Byzantine Painting*. London: The Warburg Institute, 1938.
Cardon, Bert. *Manuscripts of the Speculum Humanae Salvationes in the Southern Netherlands (c. 1410–c. 1470): A Contribution to the Study of 15th Century Book Illumination and of the Function and Meaning of Historical Symbolism*. Lovania: Uitgeverij, 1996.
Costley, Claire L. 'David, Bathsheba and the penitential psalms'. *Renaissance Quaterly* 57, no. 5 (2004): 1235–77.
Cutler, Anthony, and Nicolas Oikonomides. 'An imperial Byzantine casket and its fate at a humanist's hands'. *The Art Bulletin* 70 (1988): 77–87.
Daley, Brian E. *Gregory of Nazianzus*. New York: Routledge, 2007.
De Hamel, Christopher. *A History of Illuminated Manuscripts*. London: Phaidon Press, 1986.
Der Nersessien, Sirarpia. 'The illustrations of the Homilies of Gregory of Nazianzus, Paris gr. 510'. *Dumbarton Oaks Papers* 19 (1969): 157–63.

'Descriptions of medieval and renaissance manuscripts. MS. 739', *Corsair: The Online Research Resource of the Pierpont Morgan Library*. Available online: http://corsair.morganlibrary.org/msdescr/BBM0739.htm (accessed 10 July 2021).

Gunn, David M. 'Bathsheba goes bathing in Hollywood: Words, images, and social locations', in *Biblical Glamour and Hollywood Glitz*, edited by Alice Bach, 75–101, Semeia 74. Atlanta, GA: Scholars Press, 1996.

Harrison, Everett F., Geoffrey W. Bromely and Carl F. H. Henry. *Baker's Dictionary of Theology*. Grand Rapids: Baker Pub Group, 1987.

Harthan, John. *The Book of Hours*. New York: Thomas Y. Crowell, 1977.

James, Montagne Rhodes. *Illustrations of the Old Testament*. London: Roxburghe Club, 1927.

Kantorowicz, Ernst H. *The King's Two Bodies: A Study in Medieval Political Theology*. Princeton: Princeton University Press, 1957.

Kunoth-Leifels, Elisabeth. *Über die Darstellungen der "Bathseba im Bade": Studien zur Geschichte des Bildthemas; 4. bis 17. Jahrhundert*. Essen: Verlag Richard Bacht, 1962.

Labriola, Albert C., and John W. Smeltz. *The Bible of the Poor: A Facsimile and Edition of the British Lirary Blockbook C.9 d.2*. Pittsburgh: Duquesne University Press, 1990.

Panofsky, Erwin. 'Iconography and iconology: An introduction to the study of Renaissance art', in *Meaning in the Visual Arts Papers in and on Art History*, 51–67. New York: Doubldeday Anchor, 1955.

Réau, Louis. *Iconografía del arte cristiano: Iconografía de la Biblia. Antiguo Testamento, Vol. 1*. Translated by José María Sousa Jiménez. Barcelona: Ediciones del Serbal, 2000.

Réau, Louis. *Iconografía del arte cristiano: Introducción General, Vol. 3*. Translated by José María Sousa Jiménez. Barcelona: Ediciones del Serbal, 2000.

Saulnier-Pernuit, Lydwine. *Les Trois Couronnements Tapisserie du Trésor de la cathédrale de Sens*. Belgium: Mame, 1993.

Schaff, Philip, ed. *Nicene and Post-Nicene Fathers*, first series, vol. 4. Buffalo, NY: Christian Literature, 1887. Available online: http://www.newadvent.org/fathers/140622.htm (accessed 10 July 2021).

Stanton, Ann Rudloff. 'From Eve to Bathsheba and beyond: Motherhood in the Queen Mary Psalter', in *Women and the Book: Assessing the Visual Evidence*, edited by Jane H. M. Taylor and Lesley Smith, 172–88. London: British Library, 1995.

Stanton, Ann Rudloff. 'The Queen Mary Psalter: A study of affect and audience'. *Transactions of the American Philosophical Society* 91, no. 6 (2001) i–xxxiii: 1–287.

Steger, Hugo. *David Rex et Propheta: Köning David als vorbildliche Verkörperung des Herrschers und Dichters im Mittelalter, nach Bilddarstellungen des achten bis zwölften Jarhundents*. Nürnberg: Verlag Hans Carl, 1961.

Verdier, Phillipe. *Le couronnement de la Vierge: les origines et les premiers développents d'un thème iconographique*. Montréal: Institut d'études médiévales Albert-le-Grand, 1980.

Walker Vadillo, Mónica A. *Bathsheba in Late Medieval French Manuscript Illumination: Innocent Object of Desire or Agent of Sin?* Lewiston: Edwin Mellen Press, 2008.

Warner, George. *Queen Mary's Psalter: Miniatures and Drawings by an English Artist of the 14th Century Reproduced from Royal Ms. 2 B. VII in the British Museum*. London: The British Museum, 1912.

Weir, Alison. *Queen Isabella: She-Wolf of France, Queen of England*. London: Pimlico Books, 2006.

Weitzmann, Kurt. *Byzantine Book Illumination and Ivories*. London: Ashgate, 1980.

Weitzmann, Kurt. *Late Antique and Early Christian Book Illumination.* London: George Braziller, 1977.
Wieck, Roger S. *Painted Prayers: The Book of Hours in Medieval and Renaissance Art.* New York: George Braziller, 1997.

Chapter 4

STRONG WOMEN OF THE BIBLE AND THEIR PERSISTENCE IN SEVENTEENTH-CENTURY SPANISH PAINTING

Amparo Alba Cecilia and Guadalupe Seijas

The following verses are ascribed to the pen of Felix Lope de Vega y Carpio (1562–1635), one of the most outstanding authors of the Spanish Golden Age:

> A tu sangre miserable
> da remedio, hermosa Ester;
> que aunque es verdad que mujer
> fue causa de muchos males,
> yo sé que en mujeres tales
> puso Dios nuestro remedio,
> y que las toma por medio
> para el bien de los mortales.
> Si a la que es mala condeno,
> la buena me satisface;
> que de víboras se hace
> triaca para el veneno.
> Vaso de virtudes lleno
> fue Sara, Rebeca y Lía,
> Raquel, Thamar y María,
> hermana del gran Moisés,
> la que cantaba después
> que Israel del mar salía;
> Rahab, Débora y Jahel,
> ilustres mujeres son,
> y la madre de Sansón,
> con Ana la de Samuel,
> Rut y Abigail fiel,

Abela[1] y la de Tobías,
Judich, que casi en mis días
quitó la vida a Holofernes
porque a su ejemplo gobiernes,
　　Ester, las desdichas mías.[2]

In these verses, the author makes a list of illustrious women mentioned in the Bible: women who are virtuous and worthy of admiration, women who deserve the praise and consideration that the book of Proverbs (31.10-31) dedicates to the strong woman or the *eshet ḥayil* (אשת חיל).[3]

Strong women in the Bible

The Old Testament mentions many women who have played a leading role in the ancient history of Israel and are worthy, therefore, to deserve the praise that was made in the book of Proverbs of the ideal woman or *eshet ḥayil*. The Hebrew noun *ḥayil* is related semantically to the qualities of a warrior: courage, strength, power; that is why, when it appears adjectivally in the biblical text, it almost always accompanies a masculine name; thus, it appears sixteen times with 'man, men' (*ish, anashim*) and twelve with 'son, sons' (*ben, benei*); only on three occasions does it accompany the feminine noun 'woman' (*eshet*). In Ruth 3.11, Boaz says of her that everyone knows she is a 'worthy woman'; in Prov. 12.4, it is said that 'a good wife is the crown of her husband', where 'virtuous' is opposed to 'shameless', and in Prov.

---

1. She is the intelligent woman of the city of Abel Beth-maacah (2 Sam. 20.14-22); that of Tobias alludes to his wife Sarah.

2. In *The Beautiful Esther*, Act II, verses 680–705, a tragicomedy inspired by the biblical Book of Esther. Written in 1610, it was not published until 1621. Translation:

> To your miserable blood / gives remedy, beautiful Esther, / that even though it is true that a woman / was the cause of many evils, / I know that in women like you, / God put our Salvation / and used them as vessels / for the good of all mortals. / While I condemend the despicable woman, / the good one satisfies me, / since theriaca for poisons / is made from vipers. / A full glass of virtues / were Sarah, Rebecca, and Leah, / Rachel, Thamar and Miriam, / sister of Moses, / the woman who sang / as the Israelites came out from the Sea; / Rahab, Deborah and Jael / were illustrious women, / and Samson's mother, / with Samuel's Hannah, / Ruth and loyal Abigail, / Abela [cf. n. 2] and the woman of Tobias, / Judith, who almost during my times / took the life of Holofernes, / may their example, / Esther, help you govern my misfortunes.

3. The preparation of this work has been possible thanks to the financing of the Ministry of Science and Innovation (R+D Projects: *Unified Analysis of the Hebrew Texts with Computer* FFI2012-37226 and *Written Cultural Heritage of the Jews in the Iberian Peninsula*, FFI2008-01863).

31.10-31 the praise is performed by a woman – the mother of Lemuel – as she teaches her son to learn to choose the right woman: that is the *eshet ḥayil*. Because of the development it has in vv. 10–18, the Hebrew expression has the meaning of industrious woman, tireless and skillful worker. To these qualities are added, in the last verses, other moral characteristics, such as generosity, wisdom and prudence. It is, in short, according to a very literal translation of the Hebrew expression, a woman of value or values.

Throughout the centuries, rabbinic exegesis has given biblical women new nuances and contours with respect to the biblical text itself and has brought them together in homogeneous groups to highlight some of their main qualities: matriarchy, beauty, gift of prophecy or courage. These groups are not closed or exclusive, and thus, we often find several names that are repeated or alternate in each of the groups. We will give a brief summary of the main ones here.

The matriarchs

Also called *women in the tent*, it is the most fixed group, formed by the wives of the three patriarchs: Sarah, Rebecca, Rachel and Leah (*Berachot* 16b). Jael, the wife of Heber the Kenite (Judg. 4.21), always appears in this group of women in the tent, who, according to several Talmudic texts, 'blessed shall she be above women in the tent' (*Nazir* 23b, *Sanhedrin* 105b and *Horayot* 10b).

Women of unparalleled beauty

This group consists of four women whose names vary from one text to another: Sarah, Rahab, Abigail and Esther. An anonymous rabbi proposes to substitute Esther for Vashti, the first wife of Ahasuerus, because Esther 'had a sallow face' (*Megillah* 15a). Other candidates to hold the title of the most beautiful woman instead of any of the above are Jael, Michal, Abishag and, of course Eve, from which another Talmudic text says that 'compared with Eve, Sarah was like a monkey to a human' (*Baba Batra* 58a).

The prophetesses

This group is formed by seven women: Sarah, Miriam, Deborah, Hannah, Abigail, Huldah and Esther. The biblical text gives this title only to three of them: Miriam, 'the prophetess, Aaron's sister' (Exod. 15.20); Deborah, 'a prophetess, wife of Lappidoth' (Judg. 4.4); and Huldah, 'the prophetess, the wife of Shallum' (2 Kgs 22.14). The Talmud (*Megillah* 14a) attributes this title to the other four. Sarah, identified with Yisca,[4] had the gift of discernment (from the Hebrew *sakah*, 'to discern'), which is why God ordered Abraham to do everything she said;[5] Hannah,

---

4. Haran's daughter; cf. Gen. 11.29.
5. Cf. Gen. 21.13.

the mother of Samuel, was prophesying the survival of the royal line of David and Solomon and the disappearance of the dynasty of Saul and Jehu when she said, 'My heart exults in the LORD; my strength is exalted in my God' (1 Sam. 2.1);[6] Abigail's prophetic ability is deduced from her conversation with David when she made him desist from killing her husband Nabal and announced that he would soon be king of Israel.[7] Esther's relationship with prophecy comes from the exegesis applied to the verse 'On the third day, Esther put on her royal robes' (Est. 5.1); the passage does not say that she put on the queen's costume, but that she 'dressed in royalty' using the same verb *labash* as in 1 Chron. 12.19 in relation to the spirit of prophecy: 'Then the spirit came upon Amasai.'

The strong women

Midrashic literature[8] has brought together twenty-two biblical women who exemplify the ideal woman described in Prov. 31.10-31. The number and name of these women is provided by the *Midrash ha-Gadol*, a commentary on the fourteenth-century Pentateuch,[9] based on much older references that mention them individually as a model of a strong woman in the last chapter of Proverbs. These are Noah's wife; the four matriarchs: Sarah, Rebecca, Leah and Rachel; the two mothers of Moses: Jochebed and Bithiah, the daughter of the Pharaoh; Miriam; Hannah; Jael; the widow of Zarephath; Naomi; Rahab; the two wives of David: Bathsheba and Michal; Hazzelelponi, Samson's mother; Elisheba, wife of Aaron; Serah,[10] Asher's daughter; the wife of the prophet Obadiah,[11] the

---

6. Exegesis is based on the interpretation of the Hebrew term *keren* (which in that verse means 'power') as 'horn', a vessel to store the oil. David and Solomon were anointed with the oil in a horn; Saul and Yehu, with the oil from another vessel.

7. Cf. 1 Sam. 25.20-31.

8. Cf. Louis Ginzberg, *The Legends of the Jews* (Philadelphia: The Jewish Publication Society, 2003 [1913]), vol. 1, 238 n. 271.

9. O: *Midrash ha-Gadol*, ed. Solomon Schechter (Cambridge: Cambridge University Press, 1902), 334–39.

10. Cf. Gen. 46.16. According to the tradition contained in the midrash *Sefer ha-Yasar*, God gave her beauty, wisdom and prudence. She was commissioned by Joseph's brothers to anticipate the news that Joseph was alive to the elderly Jacob; she did it by playing the harp and repeating this song: 'My uncle Joseph, my uncle, is alive, and reigns in all the land of Egypt, and is not dead.' Jacob blessed her wishing that death would never destroy her; that is why she appears mentioned in an anonymous midrash among the twelve people who did not die, next to Methuselah, Enoch, Elijah and others.

11. It refers to the widow of 'of a member of the company of prophets' who was the object of a miracle by Elisha (2 Kgs 4.1-7); ancient sources, both Jewish (Flavius Josephus, *Antiquities of the Jews* IX, 4,2, *Pesiqta of Rab Kahana* 2,13b) and Christian (Pseudo-Epiphanius, *De Vitis Prophetarum, Obadiah,* Saint Ephrem of Syria, *Opera Omnia* I, 526c),

Shunammite; Ruth; and Esther. The main strong woman of them all is Sarah; that is why she is the only 'brave woman' whose age is mentioned in Scriptures.[12]

The number of women who bear this title, twenty-two, coincides with the number of verses dedicated to describing the strong woman in Prov. 31.10-31.

The representation of groups of strong women

The representation of the women of the Old Testament acquired great prominence in the Baroque period. Judith, Esther, Jael or Deborah, among others, were represented in numerous paintings.[13] Less well known are the iconography models that included portraits of several biblical heroines as a group. Without wishing to bring together an exhaustive list, we will cite a large number of iconography examples found in chapels, hermitages and churches, which appeared mainly from the Baroque period, although they were still being represented later on. Basically, we can distinguish two types of groups: a series of four characters distributed in pendentives and a series of eight or more than eight sculptures or frescoes.

Fray Manuel Bayeau y Subías (1740–1808) is the artist of two very similar series that included Judith, Esther, Jael and Deborah. They are found in the Carthusian monastery of Our Lady of the Fountains (Huesca, 1775) and in the Royal Carthusian monastery of Jesus of Nazareth in Valldemossa (Mallorca, 1805). José Vergara Gimeno (1726–1799) painted Judith, Esther, Ruth and Miriam in the Seo of Xátiva (Valencia, 1744–45), and Judith, Esther, Jael and Ruth in the Basilica of Our Lady of the Forsaken (Valencia, 1765). José Sánchez Villalmantos (1767–?) is credited as the artist who painted the pendentives of the Chapel of the Christ of the Redemption in the Church of Saint Genesius of Arles (Madrid) with Judith, Jael, Ruth and Rachel,[14] and José Camarón Bonanat (1731–1803) those of Judith, Esther, Deborah and Abigail of the parish Church of Saint Mary (Valencia). Of the same period are the frescoes of Judith, Esther, Jael and Deborah of the Church of Our Lady of Portillo (Zaragoza), the lunettes of the dome of the transept of the new Hermitage of the Virgin of the Fields in Camarillas (Teruel) with Judith, Esther, Jael and Ruth, and those of the Shrine of the Virgin of the Olive of Ejea

---

identified the minor prophet Obadiah with the royal official Obadiah at the court of Ahab who protected the prophets from the persecution of the evil Jezebel.

12. Cf. Gen. 23.1.

13. See Erika Bornay, *Mujeres de la Biblia en la pintura del Barroco: imágenes de la ambigüedad*, Ensayos Arte Cátedra (Madrid: Cátedra, 1998); and Bettina Baumgartel and Silvia Neysters, *Die Galerie der Starken Frauen* (Munchen: Klinkhardt & Biermann, 1995). The discussion of strong women, especially on Judith and Susannah, also deserves attention in Mary D. Garrard, *Artemisia Gentileschi: The Image of the Female Hero in Italian Baroque Art* (Princeton: Princeton University Press, 1989).

14. Along with them, the patriarchs Jacob, Joseph, Abraham and Isaac are represented on the drum.

de los Caballeros (Zaragoza), where Luis Muñoz painted Judith, Esther, Jael, and Deborah at the end of the century. From a later period are the frescoes by Vicente Castelló Amat (1787–1860), which he painted in the Chapel of the Virgin of the Forsaken of Alcoy (Alicante, 1852) in whose pendentives are represented Judith, Jael, Ruth and Miriam.

Among the iconography series composed of eight or more heroines we must mention the vault of the Triumph of the Virginal Purity of Mary in the Church of El Escorial (Madrid, 1693), in whose complex iconographic programme Luca Giordano represented in the pendentives and in the intermediate spaces of the angles of the vault ten women of the Old Testament: Judith, Esther, Jael, Deborah, Ruth, Abigail, Rebecca, Rachel, Abishag and Susannah.[15] Likewise, the sculptures of the Chapel of the Virgin of Guadalupe of Cáceres, attributed to the circle of Duque Cornejo (1736–39), represented the first six heroines but incorporated Miriam and Sarah. These eight women will also be represented in the Hermitage of the Virgin of the Snows in Zarza (Badajoz, eighteenth century) in whose vault each one of them is surrounded by a niche and with a legend in the Rococo style placed at their feet.

On the other hand, there is also evidence of other representations that have been lost, such as the pendentives of the dome of the Chapel of the Buen Suceso in the Church of Saint Isidore (Madrid) with Judith, Esther, Deborah and the mother of Samson, as well as the frescoes of the Church of Saint John of the Market (Valencia, 1699), destroyed in the Spanish Civil War, with Judith and her servant, Esther, Jael, Deborah, Ruth, Abigail, Miriam and Rachel. The artist himself, Antonio Palomino de Castro y Velasco (1655–1726), wrote one of the main sources for the study of Spanish Baroque painting, which includes a detailed description of this iconography programme and its symbolic and allegorical meaning.[16]

The analysis of the data allows us to conclude that the most represented group is formed by Judith, Esther, Jael and Deborah, and in the other series we include two or three heroines of this group, completing the quartet with images of Ruth (five times) and, to a lesser extent, Miriam (two times), Abigail, Rachel and Samson's mother, who appeared only once:

Judith, Esther, Jael and Deborah: 4
Judiht, Esther, Jael + 1 heroine: 2
Judith, Esther, Deborah + 1 heroine: 2
Judith, Esther + 2 heroines: 3
Judith, Jael + 2 heroines: 1

---

15. In close connection with the paintings he made in 1690 for the Cartuja de San Martino in Naples.

16. Antonio Palomino de Castro y Velasco, *El Museo pictórico y Escala óptica* (Madrid: Viuda de Juan García Infançon, 1724), vol. II, 188–90. This work also includes a description of the aforementioned work by Luca Giordano.

Esther, Judith and Jael are included in the feminine equivalents of the Nine Worthies which included pagan, Jewish and Christian characters: Julius Caesar, Hector and Alexander the Great correspond with Lucrecia, Veturia and Virginia; Joshua, David and Judas Maccabeus with Esther, Judith and Jael; and Geoffrey of Bouillon, Charlemagne and King Arthur with St. Helena, St. Elizabeth of Thuringia and St. Bridget of Sweden.[17] In the iconography programme that contain eight women, seven are repeated heroines in all the series: Judith, Esther, Jael, Deborah, Ruth, Abigail and Miriam, with the eighth woman being represented by one of the matriarchs, Sarah or Rachel. In the iconography programme of El Escorial, Luca Giordano dispensed with Miriam and incorporated Rebecca, Rachel, Susannah and Abishag.

All these iconography programmes, except for Saint Genesius of Arles and Saint John of the Market, are found in chapels dedicated to the Virgin Mary and often located around her. The verification of this reality is not anecdotal but has a great dogmatic and doctrinal importance since these iconography cycles were closely related to the important Trinitarian controversies of the period and the struggle against the Protestant Reformation. The Baroque was a time of great Marian devotion in clear contrast to the position held by the Protestants. Frequently, the representation of the biblical heroines appeared in a context of glorification of the Virgin Mary, as her precursors and prefigurations, especially in relation to her purity and virginity. The tradition of representing two biblical passages together, one from the Old and the other from the New Testament, where the first is presented as a prefiguration of the second, goes back to the Middle Ages, as can be seen in the *Biblia Pauperum* and the *Speculum Humanae Salvationis*. In this sense, Judith represents the victory of chastity and humility. Esther prefigures the crowned and mediating Virgin. Jael, who killed the enemy general with a stake, is the symbol of Mary, who wounded the head of the serpent, an enemy of the people of God and of all mankind. Deborah is the mother of Israel, just as Mary is the mother of the Church. Ruth is the origin of the lineage of Christ. The miraculous motherhood of Rachel is associated with that of the Virgin, while Miriam prefigures her death. Sarah is the mother of Isaac, whose name means laughter and resembles Mary, mother of Christ, the joy of the world. Abigail, whose discretion and beauty appeased David's jutified indignation against her husband Nabal, is the symbol of the Virgin, who with her beauty, fullness of grace and prudence defends and protects believers from the just indignation of God. Some of them are also a symbol of the Church and of Christ.[18]

---

17. Ángela Franco, 'Reyes, héroes y caballeros en la literatura en la literatura y el arte en el ocaso de la Edad Media y pervivencias', in *Arte, poder y sociedad en la España de los siglos XV-XX*, coord. Miguel Cabañas, Amelia López-Yarto Elizalde and Wifredo Rincón García (Madrid: CSIC, 2008), 417–34, 434.

18. Like the wheat, the ears of Ruth are the symbol of the Eucharist or Esther is the prefiguration of Christ interceding before God, the Father. About this issue, cf. Antonio Palomino de Castro y Velasco, *El Museo pictórico*, vol. II, 188–90; Santiago Sebastián,

Together with these strong women, the iconography programmes in which they are part of also included the allegorical Virtues (Charity, Prudence, Temperance, Strength, etc.) and other saintly women.

The Guadalupe Chapel in the Convent of Las Descalzas Reales

Undoubtedly, the most interesting iconography programme, due to the exceptional conditions that occur in it, can be found in the Chapel of the Virgin of Guadalupe of the Convent of Las Descalzas Reales[19] founded in 1557. It is an interesting example of fusion between the word (*Elogios de mujeres ilustres del Viejo Testamento*, see below) and the image, which were the means used during the time of the Counter-Reformation to transmit the content of the Bible. The word commented, explained and facilitated, and the image was the instrument of transmission of knowledge and feelings, since through the senses the iconographic representation can touch and move both piety and delight.[20]

The chapel is in the gallery on the top floor of the cloister, next to other small chapels. The paintings are the work of Herrera Barnuevo (1619–1671), one of the most outstanding painters of the Spanish Baroque, and are dated to 1653. The programme is composed of sixty-eight scenes painted in oil, mirroring each other and surrounded by decorated moldings arranged around the image of the Virgin who occupies the centre. The forty-six allegorical scenes are arranged over the altar and the twenty-one scenes that represent women from the Old Testament

Contrarreforma y barroco: lecturas iconográficas e iconológicas (Madrid: Alianza Editorial, 1981), 227–28; and Harold E. Wethey and Alice Sunderland Wethey, 'Herrera Barnuevo and his Chapel in the Descalzas Reales', *Art Bulletin* 48, no. 1 (1966): 15–34; 26, 28.

19. On this convent see also Chapter 22, 33–34. This chapel was not known until 1961 after some repair works were made in the convent. We would like to thank Mª Leticia Sánchez Hernández, specialist in female monasteries of the Madrid of the Austrias and in the conventual life of these communities, her valuable suggestions and, especially, the fact that she personally showed us this chapel. For reasons of space, we will limit ourselves to pointing out two of her extensive bibliographical productions: *Patronato regio y órdenes religiosas femeninas en el Madrid de los Austrias: Descalzas Reales, Encarnación y Santa Isabel* (Madrid: Fundación Universitaria Española, 1997) and 'Mujer y Biblia: visión iconográfica de una relación fascinante', ponencia presentada en el Primo Congresso Internazionale, *La donna e i luoghi della memoria*, organized by the Fondazione P. Valerio per la Storia della donne (27 Ginebra–29 junio 2007), where an image of the Chapel of Guadalupe was included. The text was accessible through http://www.efeta.org/ES/gpermanente007.php (accesed 26 April 2014), even though the page no longer exists. The quotes that I reproduce were taken from said website.

20. 'A clear example of how Catholics accessed the Bible through a spiritual book, and how the text is transformed into an image to be viewed in a pedagogical way by a community' (Sánchez Hernández, *Mujer y Biblia*).

are placed in the walls in two vertical columns that are united in the upper part forming an arch.

In this work we will focus exclusively on the representations of the biblical heroines, leaving aside other questions related to this chapel.

All the scenes are arranged around a vertical axis with Day or morning,[21] one of the daughters of Job, who is holding the solar disk in her hands, located on the upper part; the sculpture of the Virgin of Guadalupe with the Child can be seen on the centre, and an Immaculate Conception surrounded by light, sitting on the moon and stepping on a dragon – imagery taken from the Apocalypse – is located at the bottom. With the exception of the Day image that heads the aforementioned vertical axis, the remaining twenty images are distributed in pairs, which show some conceptual affinity: Abishag and Miriam, Moses's sister, were both single and virgins; Abigail and Rebecca appeared in their role as intercessors; Judith and Jael were women who brought down their enemies; the Queen of Sheba and Esther were queens; the matriarchs Sarah and Rachel were sterile mothers surrounded by children; the mother of Samson and Deborah were both represented as Roman matrons, symbol of direction, government and wisdom; Achsah and Naamah[22] symbolized purity and domestic virtues, respectively; the widow of Zarephath and the Shunammite were connected by the same experience of suffering for the death of their sons and the joy they experienced after their resurrection, since both of their children came back to life through the intervention of a prophet; Ruth, along with Naomi, and Hannah, Samuel's mother, both represented in an offering attitude; and, finally, Bathsheba and Alcohol, the daughter of Job. Arranged around the image of the Virgin at the centre of the altar, the virtues and the attitudes of these biblical women become prefigurations of the Virgin and are oriented to emphasize her glorification (Figures 4.1 and 4.2).

In the opinion of Harold E. Wethey, this chapel was a tribute made by Ana Dorotea (1612–1694)[23] for her deceased aunt, Sor Margarita de la Cruz (1567–1633), a great devotee of the Virgin, to whom she professed great affection and admiration. The daughter of Emperor Maximilian II and aunt of Philip III, Ana Dorotea was strongly attracted by the religious life and very early manifested her inclination for monastic life. While living in the convent as a nun, she intervened in political issues; she was asked for advice and support in specific situations; she exercised great influence over his nephew Philip III, and she maintained an abundant epistolary relationship. Her influence and importance were such that

---

21. On the differences/variants of the names of the daughters of Job with respect to the Bible (Jemimah, Keziah, and Keren-Happuch) cf. *infra*.

22. Naamah is the name that appears in the biblical text. In the Chapel of Guadalupe, as well as in the *Elogios* by Martín Carrillo (cf. *infra*) she is known as Noemá.

23. Natural daughter of Emperor Rudolph II and Catherine Strada, she soon became an orphan. Her aunt, Sister Margarita de la Cruz, a nun in the Convent of Las Descalzas Reales, took charge of her. She entered the monastery at twelve years; at sixteen she professed her faith and spent the rest of her life in this convent.

94 Women of the Bible

Figure 4.1 Chapel of the Virgin of Guadalupe, Convent of Las Descalzas Reales, Madrid. Source: Patrimonio Nacional, PDP220.

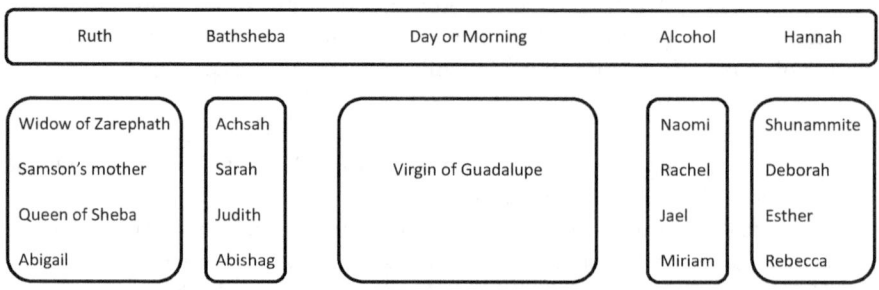

Figure 4.2 Iconography Scheme of the Chapel of the Virgin of Guadalupe.

she even received a personal letter from Pope Urban VIII, delivered in hand by the papal nuncio, Francesco de Barberini. It is, then, a woman who played a prominent role in the political context that she lived in.

Ana Dorotea arranged the iconographic programme of the chapel,[24] all of it oriented to the glorification of the Immaculate Conception, for which she used the work *Elogios de mujeres ilustres del Viejo Testamento* written by Martín Carrillo and published in Huesca in 1627, a work that had great diffusion and was re-edited several times.[25] This eulogy to illustrious women from the Old Testament was a genre that acquired great prominence from the Counter-Reformation onwards, since after the Council of Trent access to the biblical text was greatly restricted. The common people and especially women only reached the Sacred Text through devotional readings, sacred stories and the lives of saints.[26] Carrillo told the stories of biblical women with a clear orientation, showing the virtues that characterized these characters and served as an example of conduct. In this way, what the Bible narrates and the teachings that derived from it were combined. Bible and interpretation were merged into a single text. In short, it was a guided and directed reading, with an edifying character.

Elogios de Mujeres ilustres consists of forty-seven chapters in which fifty-four women are described. Most of these chapters are dedicated to a single woman, although sometimes the author treats two in the same chapter, as it happens with Ruth and Naomi or with Hannah and Penninah. Carrillo mentions the sources (Fathers of the Church and authors from different times and origins) that he has used to compose the *Elogios* and justifies the opinions he puts forward. Sometimes he includes quotations from the Bible in Latin and concludes each of the compliments with one or several sonnets. The author incorporates aspects that are not contemplated in the biblical story. Thus, for example, he presents Hannah, the mother of Samuel, as a model wife, who silences her suffering so as not to bother her husband, to Bathsheba in her role

---

24. For a complete description of this chapel, I recommend two excellent chapters: Wethey and Sunderland Wethey, 'Herrera Barnuevo and his Chapel', which includes a complete iconography guide with the description of all the biblical heroines and the allegorical scenes; and Harold E. Wethey, 'Barnuevo y su Capilla de las Descalzas Reales', *Reales Sitios* 4, no. 13 (1967): 13–21. See also Mª Leticia Sánchez Hernández, 'La capilla de Guadalupe en el monasterio de las Descalzas Reales de Madrid', in *Herederas de Clío: Mujeres que han impulsado la Historia*, coord. Gloria Franco Rubio y María Ángeles Pérez Samper (Sevilla: Mergablum, 2014), 493–514; and Begoña Álvarez Seijo, 'Cerrando un programa iconográfico: Las hijas de Job en la Capilla de la Virgen de Guadalupe en las Descalzas Reales de Madrid', *Imago: Revista de emblemática y cultura visual* 11 (2019): 97–110. Available online: https://ojs.uv.es/index.php/IMAGO/article/view/14248 (accesed 12 February 2021).

25. Re-edited in 1783 and 1792 in Madrid by the publisher Joseph Doblado. A digital version exists available in Google Books.

26. Cf. José Manuel Sánchez Caro, *La aventura de leer la Biblia en España* (Salamanca: Universidad Pontificia de Salamanca, 2000), 38–40.

Figure 4.3 Cover of the *Elogios de mujeres ilustres del Viejo Testamento* by Martín Carrillo, 1627.

as a mother, because she attributes the wisdom of Solomon to the education he received from her or Abigail as 'an example for women to learn to amend the faults of their husbands'.

Carrillo had in mind his potential readers: a female audience.[27] He presents the biblical episodes in a pleasant, dynamic and attractive way. He transformed narrative fragments into dialogues; he dealt with women's issues; he payed attention to details that women noticed and develop aspects that were barely insinuated or silenced in the biblical story. Thus, in the eulogy to Bathsheba, he deals with the question of the duration of pregnancy (folio 136), the convenience of mothers nursing their babies (folio 137) or the importance of the mother in the education of the children (folios 138–39). And to illustrate the reasons why Rebecca preferred Jacob, he says that he was more collected – Esau preferred to go out to the countryside to hunt – since he entertained himself with housework and kept his mother company (folio 27) (Figure 4.3).

27. Although it is possible that he also had in mind priests, chaplains and confessors, men in charge of guiding the readings and piety of women in general and of religious women in particular.

The work of the *Elogios* was directed to a certain type of woman. It was written for educated women, who came from royalty or nobility,[28] ladies who read and who received training. Only in this way can it be explained that in Abigail's praise he analysed the discourse she utters before David following the elements of rhetoric or that he made references to examples taken from Classical mythology. He also alluded to the exegetical problems posed by the text and even exposed his own doubts. For example, he questions whether Jael sinned by lying and deceiving Sisera (folio 71) or whether it was lawful for Esther, being a Hebrew, to marry a Gentile (folio 230).

Bearing in mind the work of Carrillo, Herrera Barnuevo painted strong and robust women. They are dressed in costumes from the painter's time, a custom that began in the Renaissance and continued into the Baroque. Sometimes, he incorporated turbans, striped fabrics and other exotic elements, as in the representation of the prophets Elijah and Elisha, who responded to the stereotype of the Jews: old men, with the head covered and with a beard. The dresses, the fabrics, the lace and the jewels show us richly dressed women, which reflects their importance.[29] The movement is perceived through the gesture of the hands, the body posture and the looks which establish visual contact between the women in the painting. All this contributes to highlighting that we are faced with active women, women with initiative, who do not remain impassive before what happens. That sensation of movement is also accentuated in the paintings that like a wave surround some women and the bows that held the hair and that the wind seems to suspend in the air, a specific detail of this artist. They are paintings in which all details have been taken care of as in the posture of Miriam's hand playing the lute and marking the chords, the limp body of the dead child in the arms of the Shunamite or the transparency of the glass cup held by the widow of Zarephath.

It is interesting to also take notice of the exchanged looks between the figures. As is to be expected from virtuous and demure women, none of these women look straight ahead. Those who appear alone direct their gaze to an object such as the figures of Alcohol, Naamah or the divinity that is at the top as Hannah or Miriam do;[30] while the ones that appear accompanied establish visual contact with the other protagonists of the painting: Rachel lovingly contemplates her children, the Queen of Sheba holds the gaze of Solomon and Judith and Jael fix their attention on their victims. Some of these images deal with biblical characters that have received little attention from artists. Regarding Naamah, the biblical text only indicates that she is the sister of Tubal-cain, forger of all copper and iron tools (Gen. 4.22) to

---

28. On the origin and lineage of the nuns of this monastery, cf. Karen Mª Vilacoba Ramos, 'Las religiosas de las Descalzas reales de Madrid en los siglos XVI-XX: fuentes archivísticas', *Hispania Sacra* LXII 125, no. 1 (2010): 115-56.

29. Only the widow of Zarephath (1 Kings 17), a woman who barely has anything to eat, appears without jewelry.

30. Interestingly, these two women are mentioned in rabbinical literature as 'prophetesses' (*Meguillah* 14a).

whom the origin of metallurgy is implicitly attributed. Carrillo defines her as a 'beautiful and free woman', an expert in weaving and spinning, and as such she is represented by Herrera Barnuevo. The widow of Zarephath (1 Kings 17) offered Elijah a loaf of bread and a glass, the last provisions that she had left. The scene of the Shunamite before Elisha (2 Kgs 4.8-37) is charged with emotion. The hope and the contained pain of the woman are reflected in the body posture and in the attentive look that the woman gives to the prophet, while the request of Elisha is represented in the gesture of his hands.

The case of Bathsheba is different. Her story is known and often depicted in painting,[31] and yet its absence is evident in the series of strong women mentioned at the beginning of this chapter. For Carrillo, it is a contradictory character. He begins her praise giving four reasons why her behaviour deserved to be condemned: letting herself be seen naked, the ease with which she allowed herself to be persuaded to go before the king, to consent to the death of her husband and to be dishonest and lack self-control. But then he affirms that 'sinners who turn to Him with true heart and tears are not disagreeable to God' (folio 127) and even though for that reason she should be considered bad and sinful, he maintains that 'she is considered between the prudent, wise, good and venerable women of the Old Testament because in their lives there are things worthy of praise' (folio 130). Above all, Bathsheba must be imitated in her role as mother and educator. This assessment is what allows Bathsheba to be considered a role model.

Although most of the paintings – except for Abishag, Judith, the Queen of Sheba, the widow of Zarephath and the Shunamite – have the name of the character labeled in gold letters, many of them are easily identifiable.[32] Deborah holds a scepter, which represents the baton of a general, and a palm tree, in reference to the place where she judged. Ruth holds a sheaf that she gives to Naomi; Miriam plays a lute, and Naamah has different types of textiles at her feet. Achsah sits on fertile, flowery ground watered by a water fountain, and Abishag carries flowers in her lap, which probably represent generosity, care and attention to fragility, virtues highlighted by Carrillo in this young woman who cared for an old, sick and helpless David. Samson's mother places one hand on the head of a lion[33] and with the other holds the solar disk. The name 'Samson', in Hebrew *shimshon*, is from the same root as 'sun', *shemesh*. In other cases, the scene depicted are frequently painted and are easily recognizable: Esther before Ahasuerus, Judith beheading Holofernes or Jael driving the stake into the temple of Sisera. Finally, other heroines appear in less represented scenes: Sarah separating Isaac from Ishmael, Rachel playing with

---

31. Especially in the bath scene witness by David (2 Samuel 11). See Chapter 3.

32. Each of the twenty-two scenes has an inscription in Latin that, in many cases, helps to understand which facet of the female character is to be highlighted.

33. In reference to the passage of Judg. 14.5-9, where Samson killed a lion and nested a hive on his skeleton. This fact underlies the enigma he proposed to the Philistines on his wedding day (Judg. 14.12-18).

her children, Joseph and Benjamin[34] or Rebecca with a finger to her lips before Isaac and Jacob.[35]

As already mentioned, only Achsah and the two daughters of Job, Day or Morning and Alcohol, are not included among the fifty-four women presented in the *Elogios*. Collectively, the daughters of Job are mentioned in the chapter dedicated to his wife, in relation to the recovery of Job's assets as a reward for having remained faithful. A speech about the importance of beauty in women is incorporated from the mention of the daughters. Nor are they cited in the *Libro de las claras e virtuosas mugeres* by Alvaro de Luna (1440) or in *The Gallery of Strong Women* by Pierre de Le Moyne (1647).[36] They are little-known biblical women, secondary characters and, to a certain extent, marginal, but who share the same fact, being worthy of their father's inheritance. Receiving the inheritance, that is, titles and possessions, would point to the equating of women with men.

Achsah is the daughter of Caleb and the episode in which her story appears is part of the distribution of the land of Canaan among the tribes. Her father offers her in marriage to the man who conquers the town of Kiriath-sepher. Achsah addresses her father to request water sources to irrigate the dry land that she had received,[37] to which he agrees. The story, which appears twice in the Bible (Josh. 15.16-19 and Judg. 1.12-13), recalls that of the daughters of Zelophehad (Num. 27.1-11), who requested Moses to be the recipient of their father's inheritance due to the absence of a male child and whose request is also accepted.

The three daughters of Job are only mentioned in the narrative framework of the book (Job 1.2 and 42.13-14); on the first mention, only their number is indicated; in the second, they are given names: 'The first was called *Dove* [Yemimah], the

---

34. These two scenes do not fit the biblical story, according to which the age difference between Ishmael and Isaac was great and Rachel died in childbirth after giving birth to Benjamin.

35. Rebecca is often depicted in the well scene (Genesis 24) or hidden behind a curtain in the episode of Isaac's blessing (Genesis 27). Although the iconography used by Herrera Barnuevo is striking, a similar scene can be seen in *Isaac's Blessing* by Jacob Gioacchino Assereto (Hermitage Museum, St. Petersburg, 1640).

36. Regarding these works, see Carmen Yebra-Rovira, 'French Biblical Engravings and the Education of the Spanish Woman in the XIX Century', *Biblical Reception* 2 (2013): 97–116.

37. The passage presents textual problems in relation to the word ותסיתהו (v. 18). A consecutive imperfect third-person feminine singular that would have to be translated as 'She seduced/persuaded him to ask' seems to make little sense in the context as it is not understood why Achsah would urge Othniel, her husband, to ask for the land if, then, she was the one who rides on a donkey to make the request to her father in person. Some translations read ויסיתה as 'He convinced her' by following the text of the Septuagint and the Vulgate. José Luis Sicre interprets 'she seduced [Caleb, mentioning indirectly], asking her father for arable land'. On this question, see José Luis Sicre, *Josué* (Estella: Verbo Divino, 2002), 341–42.

second *Cassia* [Qetsiah] and the third "Horn of kohl"[38] [Keren happuk].[39] There were no women in the whole country more beautiful than the daughters of Job.' Unlike Job's seven sons, his daughters have a name of their own, which gives them an obvious role.

The daughters of Job in rabbinical literature

Rabbinical literature developed some traditions about the daughters of Job, which reflects the exaltedness of their behaviour, traditions that can help us understand why they were assigned a prominent role. They are recorded in a Talmudic treatise (*Baba Batra* 16b), in the *Targum of Job* 42, 14[40] and in the *Testament of Job* 1, 3 and 46–53.[41]

The first thing that draws our attention are the variants that are given in the names of the daughters with respect to the text of the Hebrew Bible. The cause of these divergences seems to start from the Greek version of the Bible of the LXX, which translates the names as *Hemera* (Day), *Cassia* and *Horn of Amalthea*; thus, the translator of the Greek text derived the name of the eldest daughter, *Yemimah* (Dove) of *Yom* (day), and adapted the name of the third daughter, *Keren happuk* (Horn, or small vessel of shavings), to the Hellenic tradition and translated it as 'Horn of Amalthea', the goat that, according to Greek mythology, nursed the baby Zeus on Mount Ida on Crete.

In *Baba Batra* 16b, the daughters of Job are put as a model of beauty, and the etymology of their names is explained by connecting their interpretation with the exegesis of the term *la-rob*, 'multiply', which appears in Gen. 6.1: 'When people began to multiply on the face of the earth, and daughters were born to them.' One rabbi explains that although Job's daughters were only three – that is, their number was not doubled as happened with the rest of Job's old riches – what multiplied was their beauty, as the biblical text states, 'In all the land there were no women so beautiful as Job's daughters.' In Talmudic discussion the meaning of their names takes centre stage:

38. According to the translation of Luis Alonso Schökel in *Biblia del Peregrino* (Bilbao: Ega-Mensajero, 1993) and Francisco Cantera in *Sagrada Biblia* (Madrid: BAC, 2000): Dove [symbol of femininity and beauty], Cassia [or cinnamon flower] and Horn [or small vessel] of shavings.

39. According to *Diccionario Bíblico hebreo-español* by Luis Alonso Schökel, (Valencia: Institución San Jerónimo, 1990–91), the noun פוך has the following meanings: (1) *antimony*, cosmetic for eye shadow in 2 Kgs 9.30: Jezebel painted her eyes, or in Jer. 4.30, 'although you enlarge your eyes with paint [NAS]'; and (2) jet black, as in Isa. 54.1 and 1 Chron. 29.3.

40. O: *The Targum of Job*, trans. and intro. Céline Mangan in *The Aramaic Bible: The Targums*, ed. Kevin Cathcart, Michael Maher and Martin McNamara, vol. 15 (Minnesota: The Liturgical Press, 1991), 1–98.

41. O: 'Testament of Job', trans. and intro. R. P. Spittler in *Old Testament Pseudepigrapha, Apocalyptic Literature & Testaments*, vol. 1, ed. James Hamilton Charlesworth (New York: Doubleday, 1983), 829–68.

And he called the name of the first Jemimah, and the name of the second Keziah, and the name of the third Keren-Happuch. Jemimah, because she was like the day [*yom*]; Keziah, because the emitted a fragrance like cassia [*keziah*]; Keren-Happuch[42] because – so it was explained in the academy of R. Shila – she had a complexion like the horn of a *keresh*.[43]

This etymology, which closely follows the translation of the Septuagint, did not seem to satisfy all those present in the discussion, who objected that 'having the waist like the horn of a unicorn' could be more offensive than praiseworthy. Therefore, another rabbi proposes an alternative explanation, based on the meaning of *puk* as a cosmetic or eye khol, as it appears in Jer. 4.30.

The *Targum of Job* (42, 14), an Aramaic translation of the book of Job, coincides with the previous texts in the explanation of the first two names but introduces another variant in the name of the third daughter, opting for a second meaning of the term *puk*, 'bluish colored gemstone':

And he called the name of the first, Jemimah for she was beautiful as the day; and the name of the second, Keziah, for she was precios as cassia; and the name of the third, Karen-happuch, for she was exceedingly provided with lustre of face like the emerald.[44]

The greatest development of the motive of the daughters of Job is undoubtedly found in the *Testament of Job*, an apocryphal work probably written in Greek in the first century of our era. The last verses of the book of Job, relating to the distribution of the inheritance and to his death, are extended with a fantastic story featuring the three daughters, whose names coincide completely with the version of the Septuagint (*T. Job* 1, 2 and 52, 4). This work apparently contradicts the biblical text of Job 42.15, which states that the daughters had a share in the inheritance of their father along with their brothers and raises the claim of the daughters:

And they brought forth the estate for distribution among the seven males only. For he did not present any of the gods to the females. They were grieved and said to their father, 'our father, sir, are we not also your children? Why then did you not give us some of your goods?'[45]

But the father assures them that the inheritance he has prepared for them is far superior to that of their brothers: it consists of the three celestial belts that God

---

42. Lit., 'horn of pigment', may refer to the container that had this cosmetic product used for make-up for the eyes, hence in the iconography she is referred to by the name of Alcohol (Khol).
43. The Hebrew *keresh* is a kind of antelope.
44. *Targum of Job* 42,14, 90.
45. *T. Job* 46, 1-2, 864.

gave to Job on the day he took pity on him and ended his sufferings. These belts had the power to heal, so that as soon as Job girt them, all his wounds and illnesses were cured and he regained strength, not only physical but also moral. When each daughter put on her belt, she underwent an amazing transformation: her heart was transformed, so that they no longer thought of earthly things, and from their mouths solemn words flowed in the language of the angels and they began to sing hymns to God like the hymns of the angels, to praise God and to speak of his greatness.

In this work, the daughters also have a prominent presence at the time of Job's death, being the only witnesses, together with their father, of a great theophany:

> After three days, as Job fell ill on his bed (without suffering or pain, however, since suffering could no longer touch him on account of the omen of the sash he wore), after those three days he saw those who had come for his soul. And rising immediately he took a lyre and gave it to his daughter, Hemera. To Kasia he gave a censer, and to Amaltheia's Horn he gave a kettle drum, so that they might bless those who had come for his soul. And when they took them, they saw the gleaming chariots which had come for his soul. And they blessed and glorified God each one in her own distinctive dialect.
>
> After these things the one who sat in the great chariot got off and greeted Job as the three daughters and their father himself looked on, thought certain others did not see. And taking the soul he flew up, embracing it, and mounted the chariot and set off for the east. But his body, prepared for burial, was borne to the tomb as his three daughters went ahead girded about and singing hymns to God.[46]

The colophon of the work underlined a quality of the daughters of Job not mentioned so far, their kindness: 'There were no daughters found on earth as fair as the daughters of Job,' so that, if the text began by pointing out their beauty, it ends with emphasizing their kindness.

The women in the Guadalupe Chapel: Various readings

It is not an easy task to make a classification of the biblical heroines represented. In her study, Rosilie Hernández[47] distinguished two general categories that, according to her opinion, guided the *Elogios*: women-mothers and women-leaders. The etchings of Eve, Sarah and Rebecca that appear on the illustrated

---

46. *T. Job* 52, 867–8.
47. Rosilie Hernández, 'The politics of exemplarity: Biblical women and the education of the Spanish lady in Martin Carrillo, Sebastián Herrera Barnuevo and María de Guevara', in *Women's Literacy in Early Modern Spain and the New World*, ed. Anne J. Cruz and Rosilie Hernández (Burlington: Ashgate, 2011), 225–42.

cover of Carrillo's work represent the domestic sphere and motherhood, while Judith, Jael, Esther and the Queen of Sheba represent political action.[48] Although she recognizes that in the *Elogios* both categories are intertwined, Hernández suggests classifying Rebecca, Deborah, Hannah, Ruth, Rachel, Samson's mother, Sarah and Bathsheba as domestic figures, while Miriam, Esther, Jael, Naomi, the Shunamite, the widow of Zarephath, Abigail and Abishag would be closer to the political and public sphere.[49] This classification, which may be more oriented to the context of the seventeenth century, seems to us, however, too rigid, since it constrains the complexity and wealth of the women represented in the chapel, while moving away from the biblical story. Greater flexibility allows adopting as a criterion the binomial 'inside–outside' in relation to the place where events take place, instead of the opposition 'domestic–public/political', because one issue is the area where they are located, the space in which the action takes place, and quite another the transcendence of the actions they undertake there. Deborah and Judith combine public space and political activity. Deborah rules, judges and calls for war, and Judith beheads Holofernes in the Assyrian camp; instead, Jael carries out the murder of Sisera inside a tent with a stake (domestic sphere); however, the consequences of her action have very marked repercussions of a political nature.[50] The palace can also be understood as the domestic sphere for the wives of kings. Once married, Bathsheba lives in the royal palace and, nevertheless, her intervention will be decisive for Solomon to become king. And the same happens in the case of Esther, who carries out her strategy of persuasion for Ahasuerus to change his decree against the Jews, or Abishag, who takes care of an old king in the royal apartments. Women like the matriarchs whose life develops within the family group will be those who have the perception of the line of promise, and the mother of Samson demonstrates a special sensitivity, which her husband lacks, to perceive the presence of the divine. The assignment of different areas to Ruth and Naomi is not evident either. Both of them act inside and outside the home and, moreover, the motherhood of Ruth is transferred to Naomi (Ruth 4.17). In addition, in most cases, these women are related in one way or another to motherhood, even in the case of Deborah, who, despite not having children, is attributed a symbolic motherhood with the title of the 'Mother of Israel'.

Because of the historical and social context of the time and the intended audience of the chapel, the contemplation of these twenty-one scenes allows for different levels of reading. The set of scenes of the chapel would be contemplated not only by the nuns but also by the royal visitors and by all those illustrious women and

---

48. Hernández, 'The politics of exemplarity', 235.

49. Hernández, 'The politics of exemplarity', 236, n. 30.

50. It is hard to understand that Deborah would be assigned to the domestic sphere. In fact, Jael cannot disengage from Deborah. The victory over the Canaanites can only be understood as the result of the action initiated by Deborah and concluded by Jael and, therefore, the space in which Deborah acts (outside) and in which Jael acts (inside) complement each other to achieve victory.

ladies who lived among the walls of the convent without being religious. Among the guests of the convent, also called 'floor ladies', there were maidens who lived there for receiving instruction and education, orphans, wives whose husbands were absent and widows.[51]

There is a reading of the scenes that can be understood using a political view that claims the equality of both sexes and defends that women have the capacity and the right to carry out the same activities as men. Teresa de Jesús, María de Zayas or María de Guevara,[52] who left their ideas in writing, were aware of the inequalities, loss of rights and marginalization they experienced because they were women. As non-conformists, they did not resign themselves to the traditional roles assigned by society, but, conscious of the difficulties they had to face, they struggled to find a space in which to develop their vocation and their talent.

The characters represented are important women, whose performance was decisive in the development of events and, consequently, in the history of salvation and who even came to act when men did not dare or could not gain power. In this sense we can understand the inclusion of Achsah and the daughters of Job, who, by obtaining part of the inheritance, are equated in rights to males. The decisive intervention of these biblical women would be interpreted as an endorsement of the participation of women in politics and in the court, a participation about which Laura Oliva affirms, 'Women were essential pieces in the political game of families in the Modern Age; their status as wives, mothers, widows (highly valued social positions) gave them great maneuverability to guarantee the political power of the male clan through strategies aimed at increasing and reinforcing patronage networks.'[53] For Hernández,[54] the *Elogios*, the paintings of the Chapel of Guadalupe and the work *Desengaños de la Corte y Mujeres Valerosas* (1664) by María de Guevara would have an educational purpose, the consequence of which would be the support of political activity carried out by the women belonging to the royalty or the nobility in the Spanish court. The lives of Sor Margarita de la Cruz and Ana Dorotea herself are clear examples of this.

A reading using the lens of religion emphasizes the pious virtues and attitudes such as the prudence of Rebecca, the meekness of Abigail, the strength of Judith,

---

51. 'It may be said that [this] monastery was instituted especially to provide the ladies of renown a welcoming retreat in which they might find themselves reunited,' in reference to the Convent of Las Descalzas Reales (Cristobal de Castro, *Mujeres del Imperio* (Madrid: Espasa-Calpe, 1943), 100).

52. See, among others, Alicia Redondo Goicoechea, *Mujeres y narrativa: otra historia de la literatura* (Madrid: Siglo XXI, 2009), and the holistic vision of Mª Isabel Barbeito Carneiro, 'Gestos y actitudes "feministas" en el Siglo de Oro español: de Teresa de Jesús a María de Guevara', in *Literatura y feminismo en España (XV–XVI)*, ed. Lisa Wollendorf (Barcelona: Icaria, 2005), 59–76.

53. Laura Oliva, *Mariana de Austria. Imagen, poder y diplomacia de una reina cortesana* (Madrid: Editorial Complutense, 2006), 140.

54. Hernández, 'The politics of exemplarity', 227.

the temperance of Esther, the care of the sick in Abishag or the faithfulness in Ruth. Humility, modesty, simplicity, prudence, strength, temperance, chastity – all virtues that converge in the Virgin and that are a connection between Mary and the biblical heroines to imitate.

The third reading would be connected to the experience of each viewer. The chapel is a kind of gallery where all sorts of women's life stages and situations are represented so that those who contemplate the images could feel identified and close to one or more of the characters that appear there. In this sense, it could be that, by being painted on a mirror, the viewer will incorporate her image to that of the represented character, creating a symbiosis between the viewer and what is seen.[55] This would allow, in some way, continuity between the biblical past and the present of the seventeenth century through the association of common experiences.

There are single women, married women and widows: maidens and virgins (Miriam, Abishag), married women who are loved by their husbands (Rachel, Bathsheba), wives whose husbands are fools (Abigail) and wives who suffer in silence so as not to distress their husbands (Anna), widows who remain in this state (Naomi and Judith) and widows who remarry (Ruth).

We find women who were never mothers (Judith, Deborah), others who suffered because of their sterility (Hannah, Samson's mother, Sarah, Rebecca and Rachel), those who experienced the pain of losing their children (Naomi) and those who fought to recover their children from death (the widow of Zarephath, the Shunammite). Along with them other family ties are represented: daughters (Achsah), sisters (the daughters of Job, Miriam), mother-in-law (Naomi) and daughters-in-law (Ruth).

There are women who dedicate themselves to specific tasks such as caring for the elderly (Abishag), spinning (Naamah) or music (Miriam); others perform leadership activities such as Judith and Deborah. There are queens (Esther) and wives of kings (Abigail, Bathsheba) but also poor and humble women (the widow of Zarephath, Naomi and Ruth). There are also wise women such the Queen of Sheba and intuitive women who know how to recognize the presence of the divinity (Samson's mother, the Shunammite).

All of them make up a tapestry of great colour, an iconography of the ordinary in feminine key. In this sense it is possible that the vertical axis of the chapel formed by Day, the daughter of Job, holding the solar disk in her hands, the Virgin of Guadalupe with the child in the centre and the Immaculate Conception will represent the Bible in its entirety, from the book of Genesis to the Apocalypse. Although the solar disk is one of the symbols that accompany the representations of the Immaculate Conception (Rev. 12.1), it could also be an allusion to the creation story since the clothes and the disposition of Job's daughter have great similarity with the way in which God is represented in the scene of the creation of the world. The Immaculate Conception is represented next to the sun, the moon

---

55. Hernández, 'The politics of exemplarity', 235.

and the dragon, elements that appear in the description of ch. 12 of the book of the Apocalypse, 'a woman clothed with the sun, with the moon under her feet, and on her head a crown of twelve stars … Then the dragon stood before the woman' (Rev. 12.1-4), and she is also represented with the usual iconographic elements of this image: uncovered head, loose hair, blue mantle and red tunic, which, although usually painted in white, can also appear in this colour, alluding to the blood shed by Christ.

Through twenty-one scenes, the intervention of biblical women in the history of salvation is shown, highlighting the contribution of each and every one of them. Renowned characters share the spotlight with women barely known or simply silenced, all of them important and necessary, all of them participants in the history of salvation.

Bibliography

Alonso Schökel. Luis, ed. *Biblia del Peregrino*. Bilbao: Ega-Mensajero, 1993.

Alonso Schökel, Luis. *Diccionario Bíblico hebreo-español*, 2 vols. Valencia: Institución San Jerónimo, 1990–91.

Álvarez Seijo, Begoña. 'Cerrando un programa iconográfico: Las hijas de Job en la Capilla de la Virgen de Guadalupe en las Descalzas Reales de Madrid'. *Imago: Revista de emblemática y cultura visual* 11 (2019): 97–110. Available online: https://ojs.uv.es/index.php/IMAGO/article/view/14248 (accessed 12 February 2021).

Barbeito Carneiro, Mª Isabel. 'Gestos y actitudes "feministas" en el Siglo de Oro español: de Teresa de Jesús a María de Guevara', in *Literatura y feminismo en España (XV–XVI)*, edited by Lisa Wollendorf, 59–76. Barcelona: Icaria, 2005.

Baumgartel, Bettina, and Silvia Neysters. *Die Galerie der Starken Frauen*. Munchen: Klinkhardt & Biermann, 1995.

Bornay, Erika. *Mujeres de la Biblia en la pintura del Barroco: imágenes de la ambigüedad*, Ensayos Arte Cátedra. Madrid: Cátedra, 1998.

Cantera, Francisco, and Manuel Iglesias, eds. *Sagrada Biblia*. Madrid: BAC, 2000.

Carrillo, Martín. *Elogios de mujeres ilustres del Viejo Testamento*. Madrid: Joseph Doblado, 1783 [1792, 1627].

Castro, Cristobal de. *Mujeres del Imperio*. Madrid: Espasa-Calpe, 1943.

Franco, Ángela. 'Reyes, héroes y caballeros en la literatura en la literatura y el arte en el ocaso de la Edad Media y pervivencias', in *Arte, poder y sociedad en la España de los siglos XV-XX*, coordinated by Miguel Cabañas, Amelia López-Yarto Elizalde and Wifredo Rincón García, 417–34. Madrid: CSIC, 2008.

Garrard, Mary D. *Artemisia Gentileschi: The Image of the Female Hero in Italian* Baroque Art. Princeton: Princeton University Press, 1989.

Ginzberg, Louis. *The Legends of the Jews*, 2 vols. Philadelphia: The Jewish Publication Society, 2003 [1913].

Hernández, Rosilie. 'The politics of exemplarity: Biblical women and the education of the Spanish lady in Martin Carrillo, Sebastián Herrera Barnuevo and María de Guevara', in *Women's Literacy in Early Modern Spain and the New World*, edited by Anne J. Cruz and Rosilie Hernández, 225–42. Burlington: Ashgate, 2011.

O: *Midrash hag-Gadol*. Edited by Solomon Schechter. Cambridge: Cambridge University Press, 1902.
O: 'The Targum of Job', translation and introduction by Céline Mangan in *The Aramaic Bible: The Targums*, edited by Kevin Cathcart, Michael Maher and Martin McNamara, vol. 15, 1–98. Minnesota: Liturgical Press, 1993.
O: 'Testament of Job', translation and introduction by R. P. Spittler in *Old Testament Pseudepigrapha, Apocalyptic Literature & Testaments*, edited by James Hamilton Charlesworth, vol. 1, 829–68. New York: Doubleday, 1983.
Oliva, Laura. *Mariana de Austria: Imagen, poder y diplomacia de una reina cortesana*. Madrid: Editorial Complutense, 2006.
Palomino de Castro y Velasco, Antonio. *El Museo pictórico y Escala óptica*, 2 vols. Madrid: Viuda de Juan García Infançon, 1724.
Redondo Goicoechea, Alicia. *Mujeres y narrativa: otra historia de la literatura*. Madrid: Siglo XXI, 2009.
Sánchez Caro, José Manuel. *La aventura de leer la Biblia en España*. Salamanca: Universidad Pontificia de Salamanca, 2000.
Sánchez Hernández, Mª Leticia. 'La capilla de Guadalupe en el monasterio de las Descalzas Reales de Madrid', in *Herederas de Clío: Mujeres que han impulsado la Historia*, coordinated by Gloria Franco Rubio and María Ángeles Pérez Samper, 493–514. Sevilla: Mergablum, 2014.
Sánchez Hernández, Mª Leticia. 'Mujer y Biblia: visión iconográfica de una relación fascinante', en el Primo Congresso Internazionale, *La donna e i luoghi della memoria*, organizado por la Fondazione P. Valerio per la Storia della donne, 27 Ginebra–29 junio 2007 (unpublished).
Sánchez Hernández, Mª Leticia. *Patronato regio y órdenes religiosas femeninas en el Madrid de los Austrias: Descalzas Reales, Encarnación y Santa Isabel*. Madrid: Fundación Universitaria Española, 1997.
Sebastián, Santiago. *Contrarreforma y barroco: lecturas iconográficas e iconológicas*. Madrid: Alianza Editorial, 1981.
Sicre, José Luis. *Josué*. Estella: Verbo Divino, 2002.
Vilacoba Ramos, Karen Mª. 'Las religiosas de las Descalzas reales de Madrid en los siglos XVI-XX: fuentes archivísticas'. *Hispania Sacra* LXII 125, no. 1 (2010): 115–56.
Wethey, Harold E. 'Herrera Barnuevo y su Capilla de las Descalzas Reales'. *Reales Sitios* 4, no. 13 (1967): 13–21.
Wethey, Harold E., and Alice Sunderland Wethey. 'Herrera Barnuevo and his Chapel in the Descalzas Reales'. *Art Bulletin* 48, no. 1 (1966): 15–34.
Yebra-Rovira, Carmen. 'French Biblical Engravings and the Education of the Spanish Woman in the XIX Century'. *Biblical Reception* 2 (2013): 97–116.

Chapter 5

MOSES'S MOTHER AND HER LITERARY AND VISUAL RECEPTION IN THE NINETEENTH CENTURY

Carmen Yebra-Rovira

Introduction

The story of a child abandoned in a basket on the bank of a river by a progenitor who seeks his or her salvation in the face of imminent danger runs through ancient oriental literature. The account in Exod. 2.1-10 is a good example of this. It narrates the birth and salvation of Moses from the waters of the river, in which the intervention of three women is significant. Scholarly research has addressed the study of the text from multiple perspectives. The most significant study was, undoubtedly, the history of the creation of the narrative and its literary genre revealing its dependence on oriental literature and the typical stories associated with the birth of heroes. This study thus gave Moses meaning within a narrative focused on highlighting his figure as the great liberator of the Hebrew people.[1] Others, more in line with the present study, have focused on the role of the three women in Moses's salvation: the mother, sister and daughter of the Pharaoh, their role in the story and their role as mediators of salvation. Gender perspectives and feminist approaches have oscillated between the high esteem they have for the presence of three women who oppose the destructive power of the Pharaoh, and, therefore, they are valued as role models of liberation and for their rejection of the perpetuation of female gender roles associated with the upbringing of children and the home, criticizing the fact that only from this context of domesticity can women be significant in society. The women in Moses's salvation narrative offer a story of great values and many ambivalences for the history of research. Their significance is unquestionable, but it is also necessary to highlight how throughout history this moment of the story has been silenced or at least considered much less relevant than other passages of Moses's life.

---

1. The preparation of this work has been possible thanks to the financing of the Ministry of Economy and Competitiveness of Spain (R+D Projects: *Reception and Transmission of the Bible: Texts and Iconography* FFI2015-65610-P).

Cultural biblical studies framed in the context of the history of reception and interpretation have allowed to approach biblical texts using new resources. Non-academic literature and visual culture have become materials worthy of study and they invite the researcher to observe biblical characters and textual passages that, although they have had their relevance in other periods of history, today may pass practically unnoticed.[2] The case study that will be addressed in this chapter is the mother of Moses and the way in which she has been interpreted in the past, especially in the nineteenth century. In this study, the sociocultural context of the nineteenth century will be briefly presented; then, I will collect data from the biblical texts regarding Moses's mother, and I will study how her figure was disseminated through literature for women and through the iconography of nineteenth-century art (sculpture, painting and engraving). I will finish this study with some conclusions aimed at highlighting how the nineteenth-century context helped to recast Moses narrative into a more feminine story. This contextualization emphasizes the value of the female figures – the mother and the sister – through their role in the domestic sphere, an emphasis that had not been so relevant in previous literary and iconographic traditions.

The metaphor of the 'angel in the house': The nineteenth-century ideal of femininity

The European Romantics of the nineteenth century shared a sublimated feminine ideal in which the virtues of obedience, silence and self-denial are clearly defined and are proposed as being part of women's own virtues. However, unlike in previous periods, this vision is not based on a negative anthropology that conceives woman as a sinful being or as the origin of sin but as something positive: the woman is an angel, a reflection of all the virtues, and a saviour not only of man but also of all humanity. This ideal is known with the metaphor of 'the angel in the house', an expression shared by all Western countries, according to which a woman is seen 'as an angel on earth'.[3] She is conceived as a pure, ethereal, celestial and delicate being with a natural tendency to care and protection.

> The ideal woman is an angel of light that illuminates the nebulosity of life. She is the mystical dove, the celestial messenger, which reflects the splendours of supreme beauty. She is a poem that thought cannot analyse and that only the

---

2. Emma England and William John Lyons (eds), *Reception History and Biblical Studies*, Library of Hebrew Bible/Old Testament Studies 615-STr 6 (London: T&T Clark, 2018).

3. A very significant and influential example is the poem written by Coventry Patmore, 'The Angel in the House', dated to 1854 and printed numerous times until the twentieth century both in Europe and the United States. In Spain, the most prominent example is the novel *El ángel del hogar* by the writer María Pilar Sinués Delgado in 1859.

heart understands. The ideal woman transmits revelations of the infinite. She is a Christian Sibyl.[4]

Female *domesticity* or life within the home is proposed as the most appropriate means to preserve those innate characteristics, that purity, and 'the special gifts of nature that have enabled the woman to be inside the house, dedicating herself to her parents, her husband, and their children. This is not because she is inferior and sinful, but because she has valuable moral and physical qualities that make her especially apt for this type of work.'[5] Her superiority shines in her natural space, the home, and is expressed through her abnegation and her capacity to love, forgive and console.[6] In addition, these aspects, clearly romantic, make her an important socializing agent affirming that, from the domestic family space, she is the one that educates society and the one that leads a nation to salvation. This role as teacher or educator will be the focus of her own upbringing, because as the first teacher of life, she must be able to educate good future leaders. She is considered the moral axis on which society turns, and her home becomes the space from which she governs everything. The abundant literature written for women's education or works that systematize the social structure demonstrate this point. Preaching and catechesis for women constantly raises and spreads these ideals. Thus, for example, in the words of the priest and later Spanish bishop Antonio María Claret, 'the philosophers in their theories say: that in the moral world the throne belongs to the woman, as the physical belongs to the man'.[7]

The new woman, always understood from the perspective of motherhood, is no longer a weak or inferior being because now she is the guarantor of the regeneration of society. There is an enormous sublimation and idealization that if she drifts or fails her mission, there will be catastrophic consequences for society or 'the nation'. The mother, a mirror in which the whole family should be looked at and the pillar that sustains them, must be strong, intelligent, conscious and responsible for the great task that has been entrusted to her. Considered the best

---

4. Concepción Gimeno de Flaquer, 'La mujer ideal', *Cádiz. Artes, Letras, Ciencias* II, no. 21 (1878): 163. The same text is published as 'La mujer juzgada por una mujer' (*El Álbum de la Mujer*, 24 July 1878) in the homonymous book published up to nine times in the nineteenth and twentieth centuries.

5. Catherine Jagoe, Alda Blanco and Cristina Enríquez de Salamanca, *La mujer en los discursos de género: textos y contextos en el siglo XIX*, Antrazyt 121 (Barcelona: Icaria, 1998), 28.

6. Colette Rabaté, *¿Eva o María?: ser mujer en la época isabelina (1833–1868)*, Acta Salmanticensia: Estudios Históricos & Geográficos (Salamanca: Universidad de Salamanca, 2007), 176.

7. Cited by Iris M. Zavala and Maryellen Bieder, *Breve historia feminista de la literatura española. 5, Literatura escrita por mujer: desde el siglo XIX hasta la actualidad (en lengua castellana)*, Pensamiento crítico/Pensamiento utópico. Serie Cultura y Diferencia (Barcelona: Anthropos, 1998), 21.

educator of her children, she must transmit the purest values to future generations. Apart from this homely and maternal ideal, there are, of course, other feminine models that struggle to make their way in this century.

The above-mentioned innate abilities must be accompanied by virtues that every woman must attain. Obedience, humility, chastity, devotion, prudence, patience or the ability to wait, industriousness and diligence should inspire private morality and the actions of the daughter, the wife and the mother of the family or the good religious woman.[8] All this contributes to the configuration of an *ethic of care*, exclusive to the female gender, which will be the constitutive elements of discretion or silence, generosity and self-denial or resignation. This is how a passive, silent and melancholic female role model is created. The home, as her exclusive sphere of action, conditions and restricts her participation and visibility in the public space, especially after she is married.

> The wife must, on the other hand, forget the worldly dissipations to direct all her solicitude towards the husband and her children, because a woman who only thinks in finery and adornments, who only dreams of parties, dances and theatres will end badly. Everything on its time: dolls for childhood, but for mothers, prudence, modesty, justice and other virtues.[9]

With everything that has been said, and although it may seem paradoxical, we cannot ignore that in this nineteenth-century context it was 'evident' for all males that motherhood satisfied all female aspirations and that their position should be safeguarded and watched over by their husbands. The reason for the natural dedication of the woman to the house and the care of the children was explained, among other reasons, by her poor intelligence or by being inferior to the man. The maternal instinct was understood and disseminated as the most primordial feeling and the most typical of a real woman.[10] Other functions or tasks performed by a woman outside the home or a motherhood not inserted in the parameter of the

---

8. These are the seven virtues that Father Claret describes in his works directed to a female audience. Cf. Antonio María Claret, *Avisos saludables á las doncellas, ó sea, Carta espiritual que escribió a una hermana* (Barcelona: Imprenta de los Herederos de la Viuda Pla, 1845); Antonio María Claret, *Instrucción que debe tener la mujer para desempeñar bien la misión que el Todopoderoso le ha confiado* (Barcelona: Librería Religiosa, 1863).

9. Antonio María Claret, 'Las delicias del campo', in *Escritos pastorales* (Madrid: BAC, 1997), 319.

10. María López Fernández, *La imagen de la mujer en la pintura española, 1890–1914* (Madrid: A. Machado Libros, 2006), 309:

> Schopenhauer declared, in *De las mujeres* (1815), that if the ladies were prepared to be the nurses and teachers of our early childhood, it was due to the fact that they themselves were 'childish, frivolous, and low-minded'. By defining them as 'girls grown up throughout their lives, in a kind of intermediate state between the child and the adult man', he definitively assimilated them to their children.

family were harshly criticized and reviled in bourgeois environments as contrary to the feminine ideal.

Biblical mothers in the nineteenth century

The idea of the *angel in the house* is disseminated and fed back as much from the popular feminine literature of the period as from the Christian religious preaching or teaching. In fact, over the course of the century, this false theory assumes that this bourgeois ideal model is rooted in the Bible and in Christian morality. Its formulators propose an especially fertile motherhood, and for this they rely on biblical women and biblical families. This angelic categorization is applied in a special way to wives and mothers of the Bible who appear as models of behaviour to wives, mothers and daughters whose functions are restricted to the care of the husband and children, and to life within the family home. The image of motherhood will be the filter by the way these characters will be described, creating a very specific biblical imaginary in which figures and attitudes not frequent in other historical periods are now praised.[11] The differences between the various Christian denominations are minimized because they shared the same literary and iconographic universe due to the importation and exportation of books, illustrated stories and works of art.[12] Through these objects, as Rebeca Arce Pinedo indicates, 'a religiosity that revolves around sentimentality replaces the avenging and justifying concept of God with a protective and benevolent image that deals with everyday well-being',[13] and whose reflection must be those Christian mothers.

The biblical stories show families that are taken up in the nineteenth century to illustrate and reinforce the maternal-filial relationship and that are included in women's literature for their education. All aspects of motherhood find an echo in the sacred texts, both in how a mother should be considered and the duties owed to her, as well as her function within the family as the carer of the children or the husband. Thus, in the literature for women and in their iconography, the Old Testament examples of Eve and Abel; Sarah and Isaac; Rachel and their children;

---

11. López Fernández, *La imagen de la mujer en la pintura española*, VII.3 'La madre: el arquetipo esencial', 312–18. Emancipated women, workers, beggars and prostitutes are opposed to this maternal and homelike image. All of them were, according to this author, 'subversive stereotypes that put this ideal in danger' (308).

12. Carmen Yebra-Rovira, 'Lectura bíblica y piedad femenina en el siglo XIX: Rebeca y Raquel como modelos de virtud', in *Glorificatio Dei, Sanctificatio Hominum: Homenaje al Prf. Dr. José María de Miguel González, OSST*, ed. Gonzalo Tejerina Arias and Gaspar Hernández Peludo (Salamanca: Secretariado Trinitario, 2017), 769–98.

13. Rebeca Arce Pinedo, *Dios, patria y hogar: la construcción social de la mujer española por el catolicismo y las derechas en el primer tercio del siglo XX* (Santander: PUbliCan, Universidad de Cantabria, 2008), 37.

Figure 5.1 G. Staal, *Eve*, in Augustin Calmet and Eugène de Genoude, *Las Mujeres de la Biblia: Colección de láminas preciosísimas* (Madrid: Imprenta y Librería española, 1846).

Hannah and Samuel; Bathsheba and Solomon; Ruth, Naomi and Obed; and Sarah and Tobias are widely used (Figure 5.1). From the New Testament, Mary and Jesus, the widow of Nain who mourns the death of her son or the Canaanite woman who asks for the healing of her daughter are taken with assiduity. In this century, the figures of Anna and Mary as a model of a daughter who learns patiently from a mother who educates her with pride, as was transmitted in the apocryphal literature, take on enormous importance in Catholic countries.

All these biblical models are recreated and their stories are extended by introducing aspects of daily life and female roles that were previously absent in their representations, such as the fact that Eve or Sarah breastfed their children – an element that was used to criticize those women who in the nineteenth century used a nurse for their offspring.[14] These biblical stories helped define the functions

14. Joaquín Roca y Cornet, *Mugeres de la Biblia* (Women of the Bible) (Barcelona: Llorens Hermanos, 1850), 149. In the description of biblical women, everything that has to do with their physical aspect is accentuated in a particular way. Old traditions are recreated or retaken, or new descriptions are constructed. Thus, for example, José Zapater y Ugeda, *Compendio de las mujeres de la Biblia: obra útil e instructiva para la juventud y en particular*

that a mother must perform: caring, cleaning the home or cooking, procuring clothing, feeding and spending sleepless nights for her children who will be treated with sweetness and tenderness. Other aspects that were emphasized are obedience, respect, silence and docility towards the husband, the head of the family and on whom the woman depends. Clearly, these values of the Victorian ideal are reflected, for example, in the re-readings of this time of the story of Jephthah and his daughter (Judges 11). In this new retelling, the harshness of the story of a father who must sacrifice his daughter for a vow made to God is disregarded by offering an alternative reading where she appears as an example of an obedient and self-sacrificing young woman who peacefully assumes death in order to safeguard her father's honour.[15]

Exodus 2: The mother of Moses and the biblical story

The example of the mother of Moses, Jochebed, will serve as a paradigm of how biblical mothers are exemplified as a feminine ideal in nineteenth-century Europe and will allow us to rescue a little-known example of motherhood that surprises with its enormous development in this century compared to the scarce treatment that it received in previous periods. The story of Moses, the great biblical hero, is transmitted to nineteenth-century women from his mother and his sister's experience, who are presented as heroines. Their courage for having hidden the

para las señoritas (Valencia: Juan Fenoll Bordonado's Press, 1853), 248, describes the 'purest' Virgin Mary, stating,

> She was of medium height, with skin the colour of mature wheat, the hair was blond and golden in colour, the eyes were bright and the cheeks were a little red; the arched, black and graceful eyebrows; the nose a little long; the lips beautiful; the face longer than round; long hands and fingers; she had a serious and modest aspect, without affectation, but humble and simple; the dresses she wore were not dyed, but the colour was natural.

On the contrary, Salome's description states the following:

> The woman who stood out the most for her beauty, adornments, and ease was Salome, daughter of Herodias. She would be about fourteen to fifteen years old; she was dressed with unequalled care, but letting her curtained shapes see through the gauze that did not covered her entirely in spite of the modesty proper to every person, and much more than a girl of her age. (257)

The first presents a model of beauty and modesty, which is not described in the second, which he criticized harshly.

15. See the study of the history of the daughter of Jephtah and her interpretations in nineteenth-century Spanish literature in Carmen Yebra-Rovira, 'Interpretación bíblica y formación moral de la mujer en el siglo XIX: *El ángel del hogar*', *Moralia* 36 (2013): 418–25.

child from all danger and their attempts to save him at all costs will make them a heroic model to follow. Their story also emphasizes their pain and peaceful resignation to the events that transpired, as well as other affective elements that had been absent in the story before: love, care, sweetness or closeness. These two women are joined by the Pharaoh's daughter, known as Bithiah or Thermuthis, who assumes the role of mother from the moment that she shows compassion for the child after seeing him in the river and orders her servants to pick him up and care for him.

The origins of Moses are narrated in ch. 2 of the book of Exodus. This is a short story that follows the usual genre and structure of the hero's journey whose life from childhood is characterized by the existence of prodigious events. The story narrates how the infant, the son of a Levite family, is placed by his mother in the river in a caulked basket, since she was unable to hide him any longer. The Pharaoh had given orders to kill all the Hebrew children. His sister follows him from a distance and sees how a servant of the daughter of the Pharaoh picks him up and gives him to her lady. When this happens, the girl approaches them and offers to look for a wet nurse for him, her own mother, and the Pharaoh's daughter accepts. In this way the child is recovered by his progenitor until, once raised, he is returned to the palace to live at the court.

The names of Moses's mother, Jochebed, and his sister's, Miriam, do not appear in this chapter, but in Exod. 6.20 and Num. 26.59. Neither does this chapter discuss certain aspects that the later tradition will fill in, such as how it was possible to conceal the child before his conception and after his birth or for how long; who, when and how he was deposited in the river; how long it took the Pharaoh's daughter to retrieve him; why was the child not taken away by the current or why the vermin didn't eat him; how did he learned the Jewish traditions; and how it is possible that his older brother also survived the order of the Pharaoh. In the iconographic representation, all those details that were related to the environment in which the story takes place were added, such as what the clothes were like, who was accompanying the daughter of the Pharaoh, where the mother of Moses was while Miriam spoke to the Egyptian princess and many other details that the artist must include to construct a visually significant story.

Jochebed in the written tradition: Exegesis and parabiblical literature

Tracing the identity and facts associated with this woman throughout the literature forces the researcher to approach basically two types of works: on the one hand, the exegetical commentaries of both Jewish and Christian authors, and, on the other hand, works of parabiblical literature of very diverse genres and authors. In the first case, one may find brief comments of a more philological or moral nature, or extensive digressions on any of the issues that appear in the story.[16] The

---

16. In the Catholic tradition, this type of exegesis is carried out almost exclusively by male presbyters. In the traditions of the Reformation, the case is different. There are more biblical

protagonist of these comments is usually Moses. The comments about his mother are often reduced to what her relationship was with her husband and if it was lawful or incestuous. In the second case, the parabiblical literature, one can find retellings of the story that are transmitted through legends, plays, poems or new narrations in the form of independent stories.[17] It is not possible to fully develop the history of transmission of these stories in this chapter. Suffice to say that in the nineteenth century, books entitled *Women of the Bible* were especially significant throughout Europe and the United States.[18] These books usually presented a selection of female characters from the Old and the New Testaments as biographical stories and they were composed for the edification of women or young people or for the formation of the clergymen in charge of the formation and/or accompaniment of women. The selected stories were not only those that could 'build on the virtues' or 'be the mirror of every virtuous heart' but also those stories that were led by women of ill repute whose examples will serve 'to pity them' and 'to destroy vice even if we find it dressed in finery more resplendent'.[19] Many of these books are also accompanied by beautiful engravings, either by illustrating some of the scenes

---

comments made by women and they have received more attention from researchers. Cf. Christiana De Groot and Marion Ann Taylor (eds), *Recovering Nineteenth-Century Women Interpreters of the Bible*, Society of Biblical Literature Symposium Series 38 (Atlanta: Society of Biblical Literature, 2007); Michela Soh-Kronthaler and Ruth Albrecht (eds), *Faith and Feminism in Nineteenth-Century Religious Communities: The So-Called Long Nineteenth Century*, Bible and Women 8.2 (Atlanta: SBL Press 2019).

17. In the nineteenth century, sacred stories featuring women who follow a tradition well established since ancient times in all European countries stand out. Their most prominent precedents are Martín Carrillo, *Historias o elogios de mujeres insignes del Viejo Testamento. Dedicado a Sor Margarita de la Cruz* (Huesca: Pedro Blusón, 1627); Pierre Le Moyne, *Galería de mugeres fuertes* (Madrid: Benito Cano, 1794; original, Paris: Chez Antoine de Sommaville, 1647); Álvaro de Luna, *Libro de las virtuosas e claras mugeres* (s.l., 1436). To learn more about this type of literature, cf. Ivonne Bleyerveld, 'Chaste, obedient and devout: Biblical women as patterns of female virtue in Netherlandish and German graphic art, ca. 1500–1750', *Simiolus: Netherlands Quarterly for the History of Art* 28, no. 4 (2000–1): 219–59; Carmen Yebra-Rovira, 'French biblical engravings and the education of the Spanish woman in the XIX century', *Biblical Reception* 2 (2013): 97–116.

18. Charles Adams, *Women of the Bible* (New York: Lane & Scott, 1851); Georges Darboy, *Las mugeres de la Biblia: fragmentos de una historia del pueblo de Dios por el Abate G. Darboy adornados con estampas del célebre G. Staal traducidos del francés por Agustín A. Franco*, 1 vol., Biblioteca del Espectador (México: R. Rafael, 1851); Bonifacio Martín Lázaro y Garzón, *Semblanzas de las Mujeres de la Biblia* (Madrid: Viuda e Hijo de Eusebio Aguado, 1883); Sarah Towne Martyn, *Women of the Bible* (New York: American Tract Society, 1868); Joaquín Roca y Cornet, *Mugeres de la Biblia* (Madrid - Barcelona: Llorens Hermanos, 1850); Zapater y Ugeda, *Compendio de las mujeres de la Biblia*.

19. Zapater y Ugeda, *Compendio de las mujeres de la Biblia*, 219.

or by having portraits of the protagonists. The authors of these compilations were mostly male, although there were also some composed by women. These works, which are not exclusive to this century, were translated into different languages and helped to shape a shared collective imagination and the dissemination of very specific feminine ideals independently of the religious confession for which they could have been originally written. As feminine literature, they enjoyed great acceptance because this type of pious spiritual reading was considered the only valid one for decent women. All these books recreate the Christian and rabbinical tradition by merging them and introducing contextual elements that make the story interesting for the reader. In most of them, after the chapters on the women of Genesis, it is usual to introduce one dedicated to Miriam (or specifically to 'The Mother of Moses') and, on occasion, another one dedicated to the daughter of the Pharaoh.

In the history of reception of this story, we must mention the Jewish historian Flavius Josephus, whose interpretation has been central to later Judaeo-Christian versions. In *Antiquities of the Jews*, Book II 9,4, he narrates the birth of Moses as a family story starring the head of the family, the father (called Amran or Amaran) who is charged, by divine mandate, to hide his wife from the enemy. The author, in imitation of other biblical announcements, presents the story of Moses in the context of a revelation, presenting him as a saviour. His delivery was silent, and they kept him hidden for three months. It was the father who deposited him in the Nile.[20]

> When the vision had informed him of these things, Amram awaked, and told it to Jochebed, who was his wife. And now the fear increased upon them, on account of the prediction in Amram's dream; for they were under concern, not only for the child, but on account of the great happiness that was to come to him also. [An. 1612] However, the mother's labour was such as afforded a confirmation to what was foretold by God: for it was not known to those that watched her, by the easiness of her pains; and because the throes of her delivery did not fall upon her with violence. And now they nourished the child at home privately for three months. But after that time Amram, fearing he should be discovered; and by falling under the King's displeasure both he and his child should perish; and so he should make the promise of God of none effect; he determined rather

---

20. The scene of the father placing the child in the river also appears in the iconography, although very rarely. An example is the engraving by Bernard Solomon, *Biblia Sacra* (Lyon: Jean de Tournes), first published in 1554 and reprinted in 1558 and in 1562. This engraving was also published in *Icones Historicae Veteris et Novi Testamenti, carminibus latinis et gallicis illustratae* (Geneve: Samuelem de Tournes, 1680), 100. The striking thing about it is that in the brief text in which the story is told, it says that it is the woman who deposits the child in the water. However, in the picture she remains inside a house, peeking from the door while the father leaves the child in the river. The literary and iconographic interpretation follow, therefore, two different sources or traditions.

to entrust the safety and care of the child to God, than to depend on his own concealment of him, which he looked upon as a thing uncertain; and whereby both the child, so privately to be nourished, and himself, would be in imminent danger. But he believed that God would some way for certain procure the safety of the child, in order to secure the truth of his own predictions. When they had thus determined, they made an arch of bulrushes, after the manner of a cradle, and of a bigness sufficient for an infant to be laid in, without being too straitened. They then daubed it over with slime, which would naturally keep out the water from entering between the bulrushes and put the infant into it; and setting it afloat upon the river, they left its preservation to God: so, the river received the child, and carried him along. But Miriam, the child's sister, passed along upon the bank over against him, as her mother had bid her, to see whither the ark would be carried.

In addition, the emphasis placed on the necessity of trusting God as the only way to solve the problem is striking in this story.

The rabbinical literature that follows Josephus delves into the identity of Jochebed who is identified with Shiphrah, one of the midwives of Exod. 1.15. It was her to whom the Pharaoh orders that all male children of the Hebrews should be killed at the time of their birth. The second would be Miriam or Elisheba, wife of Aaron (*Soṭah* 11b, *Exodus Rabbah*, 1.17). She would later be known as 'the Jewish', because, by disobeying the Pharaoh's order, she founded the Jewish nation (*Leviticus Rabbah* 1.13). The midrashim greatly expanded the story of Jochebed and her husband.[21]

The subsequent Christian commentaries and stories follow Josephus's version, but they expanded or retold the story not only by introducing significant variants and filling up the silences but above all else by feminizing the narrative progressively. He accomplished this by giving more prominence to Jochebed or accentuating the feelings of the couple. Thus, for example, Martín Carrillo, a seventeenth-century Spanish author, rereading Josephus and patristic literature, speaks of the pain of the father (Amaran) when he sees his wife's suffering after losing their son, how he shares with her the revelation that he has had and the Hebrew name of the infant (Joachim). The author also highlights the pain of the Hebrew mothers when they lost their children:[22]

---

21. Cf. Emil G. Hirsch, M. Seligsohn and Solomon Schechter, 'Jochebed', *Jewish Encyclopedia*. Available online: http://www.jewishencyclopedia.com/articles/8699-jochebed (accessed 21 November 2021).

22. Carrillo, *Historias ó elogios de mujeres insignes del Viejo Testamento*, Elogio XIII, 54–56. The author justifies the inclusion of the praise of Jochebed for being the mother

of the greatest Saint, the most courageous, the friend of God, and the most distinguished and important of the many men in the Old Testament, to whom God trusted his secrets, communicated his will, made him His secretary, and messenger

[Pharaoh] He sent out and ordered that all the children who were born were to be killed by throwing them into the river: here the sorrow of the heartbroken mothers were multiplied, because after having suffered the pain of childbirth, they felt a greater pain, that of the death of their children. The silent waters, whose sweetness was entertained by the saddest and most melancholic of people, were now dark with the tongues, shouts, and cries of the children, and they saddened the most cheerful and jovial of women: and when the children deprived of vital breath, were submerged: the mothers with wailing echoes, approached the banks of the river, lamenting as another Hecuba the death of their sweet and beloved children. (55)

The tone of this fragment, dramatic and poetic, is characteristic of the time and pauses on the feelings and resounding aspects of the story. In the description of the actions of Moses's mother, the author expands the biblical account with the inclusion of the trust that she placed in the salvation of her son:

She decided to put him in the river: for this she made a wicker basket that she coated with bitumen and fish, inside and outside, and she put the child in; and in this ship he sailed on the banks of the river, between bulrush or reeds, carrying as its pilot hope and rocking into dizziness his beautiful face: she was sure that he would find free entry, and safe port, wherever he arrived, then whoever saw him would want to bring him to life. (56)

The different retellings, following the biblical text, emphasize the beauty of the infant as one of the determining factors of his salvation. In addition, the passage of the finding of the child incorporates the function of the papyrus reeds (that of protection) and his situation when he was found (pouting), giving the story more realism and thereby responding to how the child was saved from the dangers of the river and why he was found:

Thermute with her maidens, walking by the bank of the river, saw the covered basket, and that the papyrus reeds, which is a reed that found in the Nile River, shaded it from the sun ... She saw a very beautiful child, who was pouting as if complaining of his sad luck and great helplessness; and she had pity of him. (56)

The later tradition continues to retell the story but justifying its choices not so much for the pre-eminence of Moses, but for the women themselves and the repercussion of their actions later in the story. Some moral issues, such as the kinship between the parents of the child, which had already been addressed in previous comments, are again relevant and are a good example of the moralistic

and we call him Vice God; for he governed in his name, and published His Law, receiving it from His hand. (54)

perspective of the nineteenth-century interpretation. Thus, the French authors Augustin Calmet (1672–1757) and Eugène de Genoude (1792–1849) in *Las mujeres de la Biblia* try to clarify whether the relationship between Amram and Jochebed was incestuous or wrong among members of the same family.[23] It also explains who their brothers Aaron and Miriam are, and the reasons why they could not hide the child any longer: 'Maybe at that time the houses of the Hebrews were to be searched by the Egyptians.' It is striking in this account that the decision to abandon the child is attributed to both parents: 'They resolved to remove him from home, entrusting him to the care of Providence.' The mention of Providence is also characteristic of the spirituality of this moment, demonstrating how in the face of the immeasurable, trusting God must be the attitude of the believer. Resignation, joy and trust are also placed next to it. Calmet adds aspects that in our eyes are anecdotal, but they are an example of what women's activities are. The daughter of the Pharaoh 'who Josephus calls Thermuthis; Artapano, Merris; the Alexandrine chronicle Mirrina, … came to the river accompanied by her servants, to bathe or to wash some scarves or linen cloths.'[24]

Throughout this history of reception, another aspect that generates controversy and that needs to be clarified is why didn't Moses's mother speak directly to the daughter of the Pharaoh. The explanations are varied. I would like to present here, as an example, that of a Spanish author, Joaquín Roca y Cornet, who published a collection of female biblical biographies following the Calmet model but adding additional elements to the stories, for example, indicating the possible dangers that the child faced when he was deposited in the waters. After presenting Thermuthis as the guardian angel who assists and protects Moses, he says that the mother sends Miriam to watch the child because

> her love did not dare to witness the tragic scene that was to come, and therefore she wanted that a friendly eye follows and protect, so to speak, the destinies of the sad cradle; because it seems to man that the eyes encourage and sustain what they embrace with affection. She withdrew herself, leaving as the tender outlaw's only defence the innocence and weakness of a girl, as if a pigeon wanted to confront the predatory nature of the vultures. This poor mother knew how to wait even in her despair, and indeed God here under no condemnation and without appeal, what this mother recommended and consecrated for her child, embraced her with the tenderness of his soul.[25]

---

23. Cf. Augustin Calmet and Eugène de Genoude, *Las Mujeres de la Biblia: Colección de láminas preciosísimas que representan las mujeres más célebres del Antiguo y del Nuevo Testamento abiertas en acero por los mejores artistas de Londres. El texto que las acompaña contiene la Cronología bíblica pruebas de la escelencia de la historia de los hebreos* (Madrid: Imprenta y Librería española, 1846), 19–20.

24. 1 Chronicles 4.18 calls Bithiah to the Pharaoh's daughter.

25. Roca y Cornet, *Mugeres de la Biblia*, 330–1.

The author, who presents the despair of the mother, ends up showing how only God will give her comfort and tenderness. The purpose of this type of explanation is to soften the harshness that is implied in the abandonment of a child by a mother and the perplexity, therefore, that such an action arouses in readers.

These different narrations explain in detail how the child was placed in the basket, his physical characteristics, how he was deposited among the reeds during the night and how Miriam watched over him until the baby caught the sight of the Pharaoh's daughter, took her brother and how she went to meet them. Other nineteenth-century commentaries are also an example of the didactic and safeguarding functions of the tradition, typical of a mother. This emphasizes that Moses knew the Jewish tradition (language, history and religion) before the Egyptian one thanks to the training received in his home by his mother.

By way of conclusion, it can be said that the history of the transmission of the story of the birth and abandonment of Moses through the period's literature dramatizes the moment and in the nineteenth century focuses on the exposition of the feelings and actions of women, presenting them as sensitive, suffering and having an active attitude for the salvation of the precious child. They are very affective stories that, evidently, will have the complicity of all those mothers who listen to them and who join in the salvation of the child. The attitudes of Jochebed, Miriam and the Pharaoh's daughter will become role models to be imitated by them.

Jochebed in nineteenth-century painting and sculpture

This change in the conception of women occurred in the nineteenth century and the emphasis given to the maternal function, which has already been discussed, explains the growth of an abundant maternal-filial iconography in this period.[26] Paintings starred by women taking care of your children increased considerably in this century in all artistic styles. Oil paintings created to decorate the female spaces of the house, biblical paintings for competitions, illustrations in books and in the periodical press have as their focus women holding their children. These scenes appear in intimate domestic interiors in which the mother appears alone with her offspring, in family portraits or fulfilling different tasks in which she will always appear next to her husband and surrounded by their children.

There are basically two iconographic models closely related to each other. The first is that of mothers of any social condition and in any activity represented with their children attached to their body, either by being supported on their hips or 'fitted' somewhere in it (waist, back, legs). With this figuration of the 'fusion between a mother and her child', the 'natural unity' between both is transmitted and reinforced. The second model is the representation of breastfeeding, understood

---

26. López Fernández, *La imagen de la mujer en la pintura española*, 308–17.

as the best symbol of the mothers' new mission.[27] In both cases, the expression of affection, tenderness or the connection between both through their eyes is very frequent. All these images are not only a reflection of a praxis but also a means of transmitting and fixing a very specific feminine ideal.

Biblical mothers will also be regularly represented in this period, creating, even, new iconographic models and figures that did not appear in the stories. The story of Jochebed, a worried, suffering, resigned and, above all else, mediating mother in the salvation of her son, is strikingly abundant in nineteenth-century iconography in painting, sculpture, printmaking and drawing. In addition to the number of representations, the new iconographic models and the selected scenes stand out. The previous iconographic tradition had mainly represented the scene of the discovery of Moses, giving prominence to the daughter of the Pharaoh. Without discarding it, although introducing important variants, in the nineteenth century, greater prominence was given to the mother and sister by constructing some very novel and interesting scenes. These scenes were a product, no doubt, of the ideals of this period, in which, in addition, a very important change in the setting and the clothes take place. This century offers two iconography models of these familiar scenes. The first is related to what happened inside the home and the second is the moment when the child is deposited in the river by his mother, by his mother and sister, or by his mother and two siblings. Also, Jochebed's portraits with her son are not strange in this period.

The farewell and the reunion

Nineteenth-century literature reflected, as we have seen, the pain of Moses's mother for having to leave him. Paintings deal with this moment, the farewell, in a special way; it is a feminine, homelike and very affectionate story.[28]

The British painter Simeon Solomon (1840–1905), a Pre-Raphaelite of Jewish origin, presents a domestic interior scene, known as *The Mother of Moses* (1860, Delaware Art Museum) (Figure 5.2).[29] In the work that was exhibited at the Royal

---

27. The new iconography of Eve, mother of all the living, breastfeeding their children or taking care of them, is a good example of how this approach influenced the rereading of the biblical protagonists. The engravings and the texts of the chapters of women's stories highlight her maternal character as opposed to the instigator of sin by offering Adam the fruit of the Tree of Knowledge characteristic of other historical periods.

28. The domestic iconography of Moses and his mother is not entirely new. The oil painting of the Belgian Frans Floris (1517–1570), with Moses being nursed by his mother, is proof of that. Nevertheless, this scenes is more concerned with the typological interpretation of Moses being breastfed by his mother as the prefiguration of the Virgin Lactans than as a scene of domesticity.

29. This works was first exhibited as *Moses*. For the study of this work, see: Aileen Elizabeth Naylor, 'Simeon Solomon's work before 1873: Interpretation and identity', Thesis (Birmingham: University of Birmingham, 2009); Sidney Colvin, 'Simeon Solomon', in *English Painters of the Present Day: Essays. J. Beavington Atkinson, Sidney Colvin, P.G.*

Academy of Arts, under the title *Moses*, Jochebed looks tenderly at the child while holding him in her arms, tenderly grasping his right hand.[30] The baby, to our contemporary eyes strikingly blond, looks at her as he holds out his small hands to her. She is also accompanied by her daughter, located on the right of the scene, close to her mother, whom she holds on to the arm, while contemplating the child enthralled. In the other hand, she holds the basket covered with a canvas, where she will put the baby. The three figures, without any space between them, constitute a unit, apparently indissoluble. It is an interior scene, domestic, and clearly intimate and melancholic, which fits with the taste of the time for the family values it entails and the expression of affective feelings that it reflects. To the left of the image, on a wooden table, covered with a beautiful coloured cloth is a clay pot with green branches. In the background, through a window in which two pigeons alight, a cloudy sky is perceived and provides a stormy and uncertain environment that contrasts with the peace of the birds and the hope provided by the tree branch with green leaves that highlights the background. In addition, according to the painter's approach, the image tries to be historic; all the details of that interior – the vessel, the harp or the furniture, as well as the dresses, excellently well designed – try to reproduce those of the time and thus they are also used in other works. A better understanding of the East and the pieces deposited in Western museums allowed this search for realism that can also be seen in female models. They are not the usual Western white women, but the artists tried to portray women as more oriental as they were seen in the European imagination, especially reflecting the darker colour of their skin and hair. The author uses, possibly, as a model Fanny Eaton (1835–1924), a Jamaican of African descent, the offspring of slaves who worked in London as a servant and who was a model for several of the Pre-Raphaelite artists.[31] The inclusion of a racial model different from that which British society was accustomed to earned Simeon Solomon harsh criticism, but it was a sign of the change that was taking place in the aesthetic parameters of the time and it helped to create a new way of imagining biblical stories. The characters are no longer dressed in the Western way, but they are following the oriental aesthetics so in vogue at the time, with their dark skin and their facial features mimicking or copying the Egyptians or

---

Hamerton, W.M. Rossetti and Tom Taylor (London: Seeley, Jackson and Halliday, 1871), 13–19; Carolyn Conroy and Roberto C. Ferrari, 'Simeon Solomon', http://www.simeonsolomon.com/; Ray Anne Lockard, 'Solomon, Simeon (1840–1905),' *Glbtq* (2015). Available online: http://www.glbtqarchive.com/arts/solomon_s_A.pdf (accessed 21 November 2021).

30. The importance of this subject can be verified with the fact that in 1860 were exposed in the Royal Academy four more works under a similar title. Cf. Naylor, 'Simeon Solomon's work before 1873', 38.

31. Cf. Roberto C. Ferrari, 'Fanny Eaton: The "other" Pre-Raphaelite model', *Columbia University Academic Commons* (2014). Available online: https://doi.org/10.7916/D8X92900 (accessed 21 November 2021).

Figure 5.2 Simeon Solomon, *The Mother of Moses*, 1860, oil on canvas. Source: Delaware Art Museum.

Jews. The harshest critics described the painting as representing 'two ludicrously ugly women, looking at a dingy baby'.[32]

This story of female domesticity is very similar in style, structure and purpose to others, such as that made by the same artist in *Ruth, Naomi and Obed* (1860), which shares the same sense of intimacy, child care, tenderness and Orientalism in its figures and setting.[33] The figures in *The Mother of Moses* painting are organized in a clear triangular arrangement in the manner of the Renaissance images of Sacred Families or triple saints, such as those representing Saint Anne, the Virgin Mary and Child, a theme that became fashionable again in the nineteenth century.

The importance of Simeon Solomon's version lies in its ability to iconographically broaden this story within the framework of domesticity, expanding it by showing the feelings of the two women and articulating tenderness and melancholy with

---

32. For the study of the reception of the work by English critics, cf. Naylor, 'Simeon Solomon's work before 1873', 28–35.

33. Cf. Simon Cooke, 'The biblical illustrations of Simeon Solomon', *The Victorian Web: Literature, History & Culture in the Age of Victoria*. Available online: http://www.victorianweb.org/art/illustration/ssolomon/cooke.html (accessed 21 November 2021).

drama and sadness. This painting had enormous diffusion after being copied and published in numerous illustrated Bibles and children's sacred stories as, for example, in the *Dalziels' Bible Gallery* (London: Routledge, 1881) as well as in the *Foster Bible* (1897).[34]

The interest of this British Pre-Raphaelite artist in this particular subject, which he already approached in his youth, is highlighted again in 1862 when he made the oil painting known as *The Finding of Moses* (Dublin City Gallery, The Hugh Lane, oil on canvas). In this painting, a girl and a woman with a child are placed against a background of palm trees between which the river is glimpsed. The first woman, dressed in white and red and looking directly at the viewer, is playing the cymbals while dancing and leading the march. The presence of a musical instrument and dance, new elements for this iconographical representation, allow her identification, because in Exod. 15.2 Miriam is presented as a prophetess and guide of the group of women who sing and dance praising God after the crossing of the Red Sea. Next to the girl, also barefoot, is a woman holding a baby in her arms while kissing him. He, with his little hand, touches her mouth. The woman, dressed in dark, with an apron decorated in red tones and with her head covered with a white scarf with black stripes, can undoubtedly be identified as the mother of Moses. The dance of the girl, the maternal and extremely tender gesture of the other woman and especially the *tallit* with which she covers her face, leads us to affirm that, despite what the commentators of this work indicated in the past, this is not the daughter of Pharaoh but of Jochebed. Simeon Solomon has opted to represent not the classic discovery of the child among the reeds of the river but the moment when his mother and sister return home to fulfil the task given to them by the Pharaoh's daughter to take care of the child (Exod. 2.9b). Both act as precursors of the saving deeds of Moses, who, as an adult, will save the people from the waters. It is a new iconography, very typical of the sensibility of Simeon Solomon and the taste of the time.

Nineteenth-century criticism positively values this painter as much for his imagination as for his creative capacity. Critics said, commenting on his biblical paintings, that he was able to recreate scenes that have not yet been imagined. These two familiar images of complicity between the child, his mother and his sister are a good example of this.

---

34. *Bible Pictures and What They Teach Us: Containing 400 Illustrations from the Old and New Testaments: With Brief Descriptions by Charles Foster* (Philadelphia: Foster, 1897). The importance of children's Bibles in the configuration of the collective biblical memory cannot be ignored. Their stories were accompanied by images widely disseminated through school, catechisms and reading in homes. Cf. Ruth B. Bottigheimer, *The Bible for Children: From the Age of Gutenberg to the Present* (New Haven: Yale University Press, 1996); Caroline Vander Stichele and Hugh S. Pyper (eds), *Text, Image, and Otherness in Children's Bibles: What Is in the Picture?*, Semeia Studies 56 (Atlanta: Society of Biblical Literature, 2012).

Moses deposited in the Nile

The second moment of this story, full of intimacy, with important family and religious values and framed within the ideology of the angel of the home, is that of the child being deposited in the river. The sculptures of Henri de Triqueti, a French sculptor who dedicated several of his works to this theme, are enormously revealing for their delicacy and sweetness. In his version of *La Mère de Möise* (1867, Musée Girodet), he sculpts in plaster the moment in which the child is deposited in the waters.[35] Not only is the foreshortening of the mother surprising but also, above all, the motherly farewell kiss that reflects the affections expected between a mother with her son in this century, which follows what he did in his terracotta version of 1852 (*La mére de Möise embrasse son fils dans un berceau*, Orleans, Musée des Beaux Arts) and Simeon Solomon's previous example.[36] Both sculptures, of great delicacy, obviate the drama of abandonment, narrating a tender, very delicate and affective story. In both cases the infant rests with absolute tranquillity.

The woman painter of North American origin but of European artistic formation, Elisabeth Jane Gardner Bouguereau, interprets the abandonment in a different way which includes, in addition to Jochebed, Miriam, capturing the moment in which both leave the child in the river. The artist made the oil on canvas, known as *Moses in the Bulrushes*, in 1878 to present it at the Paris Salon competition. In this painting, Moses's sister appears already as a young girl, standing dressed in white and looking among the reeds to the daughter of the Pharaoh. Jochebed, on her knees, with darker clothes and her head covered by a veil, turns her head to the right, looking towards the sky as if asking God for protection for her child. At the same time, her left hand is raised towards the heavens while her right hand gently holds the basket in which her son sleeps peacefully on white sheets and tied with a blue ribbon. The clearly melancholic atmosphere seems to distance the eyes of the current spectator from all the drama and make it a scene of resigned prayer. At that time, the expression of anguish on the mother's face and the fine colouring of the work were highly valued. It was understood as a realistic work especially for the colour of the skins. To the eyes of the contemporary spectator, however, that anguish is not perceived; only the blond child and his placid rest and the heaviness of the environment are surprising.

Joseph Baume's engraving published in *The Children's Bible* (*c.* 1883) introduces a significant variant by introducing Moses's brother, Aaron, with Miriam. The

---

35. This French sculptor has addressed this issue at least five times. Cf. Leticia Azcue Brea, 'Moisés: de las aguas al mármol', in *Las imágenes de la Biblia*, ed. Francisco Calvo Serraller and Jesús María González de Zárate (Madrid: Fundación Amigos Museo del Prado, 2016), 206–7.

36. Jacqueline Banerjee, 'La Mère de Möise', *The Victorian Web. Literature, history & culture in the age of Victoria* (2009/10). Available online: http://www.victorianweb.org/sculpture/triqueti/6.html (accessed 21 November 2021).

family history of mother and children is completed by answering the question of where Aaron was while his brother was being abandoned.[37]

Jochebed and her son

A final variant in the representation of Moses and his mother is the portraits. The marble sculpture of the American artist Franklin Simmons *Jochebed (Mother of Moses)* (1873, Museum of Fine Arts, Boston) is a good example of this.[38] In this sculpture, Jochebed, seated as a Roman matron, holds her son on her lap. She holds her son with her left arm with sweetness, which contrasts with the strength of her right hand resting on the seat and ready to stand up. The child, with a new gesture of tenderness, touches his mother's breast with his left hand demanding her attention. The woman's serious expression shows concern. The simplicity of the sculpture is enriched by the details on the bracelets, the folds of the dress that leave her left shoulder exposed and the final fringe of the veil or the detail of the sandals. It might be surprising to include this North American artist when talking about these artistic representations in a European context. However, his presence is justified because his work was disseminated throughout the European continent through engravings, such as the one made by W. Roffe. The British version of Philip Richard Morris (1836–1902), *The Infant Moses and His Mother*, which depicts the moment in which she deposits the cradle in the water, reproduces the same iconographic type and the same decorative details and clothing.

The Brazilian painter, but of Roman formation, Pedro Américo de Figueiredo offers a version following the same ideas. In his portrait, *Jochebed* (1884, National Museum of Belas Artes, Rio de Janeiro), he emphasizes her strength both in the way he represents her face and in the way in which she holds her son on her hip. The concern is expressed by her hand resting on his cheek, by her wind-blown hair and by the many tears that run down her cheeks.[39] The drama, which contrasts with the stillness of the child who is peacefully asleep, wrapped between thin linens, is reinforced by the movement of the waters of the river and the darkened sky. Jochebed appears as a worried woman, but strong. The artist treats all the details

---

37. Very similar to the work of Gardner is the oil painting by the Russian artist Alexey Tyranov, *Moses's Mother* (1839–42, Tretyakov State Gallery, Moscow), in which he emphasizes the careful and academic disposition of the figures following a triangular composition which mimics those of the pyramids that appear at the bottom of the image and shows extreme calm in the action.

38. Azcue Brea, 'Moisés: de las aguas al mármol'. To this one we can add the sculptures of Charles Cumberworth and Heinrich Imhof (1848, Hermitage Museum, Moscow).

39. This Brazilian artist offers the possibility of reflecting on the expansion and influence of European works and trends in Latin America. He also paints another full-length portrait of the figure of Judith. The collections of portraits of biblical women were very frequent in this century connected, above all, to the movement of Orientalism with the idealization of the beauty of Oriental women.

with mastery, but especially the decoration of the feminine dress. Fringes, tassels, shells and inlays draw a decoration that the current spectator would identify more with Indian dresses than Egyptian or Hebrew. The multicoloured striped veil that covers her head is undeniably Hebrew.

This scene of the abandonment of Moses on the Nile is approached by numerous commentators and artists in the century and, with the exception of the Brazilian one, they all reflect sadness, but also resignation and peaceful acceptance.[40] They are works that convey great melancholy and in which the two women present themselves as sad heroines who seek an impossible salvation wrapped by an angelic halo.

Conclusions

The contemporary domestic space and the conception of women contributed to the nineteenth-century biblical reinterpretation reflecting elements and questions that had not been contemplated before, and they demonstrate that reinterpretations are always dynamic and subject to the different contexts in which the stories take on new life. The socio-religious context of the nineteenth century conditioned the transmission of female figures and brought to light women that may have been invisible or insignificant at other times in history such as the mother of Moses. On the other hand, due to the particular prism from which they are interpreted, with the angelic conception of women and their virtues praised in an idealized, almost celestial home, their stories are recreated and expanded from the perspective of the values of the time. The centrality of the home makes biblical family stories of special relevance, and their spaces and contexts are enriched and filled with everyday details, alien to the sacred texts but necessary for their dissemination and understanding in this century. This allows the inclusion of characters and attitudes that fit well in this context. The development of the biblical stories is enormously imaginative, configuring a feminine literature of great interest.

Biblical mothers are models for a feminine ideal whose ethics of care taken to heroism transforms a sinful and lost society into a new 'heaven on earth'. These women nourish the ideal of the 'angel of the home' and build a home in which motherhood is extolled in the face of other values such as freedom, paid work or external visibility, typical of other moments in history. This view risks the transformation of the ideal space of domestic heaven into the only model of female life by rejecting different approaches to life that are also possible in that same century, which in the end might lead towards a misunderstood resignation for women. The biblical stories, however, contain values and proposals that contradict the feminine moral conduct demanded by nineteenth-century society that

---

40. For example, the fresco of the Croatian Vjekoslav Karas, *Moses Deposited on the River Bank* (1842–43, Gradski Muzej Karlovac) or the British version of Edward Armitage, *The Mother of Moses* (1878, private collection).

questions the Bible as the basis of this ideological construction, as is frequently asserted.

There are scenes and figures, like that of the mother of Moses, that contribute to unify this image in the imaginary and show evidence of shared values independently of the Christian confessions and the countries where these interpretations originated. Engravings in illustrated Bibles and publications for women or children allowed for an enormous diffusion of some versions that, in turn, conditioned the reading and interpretation of the texts.

The analysis of the works presented in this study, both literary and iconographic, allows us to elucidate the selection criteria of these stories and their expansion processes, as well as to demonstrate how texts, in order to be meaningful, must respond to the sociocultural needs of those who listen to them. It also allows us to understand how they are used to reinforce a set of ideals and how the interpretation of these texts is never univocal or oriented in a single direction.

The study of nineteenth-century visual work and the knowledge of the criticism of the moment allow us, likewise, to appreciate how the perspectives, sociocultural contexts and pre-understandings from which the viewers approach the works continuously change through time. If the racial groups or the tonality of the skins could cause stupor at that moment, today they are not seen with the same intensity since they have been normalized, but there may be other elements that would cause shock in the paintings. The interpretation of texts and stories also changes with the transformations that have taken place in the reader/spectator and in their own context.

Bibliography

Adams, Charles. *Women of the Bible*. New York: Lane & Scott, 1851.

Arce Pinedo, Rebeca. *Dios, patria y hogar: la construcción social de la mujer española por el catolicismo y las derechas en el primer tercio del siglo XX*. Santander: PUbliCan, Universidad de Cantabria, 2008.

Azcue Brea, Leticia. 'Moisés: de las aguas al mármol', in *Las imágenes de la Biblia*, edited by Francisco Calvo Serraller and Jesús María González de Zárate, 205–24. Madrid: Fundación Amigos Museo del Prado, 2016.

Banerjee, Jacqueline, 'La Mère de Möise', *The Victorian Web: Literature, History & Culture in the Age of Victoria* (2009/10). Available online: http://www.victorianweb.org/sculpture/triqueti/6.html (accessed 21 November 2021).

Bleyerveld, Ivonne. 'Chaste, obedient and devout: Biblical women as patterns of female virtue in Netherlandish and German graphic art, ca. 1500–1750'. *Simiolus: Netherlands Quaterly for the History of Art* 28, no. 4 (2000–1): 219–50.

Bottigheimer, Ruth B. *The Bible for Children: From the Age of Gutenberg to the Present*. New Haven: Yale University Press, 1996.

Calmet, Augustin, and Eugène de Genoude. *Las Mujeres de la Biblia: colección de láminas preciosísimas que representan las mujeres más célebres del Antiguo y del Nuevo*

Testamento abiertas en acero por los mejores artistas de Londres. El texto que las acompaña contiene la Cronología bíblica pruebas de la escelencia de la historia de los hebreos. Madrid: Imprenta y Librería española, 1846.

Carrillo, Martín. *Historias o elogios de mujeres insignes del Viejo Testamento. Dedicado a Sor Margarita de la Cruz*. Huesca: Pedro Blusón, 1627.

Claret, Antonio María. *Avisos saludables á las doncellas, ó sea, Carta espiritual que escribió a una hermana*. Barcelona: Imprenta de los Herederos de la Viuda Pla, 1845.

Claret, Antonio María. *Instrucción que debe tener la mujer para desempeñar bien la misión que el Todopoderoso le ha confiado*. Barcelona: Librería Religiosa, 1863.

Claret, Antonio María. 'Las delicias del campo', in *Escritos pastorales*, 307–32. Madrid: BAC, 1997.

Colvin, Sidney. 'Simeon Solomon', in *English Painters of the Present Day: Essays. J. Beavington Atkinson, Sidney Colvin, P.G. Hamerton, W.M. Rossetti and Tom Taylor*, 13–19. London: Seeley, Jackson and Halliday, 1871.

Conroy, Carolyn, and Roberto C. Ferrari. 'Simeon Solomon'. Available online: http://www.simeonsolomon.com/ (accessed 21 November 2021).

Cooke, Simon. 'The biblical illustrations of Simeon Solomon', *The Victorian Web: Literature, History & Culture in the Age of Victoria*. Available online: http://www.victorianweb.org/art/illustration/ssolomon/cooke.html (accessed 21 November 2021).

Darboy, Georges. *Las mugeres de la Biblia: fragmentos de una historia del pueblo de Dios por el Abate G. Darboy adornados con estampas del célebre G. Staal traducidos del francés por Agustín A. Franco*, 1 vol., Biblioteca del Espectador. México: R. Rafael, 1851.

De Groot, Christiana, and Marion Ann Taylor, eds. *Recovering nineteenth-Century Women Interpreters of the Bible*, Society of Biblical Literature Symposium Series 38. Atlanta: Society of Biblical Literature, 2007.

England, Emma, and William John Lyons, eds. *Reception History and Biblical Studies*. LHBOTS 615-STr 6. London: Bloomsbury T&T Clark, 2018.

Exum, J. Cheryl. *Plotted, Shot, and Painted: Cultural Representations of Biblical Women*, JSOT. SS 215. Sheffield: Sheffield Academic Press, 1996.

Ferrari, Roberto C. 'Fanny Eaton: The "other" Pre-Raphaelite model', *Columbia University Academic Commons* (2014). Available online: https://doi.org/10.7916/D8X92900 (accessed 21 November 2021).

Gimeno de Flaquer, Concepción. 'La mujer ideal'. *Cádiz. Artes, Letras, Ciencias* 2, no. 21 (1878): 163.

Icones Historicae Veteris et Novi Testamenti, carminibus latinis et gallicis illustratae. Geneve: Samuelem de Tournes, 1680.

Jagoe, Catherine, Alda Blanco and Cristina Enríquez de Salamanca. *La mujer en los discursos de género: textos y contextos en el siglo XIX*, Antrazyt 121. Barcelona: Icaria, 1998.

Lázaro y Garzón, Bonifacio Martín. *Semblanzas de las Mujeres de la Biblia*. Madrid: Viuda e Hijo de Eusebio Aguado, 1883.

Le Moyne, Pierre. *Galería de mugeres fuertes*. Madrid: Benito Cano, 1794.

Lockard, Ray Anne. 'Solomon, Simeon (1840–1905)', *Glbtq* (2015). Available online: http://www.glbtqarchive.com/arts/solomon_s_A.pdf (accessed 21 November 2021).

López Fernández, María. *La imagen de la mujer en la pintura española, 1890–1914*. Madrid: A. Machado Libros, 2006.

Luna, Álvaro de. *Libro de las virtuosas e claras mugeres*. s.l. 1436.

Martyn, Sarah Towne. *Women of the Bible*. New York: American Tract Society, 1868.
Matthews, Victor Harold, and Don C. Benjamin. *Old Testament Parallels: Laws and Stories from the Ancient Near East*. New York: Paulist Press, 1991.
Naylor, Aileen Elizabeth. 'Simeon Solomon's work before 1873: Interpretation and identity'. Thesis. Birmingham: University of Birmingham, 2009.
Rabaté, Colette. *¿Eva o María?: ser mujer en la época isabelina (1833–1868)*, Acta Salmanticensia. Estudios Históricos & Geográficos. Salamanca: Universidad de Salamanca, 2007.
Roca y Cornet, Joaquín. *Mugeres de la Biblia*. Madrid – Barcelona: Llorens Hermanos, 1850.
Soh-Kronthaler, Michela, and Ruth Albrecht, eds. *Comunidades religiosas y Biblia en el siglo XIX*, La Biblia y las Mujeres 19. Estella: Verbo Divino, 2018.
Vander Stichele, Caroline, and Hugh S. Pyper, eds. *Text, Image, and Otherness in Children's Bibles: What Is in the Picture?*, Semeia Studies 56. Atlanta: Society of Biblical Literature, 2012.
Yebra-Rovira, Carmen. 'French biblical engravings and the education of the Spanish woman in the XIX century'. *Biblical Reception* 2 (2013): 97–116.
Yebra-Rovira, Carmen. 'Interpretación bíblica y formación moral de la mujer en el siglo XIX: *El ángel del hogar*'. *Moralia* 36 (2013): 405–26.
Yebra-Rovira, Carmen. 'Lectura bíblica y piedad femenina en el siglo XIX: Rebeca y Raquel como modelos de virtud', in *Glorificatio Dei, Sanctificatio Hominum: Homenaje al Prf. Dr. José María de Miguel González, OSST*, edited by Gonzalo Tejerina Arias and Gaspar Hernández Peludo, 769–98. Salamanca: Secretariado Trinitario, 2017.
Zapater y Ugeda, José. *Compendio de las mujeres de la Biblia: obra útil e instructiva para la juventud y en particular para las señoritas*. Valencia: Imprenta de Juan Fenoll Bordonado, 1853.
Zavala, Iris M., and Maryellen Bieder. *Breve historia feminista de la literatura española. 5, Literatura escrita por mujer: desde el siglo XIX hasta la actualidad (en lengua castellana)*, Pensamiento crítico/Pensamiento utópico. Serie Cultura y Diferencia. Barcelona: Anthropos, 1998.

Chapter 6

THE WOMEN IN THE BOOK OF JUDGES AND THEIR REPRESENTATION IN NINETEENTH-CENTURY ENGRAVINGS

Carmen Yebra-Rovira

Introduction

The story of Samson and Delilah is one of the most popular in the Bible. Its importance and repercussion can be verified by the fact that it is still present in our collective memory – even in the most secularized societies – and that its protagonists, who have been portrayed on many occasions throughout the history of art, are easily identified. When the curious reader wants to read the complete story, he or she has only to go to the book of Judges. Next to this story, the reader will discover a set of other unknown stories, full of complex plots and surprising narratives. In an attentive reading, he or she not only meets other judges, such as Othniel, Ehud, Shamgar, Gideon or Abimelech, but also might be surprised by the mention of Judge Deborah, or with the feats of Jael, or with the assertiveness of Samson's mother or with the harshness of the violence exercised, without justification, on many other women.

This chapter focuses on the study and analysis of some of these stories, particularly those whose main protagonists are women, and their representation in prints published in Spain in the nineteenth century. The choice of this artistic genre, this century and this geographical area are explained by the centrality that engraving acquired as a form of communication in this period, and by the importance that biblical models achieved for the formation of a new society, in particular the formation of women. The nineteenth-century bourgeoisie was gradually getting used to seeing the world through the engravings that were incorporated in the press or in books and, therefore, religious publications, which were experiencing a very notable growth, incorporated them progressively. These religious prints had an apparently doctrinal and moral purpose, but they were also used as a decorative element, as political tools and as objects of strong commercial value.[1]

---

1. The illustrated works were an element of consumption of a growing bourgeoisie throughout Europe in the nineteenth century and, therefore, a sign of social prestige.

The clarity and strength of these compositions catch the attention of the reader-spectator who is immediately surprised by the abundance of female characters that appear in each series, many of them almost or totally unknown. Therefore, this study aims to rescue some of these biblical women like Achsah, Deborah, Jael, the woman of Thebez, Jephthah's daughter and the concubine of Ephraim, with the intention of analysing what their role was in the history of salvation, how they were interpreted and how they modified their stories through these engravings, and what were the consequences that each one of these representations had for the spectator who contemplated them.

To accomplish this, I will first explain how these illustrated biblical works came to be in Spain, followed by an analysis of the meaning of the book of Judges and who were the women mentioned in it. Next, I will describe the types of representations of some of these women in the nineteenth century and what the causes were for their selection and the possible implications that they had for research. The study concludes with reflections on the meaning and relevance of these types of works for the understanding of the biblical message.

The collections of biblical engravings in Spain in the nineteenth century

The illustration of Bibles and Sacred Stories are part of the history of the book practically from its origins.[2] In the Middle Ages, beautiful *Biblia Pauperum* and illuminated Bibles were produced for a cultured and wealthy minority. In the Renaissance and the early modern period, with the development of the printing press and with the diffusion of the Protestant Reformation, illustrated bibles were popularized, making their reading very attractive when filled with images that very soon became part of the collective biblical memory. In the nineteenth century, these illustrated bibles reached their maximum dissemination, both in Protestant and Catholic countries, since they were created not only for wealthy minorities but also for the growing bourgeoisie and for their children's education.[3] Engravings

---

Editions are carefully crafted with special attention to illustrations and binding, which results in value increase. Each book then becomes a special artwork only accessible to a selected group. They were usually published in fascicles and sold by subscription.

2. To follow the development of this type of illustrated works, see cf. Max Engammare, 'Les Figures de la Bible. Le destin oublié d'un genre littéraire en image (XVIe-XVIIe s.)', *Melánges de l'Ecole française de Rome. Italie et Méditerranée* 106, no. 2 (1994): 549–91; Juan Carrete Parrondo, 'Iluminando la Biblia', *Descubrir el arte* 70 (2004): 86–91; Carmen Yebra-Rovira, *Las biblias ilustradas en España en el siglo XIX: Desarrollo, relevancia cultural e interpretación teológica*, Col. Tesis 64 (Estella: Verbo Divino – Asociación Bíblica Española, 2015).

3. Ruth B. Bottigheimer, *The Bible for Children: From the Age of Gutenberg to the Present* (New Haven: Yale University Press, 1996); Caroline Vander Stichele and Hugh S. Pyper (eds), *Text, Image, and Otherness in Children's Bibles: What Is in the Picture?* (Atlanta: Society of Biblical Literature, 2012).

became, between the sixteenth and nineteenth centuries, the chosen medium for the transmission of the biblical stories, which were then retold in the catechisms, textbooks, reading books, biblical novels or pious readings. Even today, Sacred Stories and illustrated Bibles are being represented through different genres and formats –such as comics – and they continue to enjoy great commercial success.

The development of the printing press, the increased literacy (thanks to educational improvements) and the concern for the laity and the religious faithful to know the Bible were the triggers for the development of engraving and printing of biblical stories in Spain in the nineteenth century. Their starting point must be placed in the complete translation into Spanish of the Bible which was made by the Piarist friar Felipe Scío de San Miguel (Valencia: Tomás Orga, 1790–93) and by Bishop Félix Torres Amat (Madrid: Luis Amarita, 1823–25). This translation allowed the Catholic reader, forced from the Council of Trent (1545–63) to read the Sacred Text only in Latin, to approach it now through his or her mother tongue.[4] In addition to this, it is important to acknowledge the development of the different techniques of engraving, the demand of the informative visual recording for periodical and scientific publications, and the rise of this discipline after its inclusion in the Royal Academy of Arts of San Fernando (Madrid) and San Carlos (Valencia). These elements encouraged the formation of Spanish engravers whose biblical creations coexisted with important foreign collections, such as Gustave Doré's and Julius Schnorr von Carolsfeld's, which show the relevance of the trade and import of books from France, Germany and Great Britain.[5]

In the Spanish production of prints, biblical collections were made for two types of documents.[6] The first was for the Sacred Stories – like that of the Master of Sacy, *Historia del Antiguo y Nuevo Testamento* (History of the Old and New Testament), illustrated by Antonio Pascual[7] – and the second, for complete Bibles – the editions of Scío and Torres Amat.[8] There were also collections of biblical prints,

---

4. On the first editions of the Bible in Castilian and its relation with the Enlightenment, cf. José Manuel Sánchez Caro, *Biblia e Ilustración: Las versiones castellanas de la Biblia en el Siglo de las Luces* (Vigo: Academia del Hispanismo, 2012).

5. The Gustave Doré collection of 1866 was published in Spain illustrating the third edition of *La Sagrada Biblia* by F. Torres Amat in 1871–73. The one by Schnorr von Carolsfeld was known thanks to the international edition of *Biblia Sacra Tabulis Illustrata* of 1857, followed by Julius Schnorr von Carolsfeld, *Gran colección de láminas del Antiguo y Nuevo Testamento por el eminente artista Julio Schnorr a Carolsfeld* (Barcelona: Faustino Paluzie, 1876).

6. To carry out a complete study, it would be necessary to also take into account the stamps that were printed in catechism books and school books. Some of the images found in these print collections were reused in these works which had a greater diffusion.

7. Isaac-Louis Le Maistre de Sacy, Vicente Boix and Antonio Pascual, *Historia del Antiguo y Nuevo Testamento: adornada con 700 láminas, según las esplicaciones[sic] sacadas de la Santa Escritura y Padres de la Iglesia* (Valencia: Imp. de Ventura Lluch, 1841).

8. Throughout the nineteenth century, there were several illustrated editions of the Scío Bible with different collections of engravings. The Torres Amat Bible is uniquely associated

with hardly any text, in which the drawings themselves constituted a narrative of a visual nature, that is, the 'bibles in images' by Pedro Lozano, *Colección de Estampas del Viejo y Nuevo Testamento* (Collection of Prints of the Old and New Testament) (Madrid: Antonio Sancha, 1786) and Schnorr von Carolsfeld, *Gran Colección de Láminas del Antiguo y Nuevo Testamento* (Great Collection of Prints of the Old and New Testament) (Barcelona: Faustino Paluzíe, 1876).[9]

Each unit consists of about 250–300 engravings through which the biblical story is visually narrated, especially the narrative parts of the books of the Pentateuch, the historical books (books of Joshua, Judges, Samuel, Kings and Maccabees), the novels (Ruth, Tobit, Esther and Judith) and the story of Daniel (including the story of Susannah). From the New Testament, the different gospels are harmonized, forming a 'Life of Jesus' that ends with the preaching of Peter and Paul, taken from the Acts of the Apostles, and which closes with some illustrations of the Apocalypse announcing the New Jerusalem.

The breadth of these series allowed for the creation of a very extensive iconographic repertoire, and they made it possible to give greater prominence to the stories played out by women which contained iconographic deviations with respect to the Bible that were not easily detected. Therefore, extra-biblical contextual aspects could be included that provided interesting information about the society that commissioned and contemplated them.

The importance of these Sacred Stories in pictures and illustrated Bibles lay in their ability to convey the history of salvation through a visual language. The aim of these visual stories was to edify the reader, clarify the biblical texts and fix certain stories or sequences. As with any artistic work, the selection of stories was never arbitrary as it transmits a set of values and meanings that had a great impact on the viewers/readers who contemplated them. The ability of these images to configure biblical visual memory, to condition the reading of the Sacred Text and to guide morality and customs should not be ignored.

The book of Judges and its female characters

The book of Judges is the sixth book of the Old Testament. The actions of charismatic leaders during the conquest and settlement of the people in the land of Canaan are narrated throughout twenty-one chapters as autonomous histories.[10] Abimelech,

---

with Doré's Montaner and Simón edition (Barcelona, 1971–76). Cf. Yebra-Rovira, *Las biblias ilustradas en España en el siglo XIX*.

9. Cf. Yebra-Rovira, *Las biblias ilustradas en España en el siglo XIX* .

10. For the exegetical and theological analysis of this book we refer to José Luis Sicre Díaz, *Jueces* (Estella: Verbo Divino, 2018); David M. Gunn, *Judges*, Blackwell Bible Commentaries (Oxford: Blackwell, 2005); Miguel Álvarez Barredo, *La iniciativa de Dios: estudio literario y teológico de Jueces 9-21*, Publicaciones Instituto Teológico Franciscano Serie Mayor (Murcia: Espigas, 2004); Miguel Álvarez Barredo, *La iniciativa de Dios: estudio literario y teológico de Jueces 1-8*, Publicaciones Instituto Teológico Franciscano Serie Mayor

Gideon, Jephthah and Samson are its undisputed protagonists. The shortcomings and successes of the Israelites in their journey to learn to be God's people are shown through the deeds and failures of these important characters, with a clear movement from falling from grace, repentance and forgiveness. This retributive sequence makes explicit the fidelity of God, his closeness to some characters and the problems that lead to the rupture of the Alliance and the deviation of the project of justice promoted by Yahweh. The conquests, battles and aggression are prominent elements of this book, one of the most violent in the Hebrew Bible.[11]

The book of Judges has been considered to be a book of men but, paradoxically, it is populated by many women without which the actions of the male protagonists cannot be understood. Twenty women appear in the development of the different narrative plots, either as individual characters or as collective subjects. This is the case of Achsah, the woman who fights for her inheritance (Judges 1); Deborah, prophetess, judge and wise woman (Judges 4–5); Jael, warrior and saviour (Judges 4); the mothers of Sisera, Abimelech, Samson and Micah (Judges 5; 9.3; 13; 17); the woman of Thebez, who defeats Judge Abimelech (Judg. 9.50-57); Jephthah's daughter (Judg. 11.30-40) and the wife of the Levite, brutally murdered (Judg. 19); the woman from Timnah, the prostitute of Gaza and Delilah, considered *femme fatales* to Samson (Judges 14–16); the daughters of Shiloh (Judges 21); the wise women who attended the mother of Sisera (Judges 4); and the companions of Jephthah's daughter (Judg. 11.37-38). Women are part of the story also when the collective character 'people' is mentioned or when its components are detailed. In this sense, it is symptomatic that the 'Canaanites, the Hittites, the Amorites, the Perizzites, the Hivites, and the Jebusites' are mentioned explicitly (Judg. 3.5) or that Abeson of Israel 'had thirty sons. He gave his thirty daughters in marriage outside his clan and brought in thirty young women from outside for his sons' (Judg. 12.8-9), with a clear denunciation of the idolatry that comes with marriages with foreigners. In the story of Gideon, his presence is remarkable because, in addition to the story of his concubine – the mother of Abimelech – there is a general reference to his women and the death of the women of Shechem (Judg. 8.30-31). Women are also victims of the destruction of the temple by Samson (Judg. 16.31). As can be seen, some women are protagonists – Deborah or Delilah – and others seem insignificant characters – foreign mothers of illegitimate children like Abimelech or Jephthah. However, their participation serves to denounce the depraved situation of the tribal system. A detailed analysis of Judges reveals in this work many of the topics that will appear in other stories of the Bible like the judge, son of a prostitute, the deceitful and insidious woman, the astute and wise woman, or the brave and determined woman.

(Murcia: Espigas, 2000); Athalya Brenner, *A Feminist Companion to Judges* (Sheffield: JSOT Press, 1993); and Lillian R. Klein, *The Triumph of Irony in the Book of Judges*, Bible and Literature Series (Sheffield: Almond, 1988).

11. Guadalupe Seijas, 'Algunas consideraciones sobre la violencia en el libro de Jueces', *Miscelánea de estudios árabes y hebraicos: Sección de hebreo* 60 (2011): 243–71.

The continued reading of the text shows that there is a notable difference in the treatment of women in the first nine chapters than in the following ones. At the beginning of the book, the participation and actions of the women demonstrate the errors and the lack of leadership of the males, as well as their decline, which will reach its peak with the story of Judge Jephthah and his daughter. In those chapters, it is the women who become the saviours, liberators and models of the true Israelites. The question that must be asked in regards to their iconographic representations is whether these images preserved this salvific value and the virtues of courage and initiative or if, on the contrary, they focus on other characters, passages or accents of their identities. In the following chapters the female protagonists are mainly victims or *femme fatales*, with the exception of Samson's mother whose performance criticizes, among other aspects, the lack of faith of her husband and his inability to perceive the signs and messages of God.

These stories have important concomitants with other biblical stories. The story of Deborah and Jael has parallels to that of Judith, Samson and Delilah to that of Esther, and the suffering of women such as the wife of the Levite, or the women of Silo, could remind the reader of dramatic current events.[12] The reading of these stories could evoke in the memory of the reader other biblical women like Rahab, who in ch. 2 of the book of Joshua allows the entry of the Israelites into Jericho and has a clear parallel in Judg. 1.22-26.

In the nineteenth century, a time of great political and social controversies, the characters of the book of Judges, both male and female, are shown in many occasions as models for the government, mainly from the criticism made in regard to its deviation from order, morality and the abundance of violence. In the reading of the book of Judges from a theological perspective, all its protagonists are interpreted as symbols that prefigure Christ, reading his exploits from a Christological perspective and not from a Mariological one as it had been more frequent in the past.

The iconography of the women in the book of Judges in the nineteenth century: Presentation and interpretation

The richness and breadth of the engraving collections have allowed for almost all of the women that are mentioned in the book to be represented in the history of visual illustration. Even though the indisputable protagonism of these series is assumed by men, as clearly seen by the cycles of Gideon and Samson, the women, as we will see below, are also narrators, protagonists and victims in these visual accounts.

---

12. Lilian R. Klein, 'A Spectrum of Female Characters in the Book of Judges', in *A Feminist Companion to Judges*, ed. Athalya Brenner (Sheffield: Sheffield Accademic Press, 1993), 24–33; Mercedes Navarro Puerto, *Violencia, sexismo, silencio: In-conclusiones en el libro de los Jueces* (Estella: Verbo Divino, 2013).

Achsah, daughter of Caleb and wife of Othniel: Silenced wisdom

The story of Achsah, daughter of Caleb and wife of Othniel (Judg. 1.12-15), is presented as an anecdote that goes almost unnoticed and is easily forgotten despite being a duplicate of Joshua 15. It is said of her that she was the prize promised by his father for whomever succeeded in the battle against Qiryat Sefer, and her story contrasts with the whole chapter. The scene begins when the young woman is sent by her future husband, Judge Othniel, to ask her father, Caleb, for a field. She, taking the initiative, asks for a gift, a blessing – the sources of water – that she gets without delay. The tradition speaks of her as a foresighted woman and the attentive reader realizes that she does not think only of the earth but also of what makes life possible –water – and, therefore, survival.[13]

The iconographic tradition usually silences this scene, since the dismemberment of Adoni-bezec is preferred (Judg. 1.1-8), but it is possible to find this scene in Spain in two engravings. The first one is the one made by the French artist, C. P. Marillier (1740–1808), which was imported, then copied in Valencia and published in the *Estampas que representan los principales sucesos de la historia sagrada* (Prints That Include the Most Important Events from Sacred History) sold between 1796 and 1799 as a visual complement for the second edition of the Bible of Scío.[14] In this scene, Achsah, seated on a donkey, is blessed by her father who, on the back of a camel, directs a retinue.

The second example is placed in the moralizing work of the Frenchman Corentin Le Guillou, *Bellezas de la Santa Biblia* (Joaquín Verdaguer, Barcelona 1845), who dedicates a chapter to the figure of Caleb, proposing him as a model of the faithful man, who is just and unbendable. This compendium reproduces an engraving of the oil painting by the British Henry Singleton (1766–1839), *Caleb et sa Fille* (c. 1800), in which the father kisses his daughter at the entrance of a house in the presence of her husband and a servant. In the scene, there is also a woman who is standing on the threshold of the door and who looks closely at the scene. Because of her disposition and location, she can be identified, without any doubt, as the mother of the girl. It is very clear in this image that the inclusion of the figure (mother) and the spatial element (house) are outside the narrative, but they are easily explained and understandable in the context of

---

13. Lilian R. Klein analyses the triple perspective from which this woman is presented in this brief fragment: as a woman object of gift, as a manipulative or shrewd wife and as a submissive daughter who receives from her father the blessing and therefore the land and the possibility to obtain offspring. Lilian R. Klein, 'Achsah: What price this prize?', in *Judges: A Feminist Companion to the Bible*, ed. Athalya Brenner (Sheffield: Sheffileld Academic Press, 1999), 17–26.

14. This collection was published in fascicles in different formats to be included in the two versions of the second edition of *La Sagrada Biblia*, Imp. Benito Cano (Madrid, 1794–97), and in the first edition of the Tomás Orga Press (Valencia 1790–93). The prints were reused in nineteenth-century editions.

Figure 6.1 H. Singleton, *Caleb and his daughter*, in C. Le Guillou, *Bellezas de la Santa Biblia* (Barcelona: Joaquín Verdaguer, 1845), 60; and A. Pascual, *The return of the prodigal son*, in Maestro de Sacy, *Historia del Antiguo y Nuevo Testamento* (Valencia: Ventura Lluch, 1841), 447.

nineteenth-century families.[15] The image is, then, an example of visual exegesis, a new text in which the silences of the narrative stories are completed – such as questions about where the story takes place or who is present – making it closer and more understandable to the reader/spectator who receives it. This provision, the absence of animals that serve as a saddle and the location in a domestic space, the door of the house, facilitate the textual connection with the story of the Prodigal Son whose illustrations can be found in Spain and where the mother of the two young boys is waiting, next to the father, for the return of their youngest son. This is the case of the engraving made by Pascual and published in the aforementioned work of the Master of Sacy, *Historia del Antiguo y Nuevo Testamento*, p. 447 (Figure 6.1).

The story of Achsah and her visual representation show, on the one hand, the possibility of rescuing and making visible forgotten stories in which the woman's right is recognized and, on the other hand, appreciating the importance of the recontextualization of the stories with the realization of substantial modifications or the inclusion of elements alien to them that are explained from the nineteenth-century context and that seek a better connection with the reader.

Deborah and Jael: Who is the protagonist?

In ch. 4 of the book of Judges, two women intervene whose actions have generated great controversy throughout history. These are the figures of Deborah (Judges 4–5) and Jael (Judg. 4.17) connected to the story of generals Barak and Sisera, respectively. Their intervention to save the people of Israel has certain nuances

---

15. For further discussion, see Chapter 5.

that have made scholars of the biblical tradition question which of the two was more important.

The biblical text presents Deborah as a prophetess and a judge. These functions and her ability to rule have made this figure misunderstood, undervalued or even silenced. Among the commentators there are very diverse opinions. The Master of Sacy in the *Historia del Antiguo y Nuevo Testamento* says of her:

> God gave the command of the people to a woman named Deborah, and she confirmed that in the hands of God all instruments are good when he pleases to use them. ... Deborah, full of the spirit of God, manifested no less courage in war than prudence in peace.[16]

Father Scío, on the other hand, in a footnote in his translation, gathered the controversies between the Fathers of the Church and valued her figure positively, but taking away most of her autonomy:

> Some believed that it was a thing unworthy of the People of God to be ruled by a woman; and so, they do not count her among the Judges of Israel. But this does not seem to conform to what the Scripture expressly declares in this place, saying: that she judged the people. And so, St. Augustine responds to this objection, that it was not a woman who ruled then the Hebrews, but the spirit of God who judged them through her (*De Civit Dei* lib., XVIII, chapter 25). And St. Ambrose, *lib. of Vid.*, says that Deborah ruled the people, went to the frontlines with her armies, elected warlords, declared war and assured victory.[17]

In the comments that Joaquín Roca y Cornet, a Catalan apologetic, made of the figure of the judge in his work *Mugeres de la Biblia* (Madrid – Barcelona: Llorens Hermanos, 1850), there is an explicit criticism of her leadership role and the degree of perfection assigned to her actions, very much in the Augustinian line. According to him, although her judgement is positive, her level is inferior to that of other judges:

> Presumably, Deborah did not exercise her magistracy as extensively as did the other judges of Israel. Her functions were to reconcile the spirits divided by interest, give advice and remember the practice of religious and civil laws. Her experience and discretion reconciled public esteem and trust, and in this way, she gave, without doubt, special proofs of submission. However, the main strength of her judgments came from the acceptance of the goodwill of the people: her resolutions could not pass through definitive regulations, because

---

16. Le Maistre de Sacy, Boix and Pascual, *Historia del Antiguo y Nuevo Testamento*, 133–4.

17. Felipe Scío de San Miguel, *La Santa Biblia* (Barcelona: Librería Religiosa. Imprenta de D. Pablo Riera, 1856), vol. 1, 648.

it is a maxim received by all the interpreters of Hebrew Law that no woman can judge and reign in Israel.[18]

This assessment, which highlights her submission, discretion and acceptance – values of the feminine ideal of the time[19] – criticizes the biblical story itself and distorts the identity of the judge and prophetess. Her leadership function is also questioned by the image that accompanies this story (Figure 6.2). While it is a beautiful image of romantic overtones wrapped in a warm atmosphere, in contrast to the other portraits in this print collection, and despite having strength and dynamism, the image presents a disarrayed woman, little contained (but retains the right arm close to her body), with her arm raised to the sky and dishevelled.[20] Her figure has nothing to do with the softness, sweetness, order, self-absorption and modesty of other heroines. A woman like her, in which there is not a lot of decorum or obedience to a man, could never be proposed as a model for the Spanish female bourgeois of the nineteenth century. Deborah is a subversive biblical figure that cannot be denied because she is a biblical character, but it is possible to silence her military, political, prophetic and cultic-liturgical skills. Her

---

18. Joaquín Roca y Cornet, *Mugeres de la Biblia* (Madrid: Llorens Hermanos, 1850), 455. This is an adaptation of the original French work written by Georges Darboy, *Les Femmes de la Bible, collection de portraits des femmes remarquables de l'Ancien et du Nouveau Testament… Les Femmes de la Bible, principaux fragments d'une histoire du peuple de Dieu. Texte imprimé* (Paris: Garnier Fréres, 1846). In two volumes, this was a set of biographies presented from a moral perspective and aimed especially at female readers, which were accompanied by a collection of female portraits. It has a first illustrated edition, with the text more adjusted to the French original, published in Madrid and Barcelona in 1846, by the Imp. Viuda de Razola, under the title *Las Mujeres de la Biblia: Colección de láminas preciosísimas*. For the study of the images of this collection and their importance in the construction of feminine ideals, cf. Carmen Yebra-Rovira, 'French biblical engravings and the education of the Spanish woman in the XIX century', *Biblical Reception* 2 (2013): 97–116.

19. Under the reign of Isabel II there was a strong sublimation of women in Spain. Therefore, a woman's behaviour strictly conformed to what is known as the Elizabethan canon or the angel of the home model. Obedience, submission, silence, patience and self-denial are some of its constituent elements. Cf. Iñigo Sánchez Llama, *Galería de escritoras isabelinas: la prensa periódica entre 1833 y 1895*, Feminismos (Madrid: Cátedra Instituto de la Mujer – Universitat de València, 2000), 13–90; Colette Rabaté, *¿Eva o María?: ser mujer en la época isabelina (1833–1868)*, Acta Salmanticensia: Estudios Históricos & Geográficos (Salamanca: Universidad de Salamanca, 2007).

20. In a very similar style, but more contained and familiar, is the portrait of Deborah made by the French artist Charles Z. Landelle (1821–1908). His drawings, which also include the portrait of Ruth, Judith and other biblical women, are characterized by a marked Orientalist style, so in vogue in the middle of the century.

Figure 6.2 G. Staal and W. H. Mote, *Deborah*, in J. Roca y Cornet, *Mugeres de la Biblia* (Madrid – Barcelona: Llorens Hermanos, 1850); and G. Doré, *Deborah*, in *La Sagrada Biblia* (Barcelona: Montaner y Simón, 1871–73).

public function contrasts with the domestic female model typical of the reign of Isabel II of Spain.

Doré has undoubtedly been one of the great creators of biblical images that have been strongly engraved in the collective imagination. In his collection of drawings made in 1865–66 to illustrate the Bible, which was published in Spain along with Torres Amat's translation (Barcelona: Montaner and Simón 1871), he made a different visual interpretation. The Frenchman places the judge on a stairway while being heard by a large group of males. She, at the centre of the image, shows strength and security, and her iconography is the same one that has been used in this collection to represent the prophets and other great biblical characters like Moses. The use of the same iconography means that the prophetess is visually identified with them and that her value as a leader of the group and as a person worthy of being heard by men is enhanced. The visual context is what gives the image new values although the iconography is very similar to the romantic version (one hand on the chest and the other extended pointing to the sky).

Jael, whom the biblical text presents as the wife of Heber, the Kenite, is undoubtedly the great heroine of the book of Judges (Judg. 4.17-22), although, like the previous figure, the explanations of her exploits have aroused many ruminations. The morality of her action, the execution of General Sisera with the tent's pickaxe, which is reached through deception, has been the subject of much controversy.[21] As the iconographer Louis Réau recalled, the theologians of the Middle Ages saw in her the symbol of the victorious Virgin over the devil or that of the Church of the Gentiles who, with the cross, nailed its enemy to the ground.[22] The art of the Middle Ages, however, presented her as a negative model of the tricks used by women. In the Renaissance, she shared with Judith the honour of symbolizing strength – one of the four cardinal virtues – and she was always on the lists of strong women widely spread during the Renaissance and Baroque periods as a symbol of Mary after destroying the enemy of her people.[23] In the nineteenth century, her figure was praised. Father Scío said of her:

> Much difficulty would cost to excuse from perfidy the action of Jael in the circumstances referred to here, if the praises given later by Deborah, inspired of God, do not assure us that she did it by an extraordinary movement of the Spirit of the Lord. [24]

The relevance of her figure is attested through the iconographic tradition, her representations being much more numerous than those of Deborah. The artists preferred to represent two scenes. The first, the moment in which Jael kills Sisera, and the second, the moment in which she opens the tent (or exits the temple) and shows the corpse of Sisera to his army. The great Baroque painters selected the first one; the engravers, however, preferred the second. The print series of the seventeenth, eighteenth and nineteenth centuries that illustrate the book of Judges usually begin with this image. With this selection, a criticism of general Sisera is proposed, reflected through the surprised faces of the soldiers that accompany him and highlighting the importance of the woman in the salvific action and the fulfilment of the prophecy made by Deborah.

The analysis of the iconography of these two heroines invites us to reflect on the causes that explain the progressive silencing of the figure of Deborah and her almost complete disappearance in the nineteenth century in favour of Jael. The early patristic identification of the latter with the Church and her presentation as a divine instrument of salvation justify, no doubt, this choice. Father Scío at the end of the eighteenth century writes, referring to Origen and St. Augustine,

---

21. The use of unconventional and non-war-related weapons is common in the book of Judges. The characters connected to God use ordinary tools or cunning. This reveals the immense contrast between the strength of God and the skill of the professionals of war.

22. Louis Réau, *Iconografía del arte cristiano: Iconografía de la Biblia. Antiguo Testamento*, trans. Daniel Alcoba (Barcelona: Ediciones del Serbal, 2007), 379.

23. Cf. Álvaro Molina Martín, 'De la mujer fuerte a ciudadana. Modelos heroicos femeninos a través del arte del grabado', in *El dominio de la realidad y la crisis del discurso: El nacimiento de la conciencia europea*, ed. Concepción Camarero Bullón and Juan Carlos Gómez Alonso (Madrid: Ediciones Polifemo, 2017), 77–111. For Judith as strong women, see Chapter 4, pages 91 and 103–4.

24. Scío de San Miguel, *La Santa Biblia*, vol. 1, 649.

The ancient Fathers contemplate in Deborah a figure of the Synagogue and Jael of the Church. The former orders the battle, gives the signal for combat and defeats the enemy troops; but the death of the general and the victory belongs to Jael, it is a victory of the Christian Church, and of the grace that comes to us by Christ.[25]

The woman in the tent defeats the judge of the palm tree, the executor defeats the announcer. Deborah announces victory but does not execute it. Along with these elements, the fact that the prophetess represents a model of government contrary to patriarchal interests cannot be ignored. Throughout history, both comments and images cast a constant criticism over her leadership. Deborah's words announce the humiliation of a man and demonstrate her ability to properly discern the development of events. She is a woman whose abilities to silence the people are even superior to those of Moses. In this sense, the Master of Sacy says that 'she had the glory of being the first sovereign that God placed at the head of His people without missing from her under His direction any of the advantages that could be promised of the most seasoned men'.[26] Deborah's leadership and government abilities collided with the female domestic functions and the virtues of silence, submission and obedience that were promoted in the nineteenth century.

The woman of Thebez and the fight against oppression

One of the great values of the biblical image is its ability to visualize secondary characters in the narrative and show their active role in the story of salvation. In this sense, a completely unknown figure today is the woman of Thebez. The artistic tradition makes it possible to discover this heroine, recover this saviour of her people and appreciate the importance she had in the nineteenth century.

Her representation is transmitted almost exclusively through illustrations and it allows us to evaluate the importance of the processes of silencing and selection of the biblical scenes and the implications that derive from the way in which these scenes are represented.

Judges 9.52 narrates the siege of the city of Thebez by Abimelech and his army and how this king was defeated by an anonymous woman who threw a millstone from the tower. She, like Jael had done before, used a strange weapon to defeat a professional soldier. Her feat, a clear antithesis to the misuse of the force he had exercised to kill his seventy brothers and thus gain power, has been collected and remembered throughout history in numerous commentaries. As Alonso de Villegas says in his *Flos Sanctorum*, in discourse *XXI On Cruelty*, this woman is 'the hand of God through which divine justice is executed'.[27] According to the

---

25. Scío de San Miguel, *La Santa Biblia*, vol. 1, 649.
26. Le Maistre de Sacy, Boix and Pascual, *Historia del Antiguo y Nuevo Testamento*, 314.
27. Alonso de Villegas, *Fructus Sanctorum y Quinta Parte del Flos Sanctorum* (Cuenca: Juan Masselin, 1594), XXI.3.

Master of Sacy, she was the instrument with which it was demonstrated that 'God's patience has its limits'.[28] According to them, God allows the ambitious ones to reach the summit so that their fall is greater. The narrative is an example to denounce the perversion caused by the ambition of men for power and its consequences: the most absolute humiliation. With her actions, an anonymous woman becomes the executor of divine prophecy and, therefore, a direct collaborator in the project of salvation.

The analysis of the history of the iconographic representation of this passage shows that it was significant during the Middle Ages – it can be found in many illuminated Bibles[29] – but it was silenced during the Renaissance and the Baroque periods. In the latter period, the moment in which the judge asks his squire to kill him is selected in order to avoid dishonour by having been defeated by a woman (Judg. 9.54). The nineteenth century recovers the death of Abimelech with clear political intentions at a time when centralist tendencies in different countries were attacking local identities and peripheral regions.

The iconic moment of the story could be represented in two different ways. The first option, followed by Gustave Doré, focused on the death of Abimelech, surrounded by his soldiers, with a stone on the ground but without showing who threw it – that is, silencing the woman and her liberating actions. The emphasis in this selection is placed on denouncing the perversion of the judges and the monarchy and on showing the alienation of the Alliance that is evident through the fratricidal struggles (Abimelech kills his brothers to remain on the throne).

There are other images, however, such as the illustration done by Schnorr von Carolsfeld for his *Gran Colección de Láminas del Antiguo y Nuevo Testamento* (1876) that prioritized the action of women.[30] Both he and James Tissot (New York: Jewish Museum, 1900), another great French draughtsman of the nineteenth century, captured the moment when the woman of Thebez, accompanied by other characters, threw the stone (Figure 6.3).

The German artist introduced important novelties in his engraving with respect to previous iconographical examples. Schnorr von Carolsfeld placed the woman in the foreground, so that she stands out because of the ascending disposition and her large dimensions. Her figure stands out above that of the king who remains in the shade, under the tower, oblivious to his future, in the moment prior to his death. The stone at the top reflects the centrality of divine action, as if it were God

---

28. Le Maistre de Sacy, Boix and Pascual, *Historia del Antiguo y Nuevo Testamento*, 144.

29. See, for example, the work kept at the J. Getty Museum, *Abimelech Killed by the Women of Thebes*, c. 1400–10, 88.MP.70.137v.

30. This German artist, who belonged to the group of German Nazarenes, made ten images for the book of Judges. One illustrated the story of Jael and Barak, two that of Gideon, one was dedicated to those of Abimelech and Jephthah, four to the story of Samson and one to the story of the rapture of the daughters of Shiloh. His drawings were well known because his work was published under different titles in 1876, 1878–79 and 1887. In addition, his prints were included in school books of different types.

Figure 6.3 J. Schnorr von Carolsfeld, *The woman of Thebez*, in *Gran Colección de Láminas del Antiguo y Nuevo Testamento* (Barcelona: Herederos de Pablo Riera, 1878–9).

himself who casts it from heaven. The illustration also highlights the expression of the feelings of the characters: fear, despair or resignation. Faced with this, the attitude of the woman in movement and with the raised stone shows her power, her resolution and her ability to fight against oppression, beyond all expectations. This makes visible the participation of women in the history of salvation and the way in which God uses unpredictable means to obtain it.

Jephthah's daughter, model of devotion and obedience: The perversion of a story

The perversion of the judges' model of government is shown with great clarity through the story of Jephthah (Judges 8–11). It includes a narrative in which a young anonymous maiden becomes the victim of the pride and errors of a man, in this case her own father (Judg. 11.34-40).[31] The story can be seen as an antithesis to the story of Caleb and his daughter Achsah from the first chapter. In this case

---

31. The text does not say the name of the daughter. Tradition, following Philo of Alexandria or Biblical Philo, refers to her as Sciola. Cf. Roca y Cornet, *Mugeres de la Biblia*, 478.

there is no blessing for the girl, but the father, due to his lack of knowledge of the law and by an unnecessary vote, leads her to her death. His honour in battle is discredited by his erroneous performance in family affairs. This story poses a critique of great importance for the nineteenth century. A man who is not able to properly manage his domestic space cannot be a good ruler. Its dramatic ending is explained in the tradition of the Church in two different ways. The first follows and assumes that Jephthah, by fulfilling his vow, sacrifices his daughter. The second, following the Jewish tradition and emphasizing the sentence which discusses the young woman's virginity, assumes that she is confined to serve God exclusively. This fulfils the vote and minimizes the cruelty of the judge's performance.[32]

In Spain, the story of the daughter of Jephthah is one of the clearest examples of the betrayal of the original meaning of the biblical stories and how they are used for the formation and deformation of the functions of women in nineteenth-century society.[33] In a context in which much of the Catholic literature is aimed at training the virtuous woman, this drama denounces the pride and wrongdoing of the father, in addition to offering the young woman as a model of obedience, submission, self-denial and love to the homeland. Assuming the destiny that others have chosen for her, it becomes a path for personal fulfilment, even if it leads to death. Therefore, in *Historia del Antiguo y Nuevo Testamento*, collecting the comments of the Master of Sacy, it is appreciated how the daughter of Jephthah is not treated as a victim but as a determined and believing woman who 'courageously exhorts her father to fulfil his promise'. Following this idea, it is affirmed:

> The Holy Fathers have looked at the vow of Jephthah as an example of the indiscreetness of some people, who by lightness or haste land in a situation of not being able to fulfil what he had offered to the Lord except by means of a crime. It is better not to promise anything, says St. Ambrose[,] than to make a vow of things that are detestable to God, and impossible to fulfil without committing a serious crime. … If the action of the father is reprehensible, there are no words of admiration of the actions of the daughter. She returned smiling after two months to find the one who should sacrifice her, without being deterred by the tears of her companions; nor the image of sterility that she always had in sight. She corrected in a certain way what was defective in the sacrifice on the part of her father. She voluntarily gave that which seemed forced, and she transformed, as the Holy Fathers say, a sacrifice of cruelty into a holocaust pleasing to God.

---

32. Cf. Phyllis S. Kramer, 'Jephtah's daughter: A thematic approach to the narrative as seen in selected rabbinic exegesis and in artwork', in *Judges: A Feminist Companion to the Bible*, ed. Athalya Brenner (Sheffield: Sheffield Academic Press, 1999), 67–92; David M. Gunn, 'Cultural criticism: Viewing the sacrifice of Jephtah's daughter', in *Judges and Method: New Approaches to Biblical Studies*, ed. Gale Yee (Philadelphia: Fortress Press, 2007), 202–36.

33. Carmen Yebra-Rovira, 'Interpretación bíblica y formación moral de la mujer en el siglo XIX: El ángel del hogar', *Moralia* 36 (2013): 405–26.

She taught all the Christian virgins born of the love of heaven and hatred to the century, to sacrifice themselves to God with joy; and if their relatives sacrifice them to their vanity, flattering themselves by saying that if they are taken from the world their remaining goods and possessions may pass to others; however, they sacrifice themselves to God with all their heart, and only try to please Him, without taking into consideration issues of justice or injustice; and these women admire the way God uses indiscretion, or hardness, or the greed of those who are most obligated to love them, to offer the realization of a sacrifice for which their humble piety makes them precious.[34]

The iconographic representation of Judges 11 is inspired by three moments. The first and most usual is the arrival and meeting between the father and the daughter; the second, the lamentation and tears of the young woman regarding her destiny, usually with her companions; and the third, the sacrifice of the young woman.[35]

The tragic nature of this story and its important sociopolitical criticism made it widely known and reproduced in the nineteenth century both through engraving and painting.[36] Thus, for example, the great painter John Everett Millet in his *Jephthah* (1867, National Museum of Wales, Cardiff) focused on the family drama and the feelings of the father. In this work, the young woman moves away from the tent while her father, seated on a chair, with his head down, is shown as an example of the great defeated warrior who must be consoled. Karl Oesterley (1835) preferred the moment in which the daughter, consoled by her friends, peacefully assumes the future that she must face.[37] Her attitude contrasts enormously with the faces and movement of the other three young women, presenting the daughter of Jephthah as a great heroine who renounces everything to safeguard the honour of her father and her people (Figure 6.4).

Of the collections of engravings published in Spain, it is worth highlighting Doré's interpretation of the story. The Frenchman decided to illustrate two antagonistic moments, both in a particular and novel way. In the first drawing, the young woman appears dancing to the father/spectator who is not present. She is the new protagonist, not the encounter as was usually the case in the previous iconography. In the second, she is surrounded by her companions on a hill lamenting her future. The dominant melancholy in this image subtracts strength

---

34. Le Maistre de Sacy, Boix and Pascual, *Historia del Antiguo y Nuevo Testamento*, 145–56.

35. This last variant is unusual in the nineteenth century. However, it is possible to see it among the engravings that accompanied the work of José Puiggarí, *Ilustraciones de la Santa Biblia: Antiguo Testamento* (Barcelona: José Ribet, 1854), 201.

36. Among the different representations that are made in Spain illustrating this topic, we cannot fail to review the oil made by Francisco de Goya, *The Sacrifice of the Daughter of Jephthah* (c. 1774, Colección Várez Fisa, Madrid).

37. The original oil painting can be found at Niedersächsisches Landesmuseum of Hannover.

Figure 6.4 C. Oesterley, *Jephthah's daughter*, in Ch. F. Horne and J. A. Bever (eds), *The Bible and Its Story Taught by One Thousand Picture Lessons*, vol. 3 (New York: Francis R. Nighutsch, 1908); and G. Staal and W. H. Egleton, *Jephthah's daughter*, in J. Roca y Cornet, *Mugeres de la Biblia* (Madrid: Llorens Hermanos, 1850).

and drama from the story. While pain is present, the climate of meditation and peaceful resignation is evident. The sweetness of the story and the loss of the denunciation that this implies are also appreciated in the portrait published in the aforementioned work *Mugeres de la Biblia* (Figure 6.4). In this portrait, the sweetness of the face and the stillness of the figure pervert the meaning of the text. It is a clear example of how the biblical illustration also silences violent situations and perverse structures exercised on subjects who cannot defend themselves.

The story of the concubine of the Levite and its consequences

The last three chapters of the book of Judges are different in theme and style to the rest of the work. They do not narrate the exploits of the judges or the history of the heroes but tell the story of domestic character that became the trigger of a great civil war between the tribes of Israel. Judges 19 refers to the shocking account of the rape and death of the concubine of the Levite of Ephraim, and chs 20 and 21 deal with how the Israelites united to avenge her death and the affront done to her husband and his tribe. All this triggered the abduction of the women of Jabesh and those of Silo in the face of the possible risk of the disappearance of their tribe.[38] The theological content of this section is, however, in line with the whole book, since, like the previous stories, it shows how the Jewish people are led to their destruction when they forget God and the Covenant.

This narrative, always present in the Sacred Stories, is surprisingly relevant in the nineteenth century. Commentaries, poetry, theatrical works and all kinds of compositions focused on this dramatic story that served as a starting point for an anthropological and political reflection of the first order, since the text is susceptible, according to the times, to clarify the nature of the internal violence of societies.[39] The commentaries do not criticize, however, the attitude of the old man and the Levite who deliver the young woman to a certain death, but focus on the anger and the desire for revenge that the Levite experiences and which leads to the dismemberment of the body and the convocation of the tribes to avenge the affront.

The artistic representations of these chapters do make it possible to visualize the consequences of violence against women, while the comments focus on the struggle between men, the consequences of wars, their excessive violence or conflicts over power. The engravings illustrate mainly three scenes: the arrival of the Levite, his concubine and his servant to the old man's house; the woman lying before the door; and the departure of the Levite from Jabesh after the discovery of the body.[40]

Pascual and Doré draw the woman's discovery at the door. Pascual, in the *Historia del Antiguo y Nuevo Testamento*, in the chapter of 'The Outrage Done to the Woman in a Frock Coat', reproduces almost exactly the oil painting of the

---

38. Ilse Müllner, 'Lethal differences: Sexual violence as violence against others in Judges 19', in *Judges: A Feminist Companion to the Bible*, ed. Athalya Brenner (Sheffield: Seffield Academic Press, 1999), 126–42; Jacqueline E. Lapsley, *Whispering the Word: Hearing Women's Stories in the Old Testament* (Louisville, KY: Westminster John Knox Press, 2005), 35–68; Carmen Yebra-Rovira, 'A violencia na Biblia: reflexión a partir do crime de Guilbeah (Xuices 19–21)', *Encrucillada: Revista Galega de Pensamento Cristián* 169 (2010): 21–34.

39. The development of this story was very significant in France from where it influenced Spain. The most successful author was Jean-Jacques Rousseau who composed *Le Levite d'Ephraïm* in 1762 with numerous editions and variations (there is a critical edition by Sèbastien Labrusse, *Les éditions de la Transparence*, 2010). At the beginning of the nineteenth century, J. B. J Auburtin wrote *Le Lévite d'Ephraïm de l'Ecriture Sainte, Imprimerie de la Veuve Verronnais* (Metz, 1812). The theme of the concubine was also chosen for oil paintings exhibited in the Salons of 1837, 1864 and 1895, a clear example of the repercussion of the biblical story and of the importance acquired by the history painting for propaganda purposes.

40. The moment of dismemberment and the distribution of the remains was also represented in the seventeenth century.

Figure 6.5 A. Pascual and R. Saez, *El ultraje hecho a la muger de un levita*, in Maestro de Sacy, *Historia del Antiguo y Nuevo Testamento* (Valencia: Ventura Lluch, 1841).

French artist Louis Charles Auguste Couder (1789–1873), who exhibited this work in Paris in 1817 and for which he obtained important recognition.[41] The surprise of the Levite leaves the spectator stunned, who discovers the dead woman on the threshold with her hands trying to reach for the door and with an idyllic background of palm trees (Figure 6.5).

Doré, as the great dramatic draughtsman that he is, opted for a very similar representation, but he also made another drawing in which the Levite is shown from the back, from the viewer's perspective, with the body of the woman on his mount. His work, in keeping with that of the Frenchman Sellier who presented the original painting for the Salon of 1864, although painted in the reverse direction, emphasizes the action of the man but focuses the image on the woman's body.[42]

41. Cf. Etienne A. Réveil and Jean Duchesne, *Museum of Painting and Sculptures* (London: Bossange Barthes and Lowell, 1834), vol. 16, 972.

42. The oil painting of the Frenchman Alexandre Caminade, Le *Lévite d'Éphraïm méditant de venger sa femme morte victim of the brutalité des Benjamites* (Musée des Beaux-Arts de Lyon, 1837), chooses the moment prior to departure, when they load the body of the young woman, while he reflects on his subsequent actions.

The encounter with all these images challenges the reader even today since they confront the reader with the violent nature of the stories of the Bible. The current believer flees from them and, as a rule, does not understand their inclusion in the canon. The criticism and denunciation that they pose towards a society in which respect for the person has been lost and in which personal honour is measured in terms of the violent response to an affront are very topical. The visual strength of the images invites us to look at realities dominated by violence against women and disadvantaged groups and helps to remember that violence is never a solution to the resolution of conflicts.

Regardless of the narrative, the story of the concubine, as has been usual throughout history, was also used as an excuse for the representation of the female nude.[43] For this, the moment in which her body lies before its dismemberment is selected. This is the case of the two versions created by Jean Jacques Henner (*c.* 1895, Musée National Jean-Jacques Henner) or by the Colombian Epifanio Garay, *The Woman of the Levite of the Mountains of Ephrain* (1899, National Museum of Colombia), practically the only nude feminine painting of the Colombian nineteenth century.

The artistic transmission of the book of Judges: Conclusions

This study has tried to establish a dialogue between the biblical stories and their artistic representations taking into consideration questions as diverse as follows: what did the images contribute to the study of the text? Which biblical women were silenced? What aspects of them are relegated to the background? And what narrative line is constructed from the survivors? A number of orientations has also been pointed out to analyse if their histories were distorted, if the salvific character of the stories was retained or if their decontextualization implied a betrayal with important consequences for the formation of women. In conclusion, the following aspects can be highlighted:

Although engravings with biblical images is a genre almost unknown and scarcely valued by scholarly research, it is offered here as a new source of study whose scope is still to be analysed and whose contributions in regards to biblical interpretation and transmission were undoubtedly extrapolated to other artistic genres. This genre, widely spread in the nineteenth century, presents a complex and rich reality. The usual thing is that text and image coexist on the same page so that reading and simultaneous viewing feed each other, complement each other and even, as we have seen with the story of the concubine, contradict each other. In any case, the illustrated biblical work, as a total work that integrates the visual and

---

43. Erika Bornay, *Mujeres de la Biblia en la pintura del Barroco: imágenes de la ambigüedad,* Ensayos Arte Cátedra (Madrid: Cátedra, 1998), clearly shows how female biblical figures have been widely used as 'legitimate models' for the representation of the female body.

textual language, has a great power in the fixation of narratives. In the interrelation between text and image, it is possible to perceive that there are differences between the selections made by the biblical commentaries and the images, although both are transmitted together. This is the case of Deborah and Jael in which the biblical text prioritizes the judge (the former), but the commentaries are directed towards the woman in the tent (the latter), for whom the images were clearly chosen.

The approach to biblical stories through images invites not only knowing the biblical story itself and with it the intertextual relationships with other stories and passages, but also deepening the rabbinical tradition, the patristic exegesis and the sacred history that fixed and, in many cases, 'corrected' the stories. Throughout the chapter, it has been confirmed how the commentaries and the images vary remarkably according to the accents and approaches from which they appeared in each moment of history. This makes it possible to know not only the original stories and see how they were interpreted progressively, but also how each society read those comments and viewed those illustrations. The stories were understood according to the social, cultural, political and religious background of the reader. Each comment conveyed a set of concrete values, which were the result of the preconceptions with which writers approached the texts. The great biblical specialists, such as the Master of Sacy or Father Scío, raised the contradictions inherent in the texts and justifiably chose one of the many interpretations they offered. Commentaries like that of Roca y Cornet, which had a clear moral purpose aimed at the containment of women, obviated part of the teachings that extolled the independence and capacity of women, and emphasized the discretion, submission and sweetness of the biblical heroines. The knowledge of the biblical text allows an adjusted interpretation of the characters and their salvific value.

The study of images can contribute to the visibility of characters that were not very relevant in the biblical text; in addition, it makes possible the preservation and transmission of the tradition of biblical women. Regarding the first issue, it has been demonstrated how the artistic representation favoured the reproduction of scenes and protagonists that were not usually present in the painting, such as Achsah, the woman of Thebez, the story of the daughter of Jephthah or the story of the concubine, giving space to silenced stories and characters. Also, these images served to recall stories that in other times have been relevant and to present characters that are unknown even today but who have had an active part in the history of salvation. With this they fulfil an important function by reminding the audience of the value of what is apparently useless or secondary and demonstrating its importance for social and ecclesiastical constructions. Their presence in these artistic collections questions the contemporary modes of biblical reading and the forms of transmission of sacred history, and invites us to ask ourselves questions regarding the reasons for their disappearance, silencing and transformation of these iconographic types. Likewise, this iconography contributes to the awareness of the importance of the selection processes and the oblivion to which certain passages and characters were subjected to. As has been shown through the last example, our current sensibility shies away from violent texts. The images, however, remain as witnesses of cruelty and injustice and denounce these realities, thus contributing to recover the prophetic sense of social criticism contained in the stories.

With respect to the second issue, this study shows that the preservation of the memory of biblical women was also important in the nineteenth century. Far from disappearing, their presence is significant at a time when there was a reconfiguration of women's roles and functions within nineteenth-century society. The Bible served as a legitimization tool for the familial, social and moral values that were associated with women, even if this implied the deformation of the meaning of the biblical narrative. An analysis from a gender perspective denounces how some interpretations use these women as a model of obedience, submission, resignation and silence. These biblical images were not neutral and they transmitted values that may have been contrary to the history of salvation. In the same way, they denounce the risks that may be incurred when using these images in the present without understanding the values that they contain. The recovery of biblical women, as well as of any character, can be betrayed by the use of beautiful images that contain values that are contrary to the identity of the subjects and the stories.

In the nineteenth century, four female characters stand out from the book of Judges: Jael as a brave woman; the daughter of Jephthah as a dedicated, obedient and submissive woman; the concubine of the Levite as a paradigm of the consequences of bad government and fratricidal struggles; and Delilah as an example of the perverse, deceptive and deceitful woman, and as a prototype of the dangers caused by women who are not subjected to (male) control. With the latter, we opened this chapter and with her we conclude. The extension of her artistic representations, the amplitude of the commentaries and the complexity of her figure and tradition persuade us to leave her study for another occasion.

Bibliography

Álvarez Barredo, Miguel. *La iniciativa de Dios: estudio literario y teológico de Jueces 1–8*, Publicaciones Instituto Teológico Franciscano Serie Mayor. Murcia: Espigas, 2000.

Álvarez Barredo, Miguel. *La iniciativa de Dios: estudio literario y teológico de Jueces 9–21*, Publicaciones Instituto Teológico Franciscano Serie Mayor. Murcia: Espigas, 2004.

Bornay, Erika. *Mujeres de la Biblia en la pintura del Barroco: imágenes de la ambigüedad*, Ensayos Arte Cátedra. Madrid: Cátedra, 1998.

Bottigheimer, Ruth B. *The Bible for Children: From the Age of Gutenberg to the Present*. New Haven: Yale University Press, 1996.

Brenner, Athalya. *A Feminist Companion to Judges*. Sheffield: JSOT Press, 1993.

Carrete Parrondo, Juan. 'Iluminando la Biblia'. *Descubrir el arte* 70 (2004): 86–91.

Darboy, Georges. *Les Femmes de la Bible, collection de portraits des femmes remarquables de l'Ancien et du Nouveau Testament… Les Femmes de la Bible, principaux fragments d'une histoire du peuple de Dieu. Texte imprimé*. Paris: Garnier Fréres, 1846.

Engammare, Max. 'Les Figures de la Bible: Le destin oublié d'un genre littéraire en image (XVIe-XVIIe s.)'. *Melánges de l'Ecole française de Rome. Italie et Méditerranée* 106, no. 2 (1994): 549–91.

Gunn, David M. *Judges*, Blackwell Bible Commentaries. Oxford: Blackwell, 2005.
Gunn, David M. 'Cultural criticism: Viewing the sacrifice of Jephtah's daughter', in *Judges and Method: New Approaches to Biblical Studies*, edited by Gale Yee, 202–36. Philadelphia: Fortress Press, 2007.
Klein, Lilian R. 'Achsah: What price this prize?', in *Judges: A Feminist Companion to the Bible*, edited by Athalya Brenner, 18–26. Sheffield: Sheffield Academic Press, 1999.
Klein, Lilian R. 'A spectrum of female characters in the book of Judges', in *A Feminist Companion to Judges*, edited by Athalya Brenner, 24–33. Sheffield: Sheffield Accademic Press, 1993.
Klein, Lillian R. *The Triumph of Irony in the Book of Judges*, Bible and Literature Series. Sheffield: Almond, 1988.
Kramer, Phyllis S. 'Jephtah's daughter: A thematic approach to the narrative as seen in selected rabbinic exegesis and in artwork', in *Judges: A Feminist Companion to the Bible*, edited by Athalya Brenner, 67–92. Sheffield: Sheffield Academic Press, 1999.
Lapsley, Jacqueline E. *Whispering the Word: Hearing Women's Stories in the Old Testament*. Louisville, KY: Westminster John Knox Press, 2005.
Le Maistre de Sacy, Isaac-Louis, Vicente Boix and Antonio Pascual. *Historia del Antiguo y Nuevo Testamento: adornada con 700 láminas, según las esplicaciones sacadas de la Santa Escritura y Padres de la Iglesia*. Valencia: Imp. de Ventura Lluch, 1841.
Molina Martín, Álvaro. 'De la mujer fuerte a ciudadana: Modelos heroicos femeninos a través del arte del grabado', in *El dominio de la realidad y la crisis del discurso: El nacimiento de la conciencia europea*, edited by Concepción Camarero Bullón and Juan Carlos Gómez Alonso, 77–111. Madrid: Ediciones Polifemo, 2017.
Müllner, Ilse. 'Lethal differences: Sexual violence as violence against others in Judges 19', in *Judges: A Feminist Companion to the Bible*, edited by Athalya Brenner, 126–42. Sheffield: Seffield Academic Press, 1999.
Navarro Puerto, Mercedes. *Violencia, sexismo, silencio: In-conclusiones en el libro de los Jueces*. Estella: Verbo Divino, 2013.
Puiggarí, José. *Ilustraciones de la Santa Biblia: Antiguo Testamento*. Barcelona: José Ribet, 1854.
Rabaté, Colette. *¿Eva o María?: ser mujer en la época isabelina (1833–1868)*, Acta Salmanticensia: Estudios Históricos & Geográficos. Salamanca: Universidad de Salamanca, 2007.
Réau, Louis. *Iconografía del arte cristiano: Iconografía de la Biblia. Antiguo Testamento*. Translated by Daniel Alcoba. Barcelona: Ediciones del Serbal, 2007.
Réveil, Etienne A., and Jean Duchesne. *Museum of Painting and Sculptures*. London: Bossange Barthes and Lowell, 1834.
Roca y Cornet, Joaquín. *Mugeres de la Biblia*. Madrid – Barcelona: Llorens Hermanos, 1850.
Sánchez Caro, José Manuel. *Biblia e Ilustración: Las versiones castellanas de la Biblia en el Siglo de las Luces*. Vigo: Academia del Hispanismo, 2012.
Sánchez Llama, Iñigo. *Galería de escritoras isabelinas: la prensa periódica entre 1833 y 1895*, Feminismos. Madrid: Cátedra Instituto de la Mujer – Universitat de València, 2000.
Scío de San Miguel, Felipe. *La Santa Biblia*. Barcelona: Librería Religiosa. Imprenta de D. Pablo Riera, 1856.
Schnorr von Carolsfeld, Julius. *Gran colección de láminas del Antiguo y Nuevo Testamento por el eminente artista Julio Schnorr a Carolsfeld*. Barcelona: Faustino Paluzie, 1876.

Seijas, Guadalupe. 'Algunas consideraciones sobre la violencia en el libro de Jueces'. *Miscelánea de estudios árabes y hebraicos. Sección de hebreo* 60 (2011): 243–71.

Sicre Díaz, José Luis. *Jueces*. Estella: Verbo Divino, 2018.

Vander Stichele, Caroline, and Hugh S. Pyper, eds. *Text, Image, and Otherness in Children's Bibles: What Is in the Picture?* Atlanta: Society of Biblical Literature, 2012.

Villegas, Alonso de. *Fructus Sanctorum y Quinta Parte del Flossanctorum*. Cuenca: Juan Masselin, 1594.

Yebra-Rovira, Carmen. 'French biblical engravings and the education of the Spanish woman in the XIX century'. *Biblical Reception* 2 (2013): 97–116.

Yebra-Rovira, Carmen. 'Interpretación bíblica y formación moral de la mujer en el siglo XIX: El ángel del hogar'. *Moralia* 36 (2013): 405–26.

Yebra-Rovira, Carmen. *Las biblias ilustradas en España en el siglo XIX: Desarrollo, relevancia cultural e interpretación teológica*. Col. Tesis 64. Estella: Verbo Divino – Asociación Bíblica Española, 2015.

Yebra-Rovira, Carmen. 'A violencia na Biblia: reflexión a partir do crime de Guilbeah (Xuices 19–21)'. *Encrucillada: Revista Galega de Pensamento Cristián* 169 (2010): 21–34.

Chapter 7

RUTH AND NAOMI: A STORY OF FRIENDSHIP IN IMAGES

Guadalupe Seijas

The book of Ruth is a short story that consists of only four chapters.[1] It tells the story of Ruth, a foreign widow from Moab, who by her generous attitude towards Naomi, her mother-in-law, and by her faithfulness to Yahweh ends up becoming the mother of Obed and the great-grandmother of King David, from whose family the Messiah will be born.

Jewish and Christian exegeses have underlined values such as fidelity, obedience, modesty, humility and industriousness in Ruth. She has been seen as a model of family values and, especially in Judaism, the prototype of the convert, who abandons her gods to recognize the God of Israel as her own.[2]

One of the peculiarities of this narrative is the role that women played in it.[3] Even though the book is named after Ruth, one of its protagonists, Naomi, has a very prominent role in the story. Next to them is Orpah and the women of Jerusalem, on whose background the character of Ruth is built. However, the Moabite widow does not respond to the typical role of the heroine. She does not face enemies nor save her people from great danger as in the stories of Judith or Jael (Judges

---

1. The preparation of this work has been possible thanks to the financing of the Ministry of Economy and Competitiveness of the Government of Spain (R+D Projects: *Transmission and Reception of the Bible: Texts and Iconography*, FFI2015-65610-P).

2. Cf. Guadalupe Seijas, 'El libro de Rut según la interpretación rabínica', *Reseña Bíblica* 71 (2011): 31–40. The medieval Christian texts can be consulted in Leslie Smith, *Medieval Exegesis in translation. Commentaries on the Book of Ruth* (Kalamazoo: Western Michigan University Press, 1996).

3. There is an extensive bibliography on the book of Ruth, although much less extensive than that dedicated to other biblical books. For an overview of this book and the main issues it raises, see Katrina J. Larkin, *Ruth and Esther* (Sheffield: Sheffield Academic Press, 1996). Among the reference comments I refer to Jack M. Sasson, *Ruth: A New Translation with a Philological Commentary and a Formalist-Folklorist Interpretation*, 2nd edn (Sheffield: Sheffield Academic Press, 1989), and Irmtraud Fischer, *Rut: Übersetz und ausgelegt*, 2nd edn (Freiburg im Breisgau: Herder, 2005).

4–5). On a first impression, Ruth may seem like a submissive and conventional woman. However, feminist exegesis developed especially from the second half of the twentieth century,[4] using the method of narrative analysis, has shown other facets to her character. These studies have emphasized her determined personality which lead her to abandon everything that she knew to follow her mother-in-law, her ability to solve the economic hardship that they suffered by resorting to the measures of solidarity for the most disadvantaged that were contemplated in the Law of Israel, and her initiative, by asking Boaz to act in her favour and urging him to be her husband. These skills allowed her to solve her problems using all the means at her disposal, but she did it in her own way, unconventionally, which contravenes the roles assigned to widows in the Israelite society of that time. She dared to decide for herself and started a new and unexplored path that was not without risk.

Ruth is the widow of Mahlon, the wife of Boaz and the mother of Obed. But above all, her story highlights the relationship that she had with Naomi. Her priority was to stay with her, and, in fact, the close bonds of unconditional love that united Ruth with Naomi will be the starting point of the narrative. It is true that the biblical text does not use the term 'friendship' to refer to them. However, and taking into consideration the different elements of the story, the current reader can interpret the relationship between these two women in this sense.[5]

The book of Ruth

In the group of books that make up the Bible, the one we are dealing with has gone unnoticed, both in terms of exegesis and in artistic representations.[6] There are very few allusions to the book of Ruth included in the repertoires and iconographic indexes as well as in reference works,[7] especially if we compare them with mentions

---

4. Athalya Brenner (ed.), *Feminist Companion to Ruth* (Sheffield: Sheffield Academic Press, 1993); André LaCocque, *The Feminine Unconventional: Four Subversives Figures in Israel's Tradition*, 2nd edn (Eugene: Wipf & Stock, 2006), among others.

5. Regarding the friendship between Ruth and Naomi, see J. Cheryl Exum, 'Is this Naomi?' in *Plotted, Shot, and Painted: Cultural Representations of Biblical Women*, 2nd edn, Journal for the Study of the Old Testament Supplement Series 215 (Sheffield: Sheffield Phoenix Press, 2012), 135, and the bibliography there mentioned.

6. An overview of the iconography of this character can be seen in Carmen Yebra-Rovira, 'El libro de Rut y su repercusión en el arte: Entre la fidelidad y la tradición', *Reseña Bíblica* 71 (2011): 41–51, and in Martin O'Kane, 'The iconography of the book of Ruth', *Interpretation: A Journal of Bible and Theology* 64, no. 2 (2010): 130–45.

7. Among others, Louis Réau, *Iconografía del arte cristiano: Iconografía de la Biblia. Antiguo Testamento*, trans. Daniel Alcoba (Barcelona: Ediciones del Serbal, 2007), 293–94; and Louis Goosen, *De Abdías a Zacarías: Temas del Antiguo Testamento en la religión, las artes plásticas, la literatura, la música y el teatro* (Madrid: Akal, 2006), 230–3.

to other female characters such as Esther or Judith. But the fact that this biblical book has been little studied makes it especially attractive for the researcher who works in a field where much remains to be done. In fact, the work done so far has proved much richer than what could have been expected *a priori*.

The most represented scenes of the book of Ruth are the *Peregrinatio*, the farewell of Orpah and the declaration of loyalty of Ruth; Ruth gleaning among the reapers; Ruth at the feet of Boaz; the negotiations between Boaz and the relative; the marriage of Ruth and Boaz; and, finally, the birth of Obed. Nevertheless, not all of them have received the same attention from artists. In the Middle Ages, the most represented scene was, without a doubt, the *Peregrinatio*, when Elimelech, Naomi and her two sons leave from Bethlehem towards Moab. It is a stereotyped image that presents few variants and that from the Renaissance onwards ceases to be represented. Scenes related to the harvest are also very frequent, not only in the Middle Ages but in all periods. In fact, the attribute with which Ruth is represented and which distinguishes her from other biblical women is precisely a bundle of wheat ears.[8] To a lesser extent and depending on the time period, the nocturnal scene in the field (Ruth 3.6-15) also receives attention and the negotiations between Boaz and the relative (Ruth 4.1-12).[9]

However, in this chapter I will focus on the diachronic analysis of the iconography of Ruth 1.7-19:

7   So she set out from the place where she had been living, she and her two daughters-in-law, and they went on their way to go back to the land of Judah.
8   But Naomi said to her two daughters-in-law, 'Go back each of you to your mother's house. May the Lord deal kindly with you, as you have dealt with the dead and with me.
9   The Lord grant that you may find security, each of you in the house of your husband.' Then she kissed them, and they wept aloud.
10 They said to her, 'No, we will return with you to your people.'
11 But Naomi said, 'Turn back, my daughters, why will you go with me? Do I still have sons in my womb that they may become your husbands?
12 Turn back, my daughters, go your way, for I am too old to have a husband. Even if I thought there was hope for me, even if I should have a husband tonight and bear sons,
13 would you then wait until they were grown? Would you then refrain from marrying? No, my daughters, it has been far more bitter for me than for you, because the hand of the Lord has turned against me.'

---

8. The wheat ears allude to bread, and, therefore, the character of Ruth has been interpreted as a prefiguration and/or symbol of the Eucharist.

9. These two scenes are key in the development of the story. In the first, Ruth, at the request of Naomi, goes at night to the fields to ask Boaz for his protection. In the second, Boaz goes to the city gate to carry out the negotiations that will allow him to marry Ruth before the elders of Bethlehem.

14 Then they wept aloud again. Orpah kissed her mother-in-law, but Ruth clung to her.
15 So she said, 'See, your sister-in-law has gone back to her people and to her gods; return after your sister-in-law.'
16 But Ruth said, 'Do not press me to leave you or to turn back from following you! Where you go, I will go; where you lodge, I will lodge; your people shall be my people, and your God my God.
17 Where you die, I will die – there will I be buried. May the Lord do thus and so to me, and more as well, if even death parts me from you!'
18 When Naomi saw that she was determined to go with her, she said no more to her.
19 So the two of them went on until they came to Bethlehem.

Let's proceed next to the analysis of the images, which I have gathered in two groups, according to the predominant element: the farewell scene with the separation of Orpah and Ruth's declaration of loyalty (adhesion), and the return journey to Bethlehem, where Ruth and Naomi are emphasized, leaving Orpah in the background. We will study their representations, the variants adopted in the different time periods and their interpretation.

The farewell scene

This scene was frequently represented in the Middle Ages, although it also appears in other periods.

Medieval iconography

The first artistic manifestations of which we have news in relation to the book of Ruth appear in the Middle Ages. However, before approaching this iconographic analysis, it is necessary to dwell on the circumstances and mentality of the time.

Before beginning it is necessary to deal with some previous considerations. Most medieval representations are found in manuscripts and codices, which establish a close relationship between image and text. This text/image interaction conditions the representation since the text inspires the image and at the same time the physical space reserved for the image conditions its format. Nevertheless, the image does not always reflect the text faithfully. Sometimes the artist will deviate from the text by incorporating variants, or conflating several scenes in one, or introducing glosses or visual commentaries as an explanation to the text, which in turn will contribute to the understanding of the meaning of the scene. In most cases, these images appear in Romanesque and Gothic Bibles, written in Latin or in vernacular languages, that were moralized or historiated. Moreover, they also appeared in manuscripts that included typological interpretations such as the *Biblia Pauperum*, the *Speculum Humane Salvationis* and the *Concordantiae Caritatis*; in manuscripts used for personal devotion such as Psalters and the

7. Ruth and Naomi 163

Book of Hours; and in commentaries such as the *Glossa Ordinaria*, the *Historia Scholastica* by Petrus Comestor or the *Postillae* by Nicholas of Lyra.

The study of this medieval iconography should begin by addressing some prior issues before proceeding to the analysis of the images. It is necessary to know the history of the book in the Middle Ages[10] and have a comprehensive view of the topic. Likewise, it would be important to have a notion of the history of illumination, as well as an understanding of the decorative preferences in the different periods, the iconographic traditions prevailing in the different geographical areas, and the procedures used by the copyists and illuminators.[11]

Only after these issues have been studied shall we turn to the location, collection and identification of the iconographic representations. This section is also not without difficulties. There are countless medieval manuscripts, which are scattered in many libraries worldwide. In many instances, the cataloguing of the manuscripts is not precise, which forces the researcher to review the works one by one even if only, as in our case, to verify that there are no miniatures or historiated initials from the book of Ruth. Other times requesting images from libraries entails bureaucratic tasks that do not always end in the desired results. Fortunately, there are more and more libraries that are digitizing their collections, which greatly facilitates the researcher's task. Unfortunately, since the book of Ruth has been of little academic interest, when a manuscript is partially digitized, its miniatures are not usually included among the selected ones.

With the localized and identified images, we shall proceed to contextualize the manuscript in time, place, historical and social context, patron and recipient, and the artistic current to which it belongs. All of these are fundamental data that are needed to adequately interpret the meaning of the chosen iconography.

As already mentioned, the representations of the book of Ruth in the Middle Ages appear mostly in codices and manuscripts in historiated initials, miniatures or engravings, except for the stained-glass windows of the Sainte Chapelle in Paris.[12]

---

10. See, among others, Ingo F. Walther and Norbert Wolf, *Códices ilustres: Los manuscritos iluminados más bellos del mundo desde 400 hasta 1600*, trans. Pablo Álvarez Ellacuría (Londres: Taschen, 2003); and Christopher De Hamel, *A History of Illuminated Manuscripts* (London: Phaidon, 1986).

11. Christopher De Hamel, *Scribes and Illuminators* (Toronto: Toronto University Press, 1992).

12. Likewise, in the Cathedral of Canterbury (twelfth century) there is a stained-glass window of Obed that is part of a series of forty-three ancestors of Jesus. For an overview of the medieval iconography of the book of Ruth, cf. Guadalupe Seijas, 'Rut', *Revista de iconografía medieval* 9, no. 18 (2017): 85–104. Available online: https://www.ucm.es/data/cont/media/www/pag-105877/6.%20Rut.pdf (accessed 15 September 2021). The scene in question is rarely represented in historiated initials. Cf. Guadalupe Seijas, 'The iconographical representations of the book of Ruth in medieval illuminated initials', *Die Bible in der Kunst/Bible in the Arts* 3 (2019): 1–18. Available online: https://www.bibelwisse

The same thing does not happen after the Renaissance, when a greater variety of techniques and supports are used. Along with the images that accompany Bibles and biblical stories, we find the iconography of the book of Ruth in frescoes in the pendentives and vaults of churches, large format paintings, sculptures, stained-glass windows, engravings, lithographs, watercolours, tabernacles and choirs; but it also appears in elements of daily life such as postcards, furniture and, more recently, magazine covers or comics.

The images representing the story of Ruth can appear isolated or as part of iconographic cycles. Some include a small number of images from her book; others, however, are part of wider cycles such as the ones found in the Munich Psalter with twelve episodes or the Moralized Bibles, whose iconographic cycles range between eight and fourteen scenes. The *Padua Bible* deserves special mention, since it depicts the entire book of Ruth in forty-six images.

The scenes that were chosen and/or omitted, the iconographic elements that received the most attention, as well as the modifications introduced by artists are aspects that must be analysed. The iconographic cycles behave as visual stories that orient the viewer in one way or another depending on their selection.

Once made these considerations, we turn to the iconography study. The maximum splendour of the history of the medieval book is reached with the Moralized Bibles. The first examples were produced in France the 1220s and 1230s. They are veritable picture books with very ambitious iconographic programmes. Each page contains eight images and eight texts arranged in four columns: text/image/ image/text, which became a characteristic and exclusive arrangement for this type of manuscript. The summarized text of each biblical passage (in Latin, in French or in both languages) is accompanied by a brief explanation that aims to facilitate its understanding by the medieval audience, so that each passage is relevant and makes sense for the men and women of said historical period. Each text is accompanied by its corresponding image that can appear inside a medallion or in a square format.

The book of Ruth in the Moralized Bibles has been studied by John Lowden in *The Making of the Bibles Moralisées II: The Book of Ruth*,[13] a work of compulsory reading in which he analyses in detail the texts and images of seven manuscripts containing this book. Two of these Moralized Bibles are in the National Library of Vienna (ÖNB 2554 and ÖNB 1179); the third is represented by three manuscripts (Oxford–Paris–London)[14] that reproduce the same texts and images; the fourth is the Bible of Saint Louis, which is in the Treasury of the Cathedral of Toledo; the

nschaft.de/fileadmin/user_upload/Bibelkunst/BiKu_2019_09_Seijas_Ruth.pdf (accessed 15 October 2021).

13. John Lowden, *The Making of the Bibles Moralisées II: The Book of Ruth* (University Park: Penn State University Press, 2000).

14. Bodleian Library, Ms. 270b, Oxford; BNF Ms. latino 11560; Londres, BL Mss. Harley 1526–27.

fifth is the manuscript in the British Library with the signature 'Add. 18719';[15] and the last two correspond to the two Bibles of the Bibliothèque nationale de France, Ms. fr. 167, the Bible of John II the Good of the mid-fourteenth century, and Ms. fr. 166, from the beginning of the fifteenth century.[16]

The scene of Naomi and her daughters-in-law appears in the seven Moralized Bibles.[17] In the two oldest ones (ÖNB 2554 and ÖNB 1179), the *Separation* is the first scene of the visual narrative, similar to the stained-glass windows of the Sainte Chapelle in Paris (1248), which appear in two images located in the centre of two small rosettes under the central rose window.[18] On the one on the left, Ruth appears with Orpah who seems to be listening to Naomi, who on the right is represented sitting on a chair (Figure 7.1). The same thing happens in the *Crusaders Bible* (see below), where the scene of the *Peregrinatio* is also not represented.[19]

In ÖNB 2554, Naomi occupies the centre of the scene, emphasized by her greater size in relation to the other characters and by her covered hair, unlike those of the other women. Next to her are Ruth and Orpah, both with their heads uncovered, the first one making a gesture as if of reaching towards Naomi, while the second makes a gesture of farewell. In ÖNB 1179, the image is similar, although the arrangement of the characters changes. Naomi, on the right, holds the dress, a detail that alludes to the trip, and speaks with Ruth, in the centre, while on the left side Orpah also holds the dress and walks away in lamentation.

The images do fit the narrative in the Bible, but the texts that accompany them, the first one in Latin and the second in French, are strange and demonstrate a surprising ignorance of the biblical story:

> Here is a woman named Boaz who has two daughters. One of the daughters holds to her, and says that she will go wherever she ['Boaz'] may go, and the other parts from her and her company. (ÖNB 2554)

> A certain Hebrew woman named Ruth had two daughters, one of whom was kind and following her wherever she might go. The other to be sure was contradicting her. (ÖNB 1179)

15. These five Moralized Bibles were created in the thirteenth century.

16. The abbreviations that have been used are as follows: ÖNB = Österreichische Nationalbibliothek; BNF = Bibliothèque nationale de France; BL = British Library. For a detailed codicological description of each one of these manuscripts, see John Lowden, *The Making of the Bibles Moralisées I: The Manuscripts* (University Park: Penn State University Press, 2000).

17. A selection of the analysed images can be found on the personal page of Guadalupe Seijas at https://ucm.academia.edu/GuadalupeSeijas with the title 'Ruth and Naomi: A Story of Friendship in Images'.

18. This rose window corresponds to the fourth window of the northern section dedicated to the book of Joshua and to some episodes of Deuteronomy, and it includes the story of Ruth in seven scenes.

19. In the other five Moralized Bibles, prior to the Farewell, five other scenes are represented: hunger in the days of Eli, *Peregrinatio*, the death of Elimelech, the marriage of Ruth and Orpah with Mahlon and Chilion, and the death of the latter.

Figure 7.1 Sainte Chapelle (1248) *Orpah and Ruth/Naomi*.
Source: Compound by Verbo Divino Publisher.

In these passages, two errors can be detected. The name of the woman is not Boaz, which is the name of a man, nor Ruth, which is the name of the daughter-in-law, it is Naomi. On the other hand, this woman did not have any daughters, but sons. These errors could be explained by the fact that the text that accompanies the images was written based on what the iconography model represents and not by what the original text said.[20] What is significant in these two Moralized Bibles is that the beginning of the story begins precisely here, taking as a starting point the feminine triangle formed by Naomi, Ruth and Orpah and silencing the previous context in which the males play an important role.

---

20. In Lowden, *The Making of the Biblées Moralisés II*, 72–6.

7. Ruth and Naomi

Figure 7.2 *The Farewell, Bible of Saint Louis*, Toledo, c. 1226, vol. 1, fol. 94r.
Source: M. Moleiro Editor (www.moleiro.com).

The representation of this scene in the *Bible of Saint Louis*,[21] Oxford–Paris–London and Add. 18719 follows the same iconographic pattern: on the left, the gates of the city that seem to allude to Moab can be seen. In the centre, two women embrace, and on the right another woman moves away, gathering her dress (except in the *Bible of Saint Louis*) and looking in the opposite direction. All of them have their heads covered and are not distinguished by their size, which makes identification difficult.[22] Lowden points out three possibilities. In the *Bible of Saint Louis*, it is said,

> Naomi returning to her land, Orpah and Ruth followed her. And when they came outside a town they all wept, and Orpah kissed Naomi and returned to her home. Ruth to be sure followed her mother-in-law.

From the text it follows that the women who embrace are Naomi and Orpah before separation, while Ruth is the furthest figure. In fact, the body of Orpah is the closest to the city gate while Ruth directs her steps in the opposite direction.

---

21. We would like to thank M. Moleiro Editor for allowing us access to the images of this Bible and its reproduction. A description of the folio as a whole can be seen in Chapter 2.
22. Regarding this issue I will follow Lowden, *The Making of the Biblées Moralisés II*, 79.

The same image is accompanied by a somewhat different text in Bodleian fol. 270b: 'And Naomi arose to go into her country with both her daughters-in-law from the land of Moab. Orpah then kissed her mother-in law and returned. Ruth to be sure clove her mother-in-law.' In this case the figures that embrace would correspond to Ruth and Naomi, while Orpah would be the one that moves away, although the direction of their steps would be the opposite of the expected one. Lowden points to a third possibility, which would entail reading the image independently of the accompanying text. In that case, it could be understood that the single woman could correspond to Naomi, while in the centre would be the two daughters-in-law. This is a possible interpretation from a point of view of the composition, but questionable with respect to the biblical story.

The same representation appears in Ms. fr. 167 and Ms. fr. 166, but now it is represented within a squared frame. In this case, some details allow to identify the characters. In Ms. fr. 167, the central figures that embrace each other have their heads uncovered, unlike the figure that moves away that has her head covered. In Ms. fr. 166, all of them have headdresses, but the woman who is about to leave carries a walking stick. In addition, the women who embrace each other are dressed differently, which distinguishes them both in their behaviour and in their status. On the left, Orpah seems to be dressed luxuriously and on the right Ruth wears more modest clothes.

In the same way that similarities can be found in the visual representation of the biblical text between the oldest Moralized Bibles and the later manuscripts, the representation of the moralizations follows a similar pattern.

In ÖNB 2554 and ÖNB 1179, the moralization is typological and interprets the image/story as representing the two types of men in the Church that correspond to Ruth and Orpah, those who follow the Church and those who leave, respectively. The visual parallelism between the lower and upper image is clearly perceived. In ÖNB 2554 the Church is the central figure wearing a white dress and a blue cloak, dressed like Naomi, who holds two clergymen under her mantle while on her right there are two others, one of whom carries a book. The monks represent those who follow the Church. On the opposite side three Jews represent those who move away from her. The spectator identifies them by the conical hats and by a bag of money that alludes to the greed with which they were characterized in the Middle Ages.

In the other manuscripts' moralizing text, of different length, the farewell of Orpah is identified with those who, after being purified by baptism, return to their vices, while the fidelity of Ruth corresponds to those who persevere in their purity and chastity. In the centre of the image, the Church baptizes two people. On the right, a monk carries a book in his hand, symbol of preaching and diffusion of the Gospel, and to the left, a Jew is shown with bags of money. However, the visual parallelism between both images is more difficult to appreciate.

Along with the Moralized Bibles we can mention other Bibles that contain this scene. In the Arsenal Bible of the middle of the thirteenth century (Biblioteca de l'Arsenal, Paris, Ms. 5211, fol. 364v), this scene appears after the *Peregrinatio*, within a cycle of six episodes. On this occasion the eye contact occurs between

Orpah and Ruth. Orpah returns to Moab, from where she has just left. Naomi insists that Ruth does not accompany her, but Ruth raises a finger upward, as a gesture of loyalty.

The *Crusaders Bible* (Pierpont Morgan Library, New York, Ms. M. 638), also known as the *Morgan Bible* (c. 1250) is another French Bible containing a large number of miniatures. The visual account of the book of Ruth includes eight double scenes (fols 17r–19r) and begins with the succession of three consecutive scenes on the same register. Naomi dismisses Orpah and she returns the gesture, while Ruth and Naomi take each other by the arm. Next, Ruth and Naomi face each other, and Ruth turns her back on Orpah. In the centre, Ruth and Naomi appear together, the hand of Ruth on Naomi's shoulder as a symbol of fidelity and arriving in Bethlehem where they are received by the women of the city. The colours of the clothes (blue cape and white dress for Ruth, red cape and blue dress for Naomi and green dress and grey cape for Orpah) allow to distinguish each of them.

In the *Munich Psalter* (Staatsbibliothek, Munich, clm 835, fol. 104r),[23] an English Psalter of the thirteenth century, the miniatures offer a plain image, lacking in movement. Three women appear with their heads covered. One of them walks to the left and puts her hand to her face in a gesture of crying. It is Orpah who leaves. The other two are dressed similarly and can only be distinguished by the gesture of their hands. It is a more neutral and descriptive representation of this scene.

The *Bible of Padua*, also known as the *Historiated Bible of Rovigo* (Accademia dei Concordi, Ms. 212, Fondo Silvestri),[24] was created at the end of the Trecento and contains forty-six scenes from the book of Ruth accompanied by text written in the Padovano dialect. These images present us with a popular visual narrative in which the story is adapted to the customs of the time and therefore it allows us to easily follow its development. The scenes were framed in red, forming squares or rectangles if they were double. The images were made first in pencil and then colour was added. This passage is developed in four scenes (fol. 41v) surrounded by a long text that reproduces the story of Ruth 1.8-14. In all the vignettes, the colour of their dresses (Orpah's in blue, Naomi's in light pink and Ruth's in plum) allows distinguishing them. In the first vignette, the three women set out on the road carrying water, crooks and blankets on their shoulders. Naomi precedes her daughters-in-law. In this image Orpah is barefoot, although in the rest of the sequence there is a road. In the second, Naomi kisses her two daughters-in-law.

---

23. Images of Sacred History are included in some Psalters. Although scenes from the book of Ruth are not included often, four scenes appear in two other English Psalters: the *Baltimore Psalter* of the thirteenth century and the *Queen Mary Psalter* of the fourteenth century.

24. Cf. Pier Luigi Bagatin and Accademia dei Concordi di Rovigo, *Mecenatismo in Polesine: 150 Anniversario della Donazione della Libreria Silvestriana All'accademia dei Concordi e alla città di Rovigo* (Canova: Treviso, 2009); and Guadalupe Seijas, 'Una Biblia en imágenes: el libro de Rut', *Reseña Bíblica* 87 (2015): 5-14.

The remaining two vignettes reproduce what could be a single scene. In the third, Orpah returns home, but while her face turns towards the women leaving, her feet move towards Moab, in the opposite direction, which suggests that it is a difficult and painful decision. In the fourth, Ruth and Naomi take the road with their backs to Orpah. The presentation of Orpah and Ruth in separate vignettes is characteristic of this Bible, since the scenes in which Mahlon and Chilion appear receive the same compositional treatment in the consummation of the marriage, death and burial. However, this Bible introduces a novelty in relation to this scene by including a vignette that reproduces an original scene at the end of fol. 41r: Naomi communicates her intention to return to her daughters-in-law who are seated in chairs. It is a domestic scene, which takes place inside the house. In Ruth 1.7-8 it is during the trip when Naomi communicates her decision to remain alone. The iconographic representation here departs from the biblical story and incorporates a new element that connects with the traditional mentality that home is the feminine sphere par excellence.

The last of the medieval Bibles that I will mention, produced closer to the Renaissance, is the *Alba Bible* (1422–30)[25] that was commissioned to Rabbi Moses Arragel of Guadalajara. It is a Romance translation with glosses, many of which contain rabbinic and medieval Jewish interpretations. The book of Ruth contains three miniatures[26] and a drawing from a different hand. Using rough black lines, this last scene shows Ruth, Naomi and Orpah in the farewell scene, following the most typical iconographic pattern. It is possible that, as it happened in other pages of this Bible, some spaces were reserved for additional decoration and would have been left empty. Subsequently, they could have been completed at a later date with less elaborate scenes and without colour. In this Bible, however, the iconographic emphasis falls on the final episodes of the story.

In addition to this scene, in the Middle Ages there were other ways of expressing the bonds that united these three women. An example can be found in the miniatures that appear at the beginning of the Book of Ruth in the *Anjou Bible*[27] (Maurits Sabbern University, Leuven), an illuminated Bible in Latin dating from the middle of the fourteenth century and produced in the Court of Naples. In the initial 'I' (*In diebus unius judicis*) located in the left margin of fol. 62r, there are three consecutive miniatures that represent the *Peregrinatio*, the death of

---

25. Sonia Fellous-Rozemblat, *Histoire de la Bible de Moïse Arragel: Quand un rabbin interprète la Bible pour les chrétiens (Tolède, 1422-1433)* (Paris: Somogy, 2001). For a description of this bible and its facsimiles, I refer to Esperanza Alfonso, F. Javier del Barco, Mª T. Ortega and Arturo Prats *Biblias de Sefarad: Bibles of Sepharad* (Madrid. Biblioteca Nacional, 2012), 179–85, a bilingual catalogue of the exhibition *Biblias de Sefarad: las vidas cruzadas del texto y sus lectores* (Biblioteca Nacional de Madrid, 27 febrero–13 mayo 2012).

26. They correspond to the night scene in the fields, the negotiations between Boaz and the relative, and Obed with Naomi.

27. Regarding this Bible, cf. Lieve Watteeuw and Jan Van der Stock (eds), *The Anjou Bible: A Royal Manuscript Revealed: Naples 1340* (Paris: Peeters, 2010).

Elimelech and the death of Naomi's children. The last two are scenes of mourning and lamentation in which the three women express through gestures the intensity of their suffering. It is striking that the widow of the deceased, along with her sons and daughters-in-law, are present before the body of Elimelech, since according to Ruth 1.3-4, the death of Naomi's husband was prior to the marriage of their children. The images represent the prolegomena of this narrative, contextualizing the story, but at the same time, they give prominence to the experiences of pain that the three have suffered together. We can perceive that it is the same reality, expressed through a different visual language. Here the shared sorrow and the lamentation are emphasized, in consonance with the medieval mentality, and not the complicity and harmony, closer to contemporary sensibility as we shall see later; but both facets are two sides of the same reality.

The analysed images behave like windows that allow us to peek into the Middle Ages. The typological interpretations of the Moralized Bibles echo the concerns and interests of the medieval man. In relation to the studied passage, the conflict between Christians and Jews, between those who follow Christ and the Church and those who deviate from it, between those who love virtue and those who live in sin emerges. They allow us to know their customs and ways of life, which they project and integrate into the representation of the biblical story. Thus, in the *Bible of Padua*, several scenes collect and transfer in the history of Ruth the contemporary practices in weddings (dances, banquets, etc.) and in deaths (wakefulness, consolation to the relatives, burial). They also allow us to know the clothing and fashions prevailing at the time. The Moralized Bibles show us slender and tall women, who cover their heads with the same headdress in fashion at the moment and who wear robes and mantles that do not cling to their bodies. Furthermore, in the *Crusaders Bible*, some mantles have the rim of another colour. On the other hand, in the *Bible of Padua*, Naomi, Ruth and Orpah are dressed as peasants and wear more modest and simple clothes. Finally, the images also reproduce the elements and clichés that allow the reader to identify the characters. The Jews are represented with a conical cap, pointed beard and often carry a bag of money, while the friars of the mendicant orders have tonsure, wear the habits of Dominicans or Franciscans and often carry a book containing the Gospels.

Other interpretations of this scene

After the Middle Ages, this scene from the book of Ruth was less represented, much more frequent being the representation of the episodes related to the harvest. It is possible that the new artistic medium, the canvas, influenced this change. These new paintings were not only decorative but also became a symbol of wealth and status. Ruth picking wheat ears in an agrarian and peasant environment would allow for representing rural and pastoral scenes, which were more in accordance with the tastes of the time. At the end of the eighteenth century, the artists showed a renewed interest for the farewell scene. Most of these iconographic representations conflates the farewell of Orpah and the loyalty of Ruth since, according to the biblical text, both events took place at the same time. Nevertheless, there is also another iconographic model in which the attention falls only on Ruth and Naomi, leaving the farewell of Orpah in the background.

The literary and artistic production of William Blake (1757–1827) is closely connected to the Bible, a book that is not only to be read but also to be imagined, visualized and interpreted. The farewell scene appears in his artistic oeuvre with great drama in *Naomi and Her Two Daughters-in-Law* (1795, Victoria and Albert Museum, London). If in the biblical text Orpah leaves in obedience to Naomi and only embarks on the way back after the repeated insistence of her mother-in-law, Blake's watercolour incorporates his own interpretation. The dark tones of the landscape and the figure of Naomi contrast with the white dresses of her daughters-in-law. Visually, the action of Ruth is positively valued while Orpah's is rejected. Both maintain an identical posture but in opposite directions. Ruth's embrace of Naomi is placed in opposition to the tears of Orpah; the blond hair of Ruth to the dark one of Orpah; the bottom of the dresses of the former are still, while those of Orpah move because she is leaving. On the other hand, the figure of Naomi is characterized by her passivity. She is static to the drama that is unfolding in front of her. She lets herself be embraced, but her arms remain extended, and her lost gaze, absorbed in her pain, does not notice any of her daughters-in-law.

It will be in his last works when Philip Hermogenes Calderon (1833–1898), an author greatly influenced by the Pre-Raphaelite painters, will be inspired by historical and biblical themes. In *Ruth and Naomi*[28] (1886, Walker Art Gallery, Liverpool), a hand-coloured lithograph transforms this episode into a disturbing and troubling situation.[29] The *mise en scène* is deliberately ambiguous (Figure 7.3). The action is set in a desert environment, with cactus and palm trees, evoking Palestine. The viewer's attention is focused on a couple that embraces with a strong erotic charge. The woman dressed in light clothes holds the gaze of her partner in which a love attraction is perceived. The dark figure has its back to the viewer and, therefore, his or her identity is hidden. The greater height, the clothes and the turban that the figure wears as well as the romantic nature of the embrace point to a male, who could be identified as Boaz. If this is the case, the feminine figure that is on the right margin could be Naomi observing the embrace of the couple, an embrace of which there is no mention in the biblical text. However, this woman has the face of a young woman, which would fit better the description of Orpah. If this is Orpah, then there should be no doubt as to who the other two embracing figures are, and some scholars have identified this scene as the one narrated in Ruth 1.8-18, which is also hinted at in the title of the painting. The artist then

---

28. Regarding this painting, cf. Exum, 'Is this Naomi?', where she studies this picture from the analysis of different texts and other cultural representations, although his main interest resides in the relationships between individuals of the same sex and between individuals of different sexes in the book of Ruth, especially in the Naomi–Ruth–Boaz triangle.

29. In this same line is another of his paintings, *The Great Act of Renunciation of St. Elizabeth of Hungary* (1881).

Figure 7.3 Philip Hermogenes Calderon, *Ruth and Naomi*, 1886.
Source: Walker Art Gallery, Liverpool.

challenges the viewer to find out the identity of that mysterious character, sowing doubts about the nature of the feelings that unite both. Could it be that Ruth's loyalty to Naomi was beyond friendship? Orpah has not yet left, although she is about to do so, which is another variant with respect to the story. The farewell, however, does not seem motivated by the insistence of Naomi but, rather, as the result of an exclusion. In the embrace that she is contemplating there is no place for her. The union between Ruth and Naomi leaves no room for anyone else and Orpah has no choice but to return.

The second model corresponds to the engraving created by Gustave Doré (1832–1883), who included two scenes of the story of Ruth in his *Illustrated Bible* (1866): *Boaz and Ruth* and *Ruth and Naomi* (Figure 7.4).

This work of art reflects the attraction that people felt for the Orient, which was characteristic of the time. The landscape is now reduced to a desert of sand. The focus of attention falls on the hug between mother-in-law and daughter-in-law, while Orpah leaves in tears. The image compares the loneliness and the pain of Orpah's separation from the mutual support that Ruth and Naomi offer. Unlike what we saw in Blake's watercolour, in this print Naomi is an active participant in the embrace.

In the artistic representations of the twentieth century, the special relationship that exists between Ruth and Naomi occupies a prominent place, a relationship that has been highlighted and valued by feminist exegesis. In the love that she feels for her mother-in-law, in that unconditional love that leads her to adopt another land, another town and another god, Ruth finds the strength to face the dangers and the uncertainty that threaten her future.

Figure 7.4 Gustavo Doré, *Ruth and Naomi*, 1866.
Source: Illustrated Bible.

The work of Marc Pynas (1887–1985) is difficult to classify. Deeply Jewish but, at the same time, capable of integrating other elements alien to his religious tradition, this Russian-born artist represents the biblical texts from his own peculiar perspective. In 1960 he painted a series of five colour lithographs[30] (Marc Chagall Museum in Nice) on the book of Ruth, the first of which depicts Naomi and her daughters-in-law embracing. At the centre stands Naomi with the two women on either side, namely her daughters-in-law, each one of them different but without any other means of identification. A red sun transmits heat and life. At the lower

---

30. As with other pictorial works in which the book of Ruth is represented, there are hardly any studies that address the relationship between text and image in Chagall's depictions of biblical themes. This shortage is especially noteworthy in relation to this series of five lithographs. The work of Esperanza Galindo (*Trasgresión y tradición en la obra bíblica de Marc Chagall: análisis e interpretación de las 17 pinturas del Museo Nacional Mensaje Bíblico Marc Chagall como signo y como hecho de comunicación* (Sevilla: Universidad de Sevilla, 2008)) can be cited, which does not include in her study those relating to the book of Ruth. For an overview of Chagall and the Bible, see the catalogue of the exhibition with the same title *El mensaje bíblico, 1931–1983* (Segovia: Obra social y cultural, 2001).

end a small animal, perhaps a lamb, appears next to them. The brown tones and the lines of the drawing that make up the volumes take us into a universe shared by the three women in which the pain of their husbands' death has been a shared experience that have united them. The Bible is characterized by describing facts, not feelings,[31] leaving gaps and lacunas that the reader must fill and reconstruct. Chagall takes advantage of these possibilities, those loopholes in the biblical story, and, faithful to his conviction that the artist, through images, must also be an interpreter and commentator of the Bible, shows us his own personal vision. It highlights the love that exists between them, the result of shared experiences, suffering, support and comfort. The artist extends to Orpah the meaning of the root *dbq* ('adhere, stick') that in the text is used only for Ruth (Ruth 1.14).

A certain similarity is seen in the painting *Ruth and Naomi* (2001) by He Qi, a Chinese artist living in the United States of America. His pictorial production focuses on Christian religious art and, especially, on pictures of biblical themes. In his works he combines traditional Chinese techniques and sensitivity with Western European iconography of the Middle and Modern Ages. In this painting there is also a red sun that transmits the strength and intensity of the moment. Bright and vivid colours, curved lines and grids make up a single central figure, in which three heads and two arms stand out. Ruth embraces Naomi, Naomi remains passive and Orpah moves away. Despite the separation of the latter, there is also a common space between the three women that is reflected in the emotional aspect of the embrace, although to a lesser extent than in Chagall's lithography. He Qi adds a detail, a basket with ears of wheat, a symbol that characterizes Ruth and that the artist adds to contextualize the episode and facilitate its identification.

The iconographic representations of the late eighteenth and nineteenth centuries emphasized the dramatic tension of the scene and the contrast between the behaviour of the two daughters-in-law. Orpah does not disappear from the scene, but her figure contributes to highlight the dominant element in the composition, the embrace between Ruth and Naomi. In contrast, in the twentieth century, this episode is approached from a different perspective. The force that emanates at this time comes from the sum of the affections between the characters, so that that loyalty is not exclusive of Ruth and Naomi, but Orpah can also participate in it.

The return journey

Often, the moment Ruth manifests her loyalty to Naomi is represented on the journey back to Bethlehem.

In the *Queen Mary Psalter*[32] (BL Royal Ms 2 B VII, fol. 47r and fol. 47v), we also find this scene forming part of a series that includes three other episodes. Ruth and

---

31. A good example of the parsimony in the expression of the sentiments of the biblical texts is the sacrifice of Isaac (Genesis 22).

32. A description of this Psalter can be seen in Chapter 3.

Naomi holding hands are at the gates of Bethlehem at the end of their journey. The two previous vignettes correspond to the *Peregrinatio* and to the marriage of Ruth and Orpah with the children of Naomi. The fourth and last represents Boaz who finds Ruth gleaning in the fields accompanied by Naomi. Unlike other medieval manuscripts, in which the second part of the story is fundamentally represented,[33] episodes from the first two chapters have been selected in this Psalter. The chosen scenes highlight the initiative and decision-making capacity of Ruth, underlining the fact that she marries a foreigner, that she travels with her mother-in-law and that she looks for sustenance by picking up wheat ears. In the Psalters and the Book of Hours, the choice of the contents of the miniatures depended, to a large extent, on the tastes of the person who ordered the manuscript and/or the preferences of the recipient. The *Queen Mary Psalter* is a book of personal devotion, intended for a woman. It represents many biblical women, who are shown as models of behaviour. Many are presented as mothers; however, in the case of Ruth there is no allusion to this facet of her character, and this absence contributes to highlight other of her qualities.

Dutch paintings of the seventeenth century, which takes the Bible as a source of inspiration for many of its works, also represent this story. Ruth becomes a popular character, a model of behaviour and piety. Painters such as Fabritius, Aert de Gelder, Drost and, in a special way, Pieter Lastman, Rembrandt and Jan Victors, among others, will represent different episodes of Ruth's story, in which typical Dutch landscapes and the customs and fashions of the time appear.

Among his more than sixty paintings on biblical themes, Rembrandt (1606–1669) was also inspired by the story of Ruth: *Boaz Deposits Six Measures of Barley on the Mantle of Ruth* (*c.* 1650, Rijksmuseum, Amsterdam). He also created an ink drawing and two oil paintings in which he portrayed Boaz and Ruth as respectable members of the bourgeoisie (1643, Berlin Gemaldegalerie). Two of his works recall this scene. In *Ruth and Naomi* (*c.* 1638–39, Museum Boijmans-Van Beuningen, Rotterdam), a pencil drawing and brown ink on sepia-coloured paper, only two elegant women appear, distinguished by wearing different headdresses and walking side by side in animated conversation. In addition, in the etching entitled *Preciosa* and subtitled *Ruth and Naomi* (*c.* 1642, British Museum, London), two women of different ages walk in what seems to be a forest. This is a more expressive than descriptive image, in which the journey of the trip is underlined. In both cases, Rembrandt focuses his attention on two women, one of whom is aware of the other, without including other elements that make it possible to relate the picture to the story of Ruth.

Two pictures of the Dutch School standout for introducing a variant to the scene, the horse of Naomi. The first is titled *Ruth and Naomi* (before 1650, private collection) and it has been attributed to Jacob Symonsz Pynas (*c.* 1592–1656), who was considered to be the precursor of the Dutch School. Naomi's declaration of loyalty takes place in a rural and costumbrist environment. But this time the words

---

33. This is the case, for example, of the *Baltimore Psalter* or the *Alba Bible*.

of Ruth are not pronounced in the solitude of the road, as is usually the case, but in a crowded environment in which men and women walk the roads going about their business. Orpah moves away, but her figure is somewhat obscured by the presence of other peasants. An added novelty is the presence of a man, who seems to be a servant, holding the reins of the colt. The scene incorporates new features in the representation, which make the words of Ruth to Naomi remain in a secondary place as the rural scene and the landscape acquire greater importance (Figure 7.5).

The second Dutch painting, *Ruth and Naomi* (1614, Niedersächsisches Landesmuseum, Hannover), is that of Rembrandt's teacher, Pieter Lastman (*c.* 1583–1633). The landscape is typical of Italy, a country he knew well from his travels. On this occasion, Naomi rides on the donkey while Ruth walks by her side. In the distance, Orpah, who also travels on the back of an animal, is hardly distinguished. The physical distance between the two and the gesture of Naomi's hands setting aside Ruth evoke Naomi's insistence that she return to her land and reject her. Some exegetes maintain that the presence of Ruth in Bethlehem would have made Naomi's situation even more difficult. To the economic precariousness, aggravated by one more mouth to feed, it would be necessary to add the presence of a foreigner, someone that would arouse the distrust between the neighbours, a Moabite, whose town was criticized for its indecorous sexual conduct.

Figure 7.5 Jacob Symosz Pynas, *Ruth and Naomi*, before 1650.
Source: Private collection.

In the oil painting by Jan Victors, *Ruth and Naomi* (1653, private collection, New York), the conversation takes place at the top of the road. Naomi's gestures are like those of the previous painting. The woman on the left, Naomi, is old and is sitting looking at Ruth, younger, who remains standing. The artist pays special attention to clothing. The dresses are displayed with great detail and highlights, especially, the hat of Ruth, the same as it appears in other paintings by this artist. Behind them there is an autumnal landscape, in which the spectator can make out with difficulty the silhouette of a woman, which could be Orpah. In the representation of this scene lies the story of *Vertumnus and Pomona* (Vertumnus and Pomona by Paulus Moreelse, Boijmans-Van beuningen Museum, Rotterdam[34]), a story included in Ovid's *Metamorphoses* (Book XIV, §§ 623–771), where the god of the seasons pretends to be an old woman to seduce Pomona, a nymph of the forest. In this same line, we can place the picture of Willem Drost, *Ruth and Naomi* (1642, Ashmolean Museum, Oxford), where Naomi and Ruth are shown like an old woman and a girl.[35]

The work of the Dutch School focused its attention on the journey of Ruth and Naomi but accentuating the difference in age between them and Naomi's rejection of the loyalty of Ruth. The scene is shown as a pretext that allows the artist to represent female fashion (dresses, headdresses), the landscape, nature and the rural environment.

We will have to wait until the twentieth century to find, again, images of this episode. Its absence in the representations of the preceding centuries points to the little relevance that this scene had. Also, representing the journey, although with a very different orientation, is the painting of the North American artist Sandy Freckleton Gagon *Where You Go* (2009), a half-length portrait of the two women. The artist stops time. Two women on the way, a middle-aged woman whose hair is still dark and another old woman, totally grey and marked by wrinkles, who leans on a cane. The difficulties of the path are reflected in the wind that inflates the cloth that Ruth holds over their heads to protect themselves. Ruth contemplates Naomi, attentive to her gestures. Naomi looks forward, focused on the path, but leans toward Ruth. Ruth holds Naomi and hugs her. Naomi lets herself be helped. One of them offers and the other one accepts. Contemporary exegesis has highlighted these values of the book of Ruth by stressing that the possibilities of change, renewal and transformation of reality and the surrounding world find a solid foundation in human relationships based on complicity, generosity and solidarity.

---

34. In *Vertumnus and Pomona* (c. 1638), whose authorship is attributed to Rembrandt or Ferdinand Bol, one of his students, the similarities are clearly perceived. Cf. Debra Miller, 'Ruth and Naomi of 1653: An unpublished painting by Jan Victors, The *Mercury Journal* 2 (1985): 19–28. Available online: http://archive.is/QFE44 (accessed 15 September 2018).

35. Ruth is widowed after ten years of marriage (Ruth 1.4), so we must deduce that she would be an adult; neither a teenager nor a young woman.

7. Ruth and Naomi

The scene of the farewell of Orpah and the loyalty of Ruth to Naomi during the trip appears repeatedly in complete visual narrative cycles. Since the twentieth century, there has been a renewed interest in the illustration of the book of Ruth, both from Christianity and from Judaism (*meguil·lat Rut* or scroll of Ruth). Among others, we can mention the stories told through images by John August Swanson (1938), author of a serotype that represents this narration in twelve episodes (1991) published in Joan D. Chittister's book, *The Story of Ruth: Twelve Moments in Every Woman's Life*;[36] Arthur Syzk (1894–1951), who illustrates the book of Ruth in eight images, with a style that imitates the illuminated medieval manuscripts, full of colour and luminosity similar to the stained-glass windows of the Gothic cathedrals; and Jakob Steinhardt (1887–1968), who made nineteen engravings that were published together with the text of the book of Ruth in Hebrew and English, handwritten by Franzisca Baruch (Jewish Publication Society, 1957), engravings heavily influenced by German Expressionism and with a marked white-and-black contrast.

This harmony and complicity between both women are also reflected in other scenes, connected to the home and the domestic sphere. The Pre-Raphaelite painters, in their search for a more natural and realistic painting in the face of the academicist demands of Victorian art, presented the birth of Obed in a familiar and feminine environment. In the triptych *The Story of Ruth* (1876–77, Tate Gallery, London), Thomas Matthews Rooke (1842–1942) selects three episodes of the story: the declaration of Ruth's loyalty on the way back to Bethlehem, the encounter in the field with Boaz, who shows a favourable attitude towards Ruth, and the birth of Obed. It is a visual sequence whose reading leads us to a sweet, harmonious story with a happy ending. Moments of tension are omitted, such as when Ruth goes to the fields at night to request the intervention of Boaz – an action not without risk, since it could be discovered and labelled as unseemly behaviour or she could have been rejected by Boaz – and the scene between the negotiations between Boaz and the relative, whose consequences would determine the future of these women. Nor are other facets of Ruth's personality shown, beyond the care and tenderness that the scenes give off with her mother-in-law and her son. In the last scene of this painting, Naomi holds Obed in the arms of Ruth. A serene and somewhat idyllic image, a familiar scene related to motherhood. The child fills Naomi's emptiness and gives meaning to their lives.

In addition to the already discussed work by Rooke, we can also mention another painter of this current, Simeon Solomon (1840–1905), who created several paintings on this subject, *Ruth, Noemi and Obed* (1860, Birmingham Museums and Art Gallery) and *Noemi, and the child Obed* (c. 1862 in Dalziel's Bible Gallery, 1881), and the French realist painter Emile Levy (1826–1890), with *Naomi, Obed and Ruth* (1859, Musée des Beaux-Arts, Rouen). In these paintings, in a domestic

---

36. Joan D. Chittister, *The Story of Ruth: Twelve Moments in Every Woman's Life* (Grand Rapids, MI: Eerdmans, 2000).

environment that is shown as the feminine space par excellence, the harmony between them is reflected.

The birth of Obed, however, has been represented using different models. Thus, Obed can appear in the company of his parents, Ruth and Boaz (ÖNB 1179, Sainte Chapelle, Sistine Chapel), but he can also be represented with Ruth in a bed (ÖNB 2554, the *Psalters of Munich* and *Baltimore*) or with Ruth and Naomi along with other women (in the *Saint Louis Bible* and in the rest of the Moralized Bibles cited by Lowden). Therefore, we can conclude that also in the iconography of other scenes in the history of Ruth, the relationship of complicity and harmony between these two women can be perceived; a detailed analysis of this scene remains pending for future work.

Final considerations

By way of conclusion, we can say that the book of Ruth has been read, interpreted and represented in each time period from its own perspective, taking into consideration the concerns and interests of each era: the present is projected every time onto the images of the past as can be seen by the typological interpretations of the Middle Ages; Ruth as a model of exemplary behaviour in Dutch paintings of the seventeenth century; the emphasis on family values of some representations of the nineteenth century; and the attention that Ruth and Naomi receive as women who help and support each other in the twentieth century. However, and comparing her with other women in the Bible, Ruth is a character of little relevance.

In the iconographic representation of the book of Ruth, not all scenes have received the same attention. In the case that concerns us and depending on the time, we find a greater or lesser diffusion of her story. In certain periods such as during the Renaissance, her story is hardly represented, being discarded for other scenes that were considered to be more significant or more appropriate, such as, for example, those related to rural life.

In the Middle Ages, the episode of Ruth 1.7-18 was the object of greater attention and in it the discursive capacity of the medieval artists stood out, be that in a folio or in several consecutive folios, as they showed in their miniatures several moments of the story in narrative cycles. In later periods, however, the images are focused on one scene or in a detail, being isolated from the rest of the story.

Throughout these pages we have analysed the relationship between text and image. In the Middle Ages, the interaction between both elements was especially significant because miniature and writing were integrated into the same page. This shows that what stands out in the representation of the story and what parts are just silenced; how the text is interpreted and updated through the images, adapting them to the mentality, customs and fashions of each period; the innovations that are incorporated, as well as the scenes that are selected to visually represent the book of Ruth, become relevant issues. While the episodes depicted in the *Queen Mary Psalter* highlight Ruth's courage and decision making, the miniatures of the *Baltimore Psalter* focus on the second part of the story and underline Ruth's role as David's great-grandmother and the origin of the Davidic dynasty. This dialogue between image and text, between Bible and art, is not limited to the Middle Ages but extends in time and space at different periods, both in the illustrated Bibles and in the Sacred Stories that include images.

On the other hand, the representation of the bonds of friendship between Ruth and Naomi is not limited to a single scene. If in the Middle Ages the harmony that unites them appears in other moments of the narration such as the mourning for the deceased or with the incorporation of scenes that do not exist in the biblical story, as in the *Bible of Padua*, in the nineteenth century this is shown in the birth of Obed, and in the twentieth century, the hug between the three women predominates and the representation of two women who walk together and support each other.

Finally, the character of Ruth is constructed in opposition to the figure of Orpah. Both are women who face a difficult decision. They must choose between returning to their village and following the road to Bethlehem with Naomi. Each option has elements for and against it. Each one of them, freely, makes a different choice, although we must remember that Orpah is the one that obeys Naomi when she insists that they return. As we have seen, in some representations (medieval moralizations, Blake) Orpah is negatively valued or left out (Calderon), but in others, she receives favourable treatment. Ruth and Orpah appear together (Sainte Chapelle, *Bible of Padua*) and say goodbye with affection (*Arsenal Bible*) or join in a shared embrace with Naomi (Chagall, He Qi). The feminist exegesis has recovered the character of Orpah and her role in the story and has contributed to a positive assessment of her character. Ruth not only stands out for her loyalty to Naomi (Dutch School), for her domestic virtues (nineteenth century), but also for being a woman capable of making decisions and facing difficulties (*Queen Mary Psalter*, Freckleton). These are some of the facets of a complex and rich character, whose iconographic representation has not yet been studied in its entirety.

Bibliography

Alfonso, Esperanza, F. Javier del Barco, Mª Teresa Ortega and Arturo Prats. *Biblias de Sefarad: Bibles of Sepharad*. Madrid: Biblioteca Nacional, 2012.

Bagatin, Pier Luigi, and Accademia dei Concordi di Rovigo. *Mecenatismo in Polesine: 150 Anniversario della Donazione della Libreria Silvestriana All'accademia dei Concordi e alla città di Rovigo*. Canova: Treviso, 2009.

Biblia de San Luis, Catedral Primada de Toledo, 3 vols. Barcelona: M. Moleiro Editor, 2002.

Bornay, Erika. *Mujeres de la Biblia en la pintura del Barroco: imágenes de la ambigüedad*, Ensayos Arte Cátedra. Cátedra: Madrid, 1998.

Brenner, Athalya, ed. *Feminist Companion to Ruth*. Sheffield: Sheffield Academic Press, 1993.

Chagall, Marc. *El mensaje bíblico, 1931–1983*. Segovia: Caja Segovia, Obra social y cultual, 2001.

Chittister, Joan D. *The Story of Ruth: Twelve Moments in Every Woman's Life*. Grand Rapids, MI: Eerdmans, 2000.

De Hamel, Christopher. *A History of Illuminated Manuscripts*. London: Phaidon, 1986.

De Hamel, Christopher. *Scribes and Illuminators*. Toronto: Toronto University Press, 1992.

Exum, J. Cheryl. 'Is this Naomi?', in *Plotted, Shot, and Painted: Cultural Representations of Biblical Women*, 2nd edn, 128–74, JSOT Supplement Series 215. Sheffield: Sheffield Phoenix Press, 2012.

Fellous-Rozemblat, Sonia. *Histoire de la Bible de Moïse Arragel: Quand un rabbin interprète la Bible pour les chrétiens (Tolède, 1422–1433)*. Paris: Somogy, 2001.

Fischer, Irmtraud. *Rut: Übersetz und ausgelegt*, 2nd edn. Freiburg im Breisgau: Herder, 2005.

Galindo, Esperanza. *Trasgresión y tradición en la obra bíblica de Marc Chagall: análisis e interpretación de las 17 pinturas del Museo Nacional Mensaje Bíblico Marc Chagall como signo y como hecho de comunicación*. Sevilla: Universidad de Sevilla, 2008.

Goosen, Louis. *De Abdías a Zacarías: Temas del Antiguo Testamento en la religión, las artes plásticas, la literatura, la música y el teatro*. Madrid: Akal, 2006.

LaCocque, André. *The Feminine Unconventional: Four Subversives Figures in Israel's Tradition*, 2nd edn. Eugene: Wipf & Stock, 2006.

Lowden, John. *The Making of the Bibles Moralisées I: The Manuscripts*. University Park: Penn State University Press, 2000.

Lowden, John. *The Making of the Bibles Moralisées I: The Book of Ruth*. University Park: Penn State University Press, 2000.

Miller, Debra. 'Ruth and Naomi of 1653: An unpublished painting by Jan Victors'. *The Mercury Journal* 2 (1985): 19–28. Available online: http://archive.is/QFE44 (accessed 15 September 2018).

O'Kane, Martin. 'The iconography of the book of Ruth'. *Interpretation: A Journal of Bible and Theology* 64, no. 2 (2010): 130–45.

Réau, Louis. *Iconografía del arte cristiano: Iconografía de la Biblia. Antiguo Testamento*. Translated by Daniel Alcoba. Barcelona: Ediciones del Serbal, 2007.

Sasson, Jack. M. *Ruth: A New Translation with a Philological Commentary and a Formalist-Folkorist Interpretation*, 2nd edn. Sheffield: Sheffield Academic Press, 1989.

Seijas, Guadalupe. 'El libro de Rut según la interpretación rabínica'. *Reseña Bíblica* 71 (2011): 31–40.

Seijas, Guadalupe. 'Una Biblia en imágenes: el libro de Rut'. *Reseña Bíblica* 87 (2015): 5–14.

Seijas, Guadalupe. 'Rut'. *Revista de iconografía medieval* 9, no. 18 (2017): 85–104. Available online: https://www.ucm.es/data/cont/media/www/pag-105877/6.%20Rut.pdf (accessed 15 September 2021).

Seijas, Guadalupe. 'The iconographical representations of the book of Ruth in medieval illuminated initials'. *Die Bible in der Kunst/Bible in the Arts* 3 (2019): 1–18. Available online: https://www.bibelwissenschaft.de/fileadmin/user_upload/Bibelkunst/BiKu_2019_09_Seijas_Ruth.pdf (accessed 15 October 2021).

Smith, Leslie. *Medieval Exegesis in Translation: Commentaries on the Book of Ruth*. Kalamazoo: Western Michigan University Press, 1996.

Walther, Ingo F., and Norbert Wolf. *Códices ilustres: Los manuscritos iluminados más bellos del mundo desde 400 hasta 1600*. Translated by Pablo Álvarez Ellacuría. London: Taschen, 2003.

Watteeuw, Lieve, and Jan Van der Stock, eds. *The Anjou Bible: A Royal Manuscript Revealed: Naples 1340*. Paris: Peeters, 2010.

Yebra-Rovira, Carmen. 'El libro de Rut y su repercusión en el arte: Entre la fidelidad y la tradición'. *Reseña Bíblica* 71 (2011): 41–51.

CONCLUSIONS

Guadalupe Seijas

The Bible is a dynamic text, a text that is alive, read and reread incessantly and a source of inspiration in artistic and cultural manifestations of all kinds. When an artist recreates a biblical scene, he or she is doing visual exegesis. He decides what he chooses to represent, to which character he gives more prominence, which elements he modifies and which he silences, and, consequently, he determines the type of relationship that is established between image and text. All of them are essential questions in the iconographic analysis of the Bible. At the same time, it is necessary to dwell on the values that are to be transmitted with the image and on how this influences the understanding of the message. The images are not neutral or 'aseptic' but reveal the artist's gaze, which, in turn, is determined by the historical, social and economic context, as well as by the prevailing mentality and the challenges of his time. Sometimes the images reflect the interpretation that is made of the text at that moment. In the medieval illustrations it is frequent to find that the characters of the Old Testament are understood as prefigurations that anticipate the episodes of the New Testament, following the typological interpretation of the Fathers of the Church transmitted in medieval compendiums such as the *Historia Scholastica* by Petrus Comestor. Other times, the representations are not directly inspired by the Bible, but rather they resort to a type of literature written for women with a clear pedagogical and moralizing intention as in the Chapel of Guadalupe, which is based on the *Elogios de Mujeres ilustres del Viejo Testamento* by Martín Carrillo, or they could refer to sacred stories and/or collections of biblical prints as in the nineteenth-century examples.

The study of biblical representation involves working from the text and from the image or, likewise, the text of the image and the image of the text. The relationship between the two is not limited to the biblical text. We are not always faced with independent paintings or representations. In the Middle Ages, the miniatures appeared in Bibles, in books for private devotion such as Psalters or the Book of Hours and in typological works such as in the *Biblia Pauperum* or the *Speculum Humanae Salvationis*, among others. The images were integrated into these codices to illustrate the text they accompany, adjusting their form to the assigned space, which greatly conditioned the possibilities of the artist. There are codices in which the text is subordinated to the image, as in the *Pierpont Morgan Bible*, and there are others in which the miniature is a secondary element, as it happens in most of the historiated initials that mark the beginning of each book in the medieval Bibles. Therefore, it is essential to determine which is the preponderant element in each manuscript and how they intervene in the reader's perception. It is equally important to integrate the representation within the iconographic programme, especially in medieval codices and stained-glass windows. Studying the isolated images decontextualized can lead us to wrong conclusions and to miss elements that are repeated regularly and that give coherence to the work in terms of its visual representation.

But artists also incorporate the trends and artistic styles of the moment. They embrace innovative iconographic traditions or recover old ones that had fallen into oblivion. They also resort to biblical scenes as a pretext to demonstrate their artistic skills in erotic or landscape scenes.

The stained-glass windows of the Gothic cathedrals represent biblical episodes with a didactic function: to make the Bible known to the illiterate and to those who did not have easy access to the texts. Other times, as in the Psalters and the Book of Hours, the images helped the religious practice of devotion and prayer.

However, it is possible to see other values present in the choice of characters and scenes. David defeating Goliath and Judith beheading Holofernes were two episodes heavily represented in Renaissance Florence, symbolizing the triumph of the weak against the oppressor. Its inhabitants perceived similarities between their vital reality and the stories of these characters, who defeated many more powerful enemies by resorting to cunning and intelligence. These scenes transmitted courage and encouraged hope in a possible victory against all odds. In the nineteenth century, Jochebed, the mother of Moses, became the subject of an unprecedented attention until the nineteenth century. If previously the scene of the discovery of Moses by the daughter of the Pharaoh predominated, at this time what stands out is the courage of Jochebed and her tireless struggle to save her son, values that make her a hero but always from her function as a mother. This projection of the present into the past facilitates the survival of the biblical characters as models to be imitated, but it also shows them as close figures with whom the viewer feels identified and can even be a source of consolation.

All this information helps us configure a complex map, which allows us to relate the origin of certain interpretations with the consequences derived from them; find out the reasons why some biblical characters are represented more frequently at certain times; and know the customs of the dress, the domestic trousseau or people's hobbies and the main human types that made up the society of an era (clergymen, knights, merchants, Jews, etc.), among others. Text and image behave like an open window into the society of a time. The Moralized Bibles are a magnificent example of this. Through its miniatures we can establish the code shared by emitter and receiver, that is, the elements that the viewer requires in order to correctly identify and interpret the scenes. At the beginning of the book of Ruth, it is very frequent to represent in miniatures or in the historiated initial of the text the first scene of the book in which Elimelech and Naomi leave Bethlehem in the direction of Moab (Ruth 1.1-2). These characters usually lean on a cane or carry on their shoulders a stick from which hangs a bundle with their possessions, details that allow the person contemplating the image to identify the moment of departure, elements that are well known to them because pilgrimages to places where the relics of saints were kept were very common at that time. That is why the results of these works constitute a significant contribution to the history of the interpretation of the biblical text.

However, the values that transmit the images can be of an opposite character, depending on the time and the context. The representation of the biblical women in the Chapel of Guadalupe of the Convent of Las Descalzas Reales of Madrid 'empower and strengthen' women to be protagonists of their lives and their time as abbesses, queens, writers and so forth. Women like Teresa of Jesus, Mariana of Austria or María de Zayas are testament of this.

On the other hand, the prints and engravings of the nineteenth century resort to the women of the Bible to reinforce the female role in the home, a compendium of domestic virtues and an essential figure in the transmission of the faith to children. The women of the Bible will be, therefore, an example of modesty, silence and self-denial, virtues that are associated with the role attributed to women in nineteenth-century society.

In the Middle Ages, the return of Orpah (Ruth 1.14) was placed in relation with those who do not accept the call of Christ and insist on returning to sin and vice, while Ruth's fidelity towards her mother-in-law was seen as a metaphor/symbol of those who persevere in the faith. However, since the twentieth century, the interpretation changed radically. It is no longer a matter of knowing which of the two women acted correctly or of choosing between the behaviour of Orpah and that of Ruth, but of perceiving the bonds that unite the mother-in-law and the daughters-in-law. The two decisions correspond to different responses to life. Their actions highlight the ability of women to decide and take charge of their lives. None is better than the other and Chagall understands this when he captures the moment of farewell in an emotional embrace between Naomi, Orpah and Ruth, where the protagonism rests in the love that unites them.

In Bathsheba and Mary of Magdala we find different evaluations of the same character. In Bathsheba, two very different facets of this woman coexist in the same spatial and temporal framework. She is seen as an immoral woman who can induce sin or, on the contrary, as an intercessor figure, in parallel with the Virgin Mary. In the case of Mary of Magdala, she evolved and acquired new attributes as the evangelical character merged with medieval legends. From a woman who was a referent to the community to the repentant prostitute, Mary of Magdala now has re-emerged once more as the woman of authority of the first centuries of the Christian era.

In short, there are several perspectives that converge in each representation. First, the meaning of the biblical text in its origins, when it is fixed. Second, the exegesis of each time period, which was conditioned by historical, social, economic, political and philosophical/thinking circumstances. Third, that of the artist who projects his own concerns, experiences and interests into the biblical character or scene and, finally, that of the current spectator who contemplates the painting from his or her own mentality (rejection of violence or of the subordination of the woman to man, to name some of the prevailing values in today's society) and his or her own personal reality. As John Berger suggests in *Ways of Seeing* (1972), every act of looking is unique. That which is seen is the result of the relationship between what one is and what one sees.

SELECT BIBLIOGRAPHY

Note: This bibliography lists a selection of the most relevant books cited in the chapters.

Barbeito Carneiro, Mª Isabel. 'Gestos y actitudes "feministas" en el Siglo de Oro español: de Teresa de Jesús a María de Guevara', in *Literatura y feminismo en España (XV–XVI)*, edited by Lisa Wollendorf, 59–76. Barcelona: Icaria, 2005.
Bornay, Erika. *Mujeres de la Biblia en la pintura del Barroco: imágenes de la ambigüedad*, Ensayos Arte Cátedra. Cátedra: Madrid, 1998.
Brenner, Athalya, ed. *Feminist Companion to Ruth*. Sheffield: Sheffield Academic Press, 1993.
Brown, Michelle P. *Understanding Illuminated Manuscripts: A Guide to Technical Terms*. Los Angeles: The J. Paul Getty Museum, 1994.
Carrillo, Martín. *Historia o Elogios de mujeres ilustres del Viejo Testamento*. Huesca: Pedro Blusón, 1627. Available online: https://books.google.es/books?id=ELy2wTaOksYC.
De Hamel, Christopher. *A History of Illuminated Manuscripts*. London: Phaidon, 1986.
De Hamel, Christopher, *Scribes and Illuminators*. Toronto: Toronto University Press, 1992.
De Voragine, Jacobus, *The Golden Legend or Lives of the Saints*. Translated by William Caxton (1483), from the Temple Classics, edited by F. S. Ellis. First issue of this edition, 1900; reprinted 1922, 1931. Available online: https://www.christianiconography.info/goldenLegend/.
England, Emma, and William John Lyons, eds. *Reception History and Biblical Studies*, LHBOTS 615-STr 6. London: Bloomsbury T&T Clark, 2018.
Exum, J. Cheryl. 'Beyond the biblical horizon: The Bible and the arts'. *Biblical Interpretation* 6, no. 3 (1998): 259–65.
Exum, J. Cheryl. ed. *Biblical Studies/Cultural Studies: The Third Sheffield Colloquium*, JSOT Supplement Series 226. Sheffield: Sheffield Academic Press, 1998.
Exum, J. Cheryl. *Plotted, Shot, and Painted: Cultural Representations of Biblical Women*. JSOT. Supplement Series 215. 2nd edn. Sheffield: Sheffield Phoenix Press, 2012.
Exum, J. Cheryl, and Stephen D. Moore. 'Biblical studies/cultural studies', in *Biblical Studies/Cultural Studies: The Third Sheffield Colloquium*, edited by J. Cheryl Exum, 19–45. Sheffield: Sheffield Academic Press, 1998.
Exum, J. Cheryl, and Ela Nutu, eds. *Between the Text and the Canvas, The Bible and Art in Dialogue*. The Bible in the Modern World 13. Sheffield: Sheffield Phoenix Press, 2007.
Gunn, David M. *Judges*, Blackwell Bible Commentaries. Oxford: Blackwell, 2005.
Harthan, John, *The Book of Hours*. New York: Thomas Y. Crowell, 1977.
Hernández, Rosilie. 'The politics of exemplarity: Biblical women and the education of the Spanish Lady in Martin Carrillo, Sebastián Herrera Barnuevo and María de Guevara', in *Women's Literacy in Early Modern Spain and the New World*, edited by Anne J. Cruz and Rosilie Hernández, 225–42. Burlington: Ashgate, 2011.
LaCocque, André. *The Feminine Unconventional: Four Subversives Figures in Israel's Tradition*, 2nd edn. Eugene: Wipf & Stock, 2006.

Le Maistre de Sacy, Isaac-Louis, Vicente Boix and Antonio Pascual. *Historia del Antiguo y Nuevo Testamento: adornada con 700 láminas, según las esplicaciones[sic] sacadas de la Santa Escritura y Padres de la Iglesia*. Valencia: Imp. de Ventura Lluch, 1841.

Navarro Puerto, Mercedes. *Violencia, sexismo, silencio: In-conclusiones en el libro de los Jueces*. Estella: Verbo Divino, 2013.

O'Kane, Martin. *Painting the Text: The Artist as Biblical Interpreter*, The Bible in the Modern World 8. Sheffield: Sheffield Phoenix Press, 2007.

Réau, Louis. *Iconografía del arte cristiano: Iconografía de la Biblia. Antiguo Testamento*. Translated by Daniel Alcoba. Barcelona: Ediciones del Serbal, 2007.

Sánchez Hernández, Mª Leticia. 'La Biblia y las mujeres: Iconografía de una relación en la Baja Edad Media', in *Medievo II (siglos XII–XV): Entre recepción e interpretación*, edited by Kari Elisabeth Børresen and Adriana Valero, 371–90, La Biblia y las mujeres 14. Estella: Verbo Divino, 2012.

Sánchez Hernández, Mª Leticia. 'La capilla de Guadalupe en el monasterio de las Descalzas Reales de Madrid', in *Herederas de Clío: Mujeres que han impulsado la Historia*, coordinated by Gloria Franco Rubio and María Ángeles Pérez Samper, 493–514. Sevilla: Mergablum, 2014.

Seijas, Guadalupe. 'Algunas consideraciones sobre la violencia en el libro de Jueces'. *Miscelánea de estudios árabes y hebraicos. Sección de hebreo* 60 (2011): 243–71.

Seijas, Guadalupe. 'Rut'. *Revista de iconografía medieval* 9, no. 18 (2017): 85–104. Available online: https://www.ucm.es/data/cont/media/www/pag-105877/6.%20 Rut.pdf (accessed 15 September 2021).

Seijas, Guadalupe. 'The iconographical representations of the book of Ruth in medieval illuminated initials'. *Die Bible in der Kunst/Bible in the Arts* 3 (2019): 1–18. Available online: https://www.bibelwissenschaft.de/fileadmin/user_upload/Bibelkunst/BiKu_2019_09_Seijas_Ruth.pdf (accessed 15 September 2021).

Sölle, Dorothee, Joe H. Kirchberger and Anne-Marie Schnieper. *Great Women of the Bible in Art and Literature*. Minneapolis: Fortress Press, 2006.

Walther, Ingo F., and Norbert Wolf. *Códices ilustres: Los manuscritos iluminados más bellos del mundo desde 400 hasta 1600*. Translated by Pablo Álvarez Ellacuría. London: Taschen, 2003.

Yebra-Rovira, Carmen. 'French biblical engravings and the education of the Spanish woman in the XIX century'. *Biblical Reception* 2 (2013): 97–116.

Yebra-Rovira, Carmen. 'Interpretación bíblica y formación moral de la mujer en el siglo XIX: El ángel del hogar'. *Moralia* 36 (2013): 405–26.

Yebra-Rovira, Carmen. *Las biblias ilustradas en España en el siglo XIX: Desarrollo, relevancia cultural e interpretación teológica*. Col. Tesis 64. Estella: Verbo Divino – Asociación Bíblica Española, 2015.

INDEX OF BIBLICAL CHARACTERS

Abela, woman of Abel Beth-maacah 86
Abigail 86, 87, 88–91, 93, 94, 96, 97, 103, 104, 105
Abimelech 133, 136, 137, 145, 146
Abishag 53, 65, 87, 90–1, 93, 94, 96, 97, 103, 104, 105
Abraham 10, 15, 36, 87, 89
Achsah 3, 99, 104, 105, 139–40
Adam 12, 37, 54, 57, 58, 123
Adonijah 52–3, 64
Ahasuerus 11, 79, 80, 87, 98, 113
Alcohol, daughter of Job 93, 94, 97, 101
Amram 118, 121

Barak 140, 146
Bathsheba 51–81, 88, 93, 94, 95, 96, 98, 103, 105, 114, 185
Benaiah 52, 53
Benjamin 99
Bithiah, *see* daughter of Pharaoh
Boaz 18, 37, 86, 160–1, 165–6, 170, 172, 173, 176, 179, 180

Caleb 99, 139, 140, 147
Canaanite woman 14, 114
Chilion 165, 170
Christ 26, 27, 29, 30, 31, 35, 40, 54–9, 60, 67, 70, 76, 77, 79, 80, 89, 91, 106, 138, 145, 171
Concubite of Levite, *see* woman of Levite

Daughter of Asher 88
Daughter of Jephthah 14, 115, 134, 137, 138, 147–50
Daughters of Job 11, 93, 99, 100–2, 104, 105
Daughters of Lot 13
Daughters of Noah 11
Daughter of Pharaoh 3, 4, 88, 109, 116, 118, 121–3, 126, 127, 184

Daughters/women of Shiloh 137, 138, 146, 151
Daughters of Zelophehad 99
David 10, 11, 26, 30, 31, 52–74, 80, 88, 91, 97, 98, 154, 180, 184
Day, daughter of Job 93, 94, 99–100, 101, 105
Deborah 2, 86, 87–90, 91, 93, 94, 98, 103, 105, 133, 134, 137, 138, 140–6
Delilah 6, 18, 19, 36–7, 75, 137, 138, 155
Dinah 14

Ehud 133
Elijah 88, 97, 98
Elimelech 27, 28, 161, 165, 171, 184
Elisha 88, 97, 98
Elisheba, wife of Aaron 88, 119
Esau 30, 96
Esther 11, 12, 14, 34, 78, 79, 80, 86–91, 93, 94, 97, 98, 103, 105, 136, 138, 161
Eve 12, 37, 40, 54, 67, 75, 87, 102, 113, 114, 123

Gideon 31, 137, 138, 146
Goliath 26, 62, 184

Haggith 52
Hannah, mother of Samuel 75, 87, 88, 93, 95, 97, 114
Hazzlelponi, *see* mother of Samson
Holofernes 15, 18, 26, 36, 86, 98, 103, 184
Huldah 87

Immaculate 16, 20, 21, 93, 95, 105
Isaac 18, 36, 89, 91, 98, 99, 113, 175
Ishmael 98, 99

Jacob 18, 88, 89, 99
Jael 2, 14, 17, 86, 87–91, 93, 94, 97, 98, 103, 133, 134, 137, 138, 140–5, 146, 154, 155, 159

Jehu 88
Jephthah 115, 137, 138, 146, 147, 148
Jezebel 12, 89
Joab 52
Jochebed 3, 4, 88, 115–30, 184
Jonah 55
Joseph 72, 88, 89, 99
Joshua 72, 91
Josiah 59
Judah 18
Judith 12, 14, 18, 26, 27, 34, 36, 37, 86, 89–91, 93, 94, 97, 98, 103, 104, 105, 128, 136, 138, 142, 144, 159, 161, 184

Lazarus 40, 41, 77
Leah 86, 87, 88
Lydia 11

Maccabees 18
Mahlon 160, 165, 170
Maid of Judith 15, 18, 36, 90
Martha, sister of Lazarus 40, 41, 44
Mary of Bethany, *see* Mary, sister of Lazarus
Mary of Magdala / Mary Magdalene 3, 12, 13, 25, 38–46, 77
Mary, sister of Lazarus 40, 41, 44
Michal 30, 31, 87, 88
Miriam 6, 11, 13, 86, 87–91, 93, 94, 97, 98, 105, 115, 116, 118, 119, 121, 122, 126, 127
Mordecai 12
Moses 10, 31, 55, 58, 99, 109, 110, 115, 117, 118, 120–3, 129, 143, 145
Mother of Abimelech 137
Mother of Samson 86, 88, 90, 93, 94, 98, 103, 105, 133, 137, 138
Mother of Sisera 137

Naamah 93, 97, 98, 105
Nabal 91
Naomi 12, 18, 27, 29, 88, 93, 94, 95, 98, 103, 105, 114, 159–62, 165–81
Nathan 52, 53, 62, 64, 65, 69, 70, 72, 73
Noah 58

Obed 114, 119, 125, 159, 160, 161, 163, 170, 179–80, 181
Orpah 12, 29, 159, 161, 162, 165–73, 175, 177–9, 181, 185
Othniel 99, 133, 139

Paul of Tarsus 55
Peninnah 95
Prostitute of Gaza 137
Puah 19

Qetsiah, daughter of Job 100
Queen of Sheba 93, 94, 98, 103, 105

Rachel 18, 75, 86, 87, 88–91, 93, 97, 98, 99, 103, 105, 113
Rahab 85, 86, 87, 88, 138
Rebecca 18, 30, 31, 35, 86, 88, 90, 93, 94, 99, 102, 103, 104, 105
Rizpah 18
Ruth 3, 12, 27, 29, 34, 37–8, 86, 89–91, 93, 94, 98, 103, 105, 114, 125, 136, 142, 159–181, 185

Salomé 115
Samuel 114
Samson 18, 19, 36, 37, 72, 98, 103, 133, 137, 138, 146
Sarah, wife of Abraham 18, 87–9, 91, 93, 94, 98, 102, 103, 105, 114
Sarah, wife of Tobias 18, 86, 114
Saul 30, 59, 88
Serah 88
Shamgar 133
Shiphrah 19, 119
Shunammite 89, 93, 94, 105
Sisera 97, 98, 103, 140, 143, 144
Solomon 51–3, 56–9, 60–70, 74, 76, 79–81
Sussanah 12, 17, 19, 34, 89, 90, 91, 136

Tabitha 11
Tamar 14, 74
Thermuthis, *see* daughter of Pharaoh
Tobias 18, 34, 86, 114
Tobit 14, 74
Tubal-cain 97

Uriah 13, 52, 62, 63, 64, 70, 73

Vashti 87
Virgin Mary 2, 6, 12, 13, 16, 18, 19, 20, 21, 30–1, 39, 42, 46, 55–8, 66–7, 75–80, 81, 90, 91, 105, 114, 115, 125, 144, 185

Widow of Zarephath 88, 93, 97, 98, 103, 105
Wife of Job 12
Wife of Noah 88
Wife of Obadiah 88
Wife of Othoniel 139–40

Woman of Levite 14, 134, 137, 138, 150–5
Woman of Potiphar 13
Woman of Thebez 134, 137, 145–50, 154
Woman with the flow of flood 19

Yiscá 87

INDEX OF REFERENCES

Hebrew Bible/Old Testament
Genesis
3	37	15.16-19	99
4.22	97	15.18	99
6.1	100		
7	37	*Judges*	
21.13	56, 87	1	137
22	36, 175	1.1-8	139
23.1	89	1.12-13	99
24	99	1.12-15	139
24.15-21	35	1.22-26	138
24.16-20	31	2	
27	30, 99	3.5	137
46.16	88	4	14, 137
		4-5	137, 140, 160
Exodus		4.4	87
1-15	27	4.17	140
1.15-21	19	4.17-22	143
2	115, 116	4.21	87
2.1-10	109	5	137
2.9	126	5.11	137
3	31	6.36-40	31
6.20	116	8-11	147
15	13	8.30-31	137
15.2	126	9.3	137
15.20	87	9.52	145
		9.54	146
Numbers		11	14, 115
12	6	11.30-40	137
12.1-2	13	11.34-40	147
12.10	6	11.37-38	137
13	37	12.8-9	137
21	6	13	137
21.5-9	5	14-16	137
21.9	55	14.12-18	98
26.59	116	15.19	99
27.1–11	99	16.1	36
		16.4	36
Joshua		17	137
2	138	19	14, 137, 150
15	139	20-21	150
		21	137

Index of References

Ruth
1.1-2	185
1.3-4	171
1.4	178
1.7-8	170
1.7-18	3, 180
1.7-19	162–3
1.14	175, 185
2	37
3.6-15	161
3.11	86
4.1-12	161
4.17	103

1 Samuel
2.1	88
17	26
19.11-12	30
25.20-31	88

2 Samuel
11	52, 98
11.2-4	62
11.5	52
12	63
12.1-14	52
12.1-19	52
12.24-25	52
13.1-19	14
20.14-22	86
21.10-12	18

1 Kings
1.11-14	53
1.11-27	64
1.11-31	52
1.15	65
1.24-27	65
1.32-35	52
2.10-12	52
2.19	52, 53, 65
2.19-20	79
2.19-25	64
17	97, 98

2 Kings
4.1-7	88
4.8-37	98
9.30	100
22.14	87

1 Chronicles
4.18	121
12.19	88
29.3	100

Esther
5.1	88
7.1-10	12

Job
1.2	99
42.13-14	99
42.15	101

Psalms
44.10	58
45.9	57
45.13	79
51	70
54.8	31

Proverbs
12.4	86
31.10-31	87, 88, 89

Songs
4.15	56

Isaiah
19	131
35.2	79
54.1	100

Jeremiah
4.30	100, 101
12.7	31

Daniel
13	12, 18

Hosea
5.6	31

Haggai
2.7	56

Apocrypha

Judith
13	26–7

New Testament

Matthew
1.1	59
1.6-7	70
2.13-16	30
5.17-18	55
12.40	55
14.6-12	36
15.23-24	14
26.6-13	40
27.56	39
28.1-10	39

Mark
5.24-34	19
6.14-29	36
14.3-9	40
15.40	39
16.1-8	39
16.9	39

Luke
7.36-50	40
8.1-3	39
10.38-42	40
23.49	39
24.1-12	39

John
3.14	55
11.1-44	40
12.1-11	40
19.25	39
20.11-18	39

Colossians
2.17	55

Revelations
12.1	105
12.1-4	106

Josephus
Antiquities of the Jews
II, 9, 4	118
IX, 4, 2	88

Rabbinic Sources
Talmud
Baba Batra 16b	87, 100
Baba Batra 58a	87
Berachot 16b	87
Horayot 10b	87
Meguillah 14a	87, 97
Meguillah 15a	87
Nazir 23b	87
Sanhedrin 105b	87
Sotah 11b	119

Targum of Job
42, 14	90, 100, 101

Midrashim
Exodus Rabbah
1.17	119

Leviticus Rabbah
1.3	119

Pesiqta of Rab Kahana
2, 13b	88

Pseudoepigrapaha
Testament of Job
1, 2	101
1, 3	100
46-53	100
46, 1-2	101
52	102
52, 4	101

Classical

Ephrem of Syria
Opera Omnia
I, 526c	88

Jerome of Stridon
Epistle LXIX
419	56

Ovid
Metamorphoses
Book XIV	14
Book XV	38

Other sources		54-56	119
Alonso de Villegas		71	97
Flos Sanctorum		127	98
XXI.3	145	130	98
		136	96
Lope de Vega		137	96
The Beautiful Esther		138-39	96
II. vv. 680-705	85–6	230	97
Martín Carrillo		Jacobo de la Voragine	
Elogios		*The Golden Legend*	
27	96	Vol. 4, 36	41

INDEX OF AUTHORS

Ackerman, S. 53
Adams, C. 117
Albrecht, R. 117
Alfonso, E. 170
Alonso Schökel, L. 100
Alpers, S. 118
Álvarez Barredo, M. 136
Arce Pinedo, R. 113
Armstrong, K. 26
Azcárate Luxán, M. 51, 57
Azcue Brea, L. 127

Backhouse, J. 65, 78
Bagatin, P. L. 169
Banerjee, J. 127
Banning, K. 81
Barbeito Carneiro, M. I. 104
Baumgartel, B. 89
Benjamin, D. C. 132
Berdini, P. 16
Bernabé, C. 39, 42, 46
Bernárdez, A. 21
Bieder, M. 111
Blanco, A. 111
Bleyerveld, I. 117
Bohn, B. 18
Boix, V. 135, 141, 145, 146, 149
Bornay, E. 9, 18, 36, 89, 153
Bottigheimer, R. B. 126, 134
Bourassé, J. J. 58
Brenner, A. 137, 138, 139, 148, 151
Bromely, G. W. 54
Brown, M. P. 67, 76
Brubaker, L. 64, 71, 73
Buchthal, H. 64, 65
Bullard, J. M. 7
Burnet, R. 39, 46

Calmet, A. 114, 121
Camacho Martínez, R. 10
Cantera, F. 100

Cao, M. F. 10
Cardon, B. 54, 55, 59, 60, 80
Carrete Parrondo, C. 134
Chittister, J. D. 179
Chordá, F. 26
Claret, A. M. 111, 112
Colvin, S. 123
Conroy, C. 124
Cooke, S. 125
Costley, C. L. 70
Cubas Martín, N. 10
Cutler, A. 72

Daley, B. E. 81
Darboy, G. 117, 142
De Castro, C. 104
De Genoude, E. 114, 121
De Groot, C. 117
De Hamel, C. 26, 30, 67, 163
Del Barco, F. J. 170
Der Nersessien, S. 81
Deepwell, K. 10
Delenda, O. 42, 44
Dubay, G. 41, 42
Duchesne, J. 152

Eco, U. 38
Engammare, M. 13, 134
England, E. 8, 110
Enriquez de Salamanca, C. 111
Estévez, M. E. 7
Exum, J. C. 8, 12, 19, 160, 172

Fellous-Rozemblat, S. 170
Ferrari, R. C. 124
Fischer, I. 159
Fontana, E. 45
Franco, A. 91

Galindo, E. 174
Giebelhausen, M. 8

Gimeno de Flaquer, C. 111
Ginzberg, L. 88
Giordano, M. L. 26
Godoy Domínguez, M. J. 10, 17
Gonzálo Hernando, I. 51
Goosen, L. 42, 160
Gunn, D. M. 51, 136, 148

Harrison, E. F. 54
Harthan, J. 7
Henry, C. F. H. 54
Hernández, R. 102, 103, 104, 105
Hidalgo Rodríguez, D. 10

Iglesias, M. 100

Jagoe, C. 111
James, R. M. 59
Jasper, D. 42

Kantorowicz, E. H. 59
Kirchberger, J. H. 10
Klein, L. R. 137, 138, 139
Kramer, P. S. 148
Kunoth-Leifels, E. 51

Labriola, A. C. 78, 79, 80
LaCocque, A. 160
Lapsley, J. E. 151
Larkin, K. 159
Lázaro y Garzón, B. M. 117
Le Maistre de Sacy, I.-L. 135, 141, 145, 146, 149
Letellier, R. I. 7
Lockard, R. A. 124
López Fernández, M. 9, 112, 113, 122
Lowden, J. 27, 29, 164, 165, 166, 167, 168, 180
Lyons, W. J. 8, 110

Maher, M. 107
McNamara, M. 107
Mangan, C. 100
Marcos, M. 46
Martínez Quinteiro, M. E. 10
Martyn, S. T. 117
Marsh, C. 11
Marrow, J. H. 76
Matthews, V. H. 132

Mayayo, P. 10, 19
Migne, J.-P. 40, 58
Miller, D. 178
Miquel, E. 39
Miró, A. 10
Molina Martín, A. 144
Moore, S. D. 8
Moreno Alcalde, M. 43
Müllner, I. 151

Navarro, M. 138
Naylor, A. E. 123, 124, 125
Neysters. S. 89

O'Kane, M. 8, 11, 12, 16, 37, 38, 160
Oikonomides, N. 72, 104
Oliva, L. 104
Ortega Monasterio, M. T. 170

Panofsky, E. 60, 61, 66
Pascual, A. 34, 135, 140, 141, 145, 146, 149, 151, 152
Plazaola, J. 14
Pollock, G. 10
Prats, A. 170
Puiggarí, J. 149
Pyper, H. S. 126, 134

Rabaté, C. 111, 142
Réau, L. 9, 42, 48, 54, 60, 65, 66, 144, 160
Redondo Goicoechea, A. 104
Réveil, E. A. 152
Roca y Cornet, J. 114, 117, 121, 141, 142, 143, 147, 150, 154
Rousseau, J.-J. 151
Ruiz López, D. 18

Sánchez Caro, J. M. 95, 135
Sánchez Hernández, M. L. 42, 92, 95
Sasson, J. M. 159
Saulnier-Pernuit, L. 67
Schaff, P. 82
Schechter, S. 88
Schmidt, G. 76, 77, 79
Schnieper, A.-M. 10
Scio de San Miguel, F. 135, 145
Sebastián López, S. 30, 91
Seijas, G. 42, 137, 159, 163, 165, 169

Sheaffer. A. M. 15
Sicre, J. L. 99, 136
Smeltz, J. W. 78, 79, 80
Smith, L. 159
Soh-Kronthaler, M. 117
Sölle, D. 10
Spittler, R. P. 100
Stanton, A. R. 74, 75, 76
Steger, H. 59
Stoichita, V. I. 12, 18
Sunderland Wethey, A. 92, 95

Taschl-Erber, A. 41
Taylor, J. H. M. 74
Taylor, M. A. 117
Torres, J. 46
Torres Amat, F. 34, 135, 143
Trebolle Barrera, J. 33

Valerio, A. 26
Van der Stock, J. 170

Vander Stichele, C. 126, 134
Vega, J. 5
Verdier, P. 57, 58
Vilacoba Ramos, K. M. 97

Walker Vadillo, M. A. 68, 70
Walther. I. F. 163
Warner, G. 74
Watteeuw, L. 170
Weir, A. 75
Weitzmann, K. 63
Wethey, H. E. 92, 93, 95
Wieck, R. S. 69, 70
Wolf, N. 163

Yarza Luaces, J. 19, 21
Yebra-Rovira, C. 12, 34, 99, 113, 115, 117, 134, 136, 142, 148, 151, 160

Zapater y Ugeda, J. 114, 117
Zavala, I. M. 111

www.ingramcontent.com/pod-product-compliance
Lightning Source LLC
Chambersburg PA
CBHW061829300426
44115CB00013B/2305